MARY LYON
Documents and Writings

Edited by James E. Hartley

DOORLIGHT PUBLICATIONS
SOUTH HADLEY, MA

Partial funding for editing Mary Lyon: Documents & Writings has been provided by Mount Holyoke College

*Copyright © 2008 by Doorlight Publications
All rights reserved*

This book may not be reproduced in whole or in part, in any form (beyond that copying permitted by sections 107 and 108 of U.S. Copyright Law and except by reviewers for the public press), without the written consent of the publishers.

*Designed by Allison Brown
Printed and bound in the United States of America*

*Cover Illustration
Joseph Goodhue Chandler (American, 1813-1884), Mary Lyon, oil on canvas, Mount Holyoke College Art Museum, South Hadley, Massachusetts*

To Mary Lyon's Students

That our daughters may be as corner stones,
Polished after the similitude of a palace
Psalm 144:12

Table of Contents

Page

I. LETTERS   3

II. FOUNDING MOUNT HOLYOKE FEMALE SEMINARY   127

1. *New England Female Seminary for Teachers (1832)*   *129*

2. *Meeting of the Friends of Female Education (September 1834)*   *133*

3. *Mount Holyoke Female Seminary (September 1835)*   *138*

4. *Fundraising Letter (November 1836)*   *150*

5. *General View of the Principles and Designs of the Mount Holyoke Female Seminary (1837)*   *161*

6. *Procuring Furniture (1837)*   *180*

7. *Circular to the Young Ladies (1837)*   *182*

8. *Prospectus of Mount Holyoke Female Seminary (1837)*   *184*

9. *First Annual Catalogue of Mount Holyoke Female Seminary (1837)*   *193*

10. *Female Education (June 1839)*   *206*

11. *Preparation for Admission (September 1840)*   *229*

12. *Report of the Teachers (date unknown, possibly 1839)*   *231*

III. A MISSIONARY OFFERING   235

CHAPTER I: Christian Sympathy—Personal Responsibility—Missionary Circular—American Board of Foreign Missions   239

CHAPTER II: Fellowship with Christ's Sufferings —View of the World of Despair —View of Heaven   247

CHAPTER III: View of Personal Responsibility— Scene of the Judgment —Scene at the Missionary House   256

CHAPTER IV: The God Covetousness becoming an Advocate for Foreign Missions—Labors of Covetousness   263

CHAPTER V: Labors of Covetousness continued—Convention of the Laboring and Uneducated Classes—Recollections of a Little Mountain Home   268

CHAPTER VI: Labors of Covetousness continued—His Speech before a Literary Assembly—Reply of Disinterested Benevolence   276

CHAPTER VII; Labors of Covetousness continued—His Newspaper Article—His Personal Advice to Friends   284

CHAPTER VIII: Power of Personal Responsibility in Behalf of Missions —Cases of Self-Denying Benevolence   292

CHAPTER IX: Reversed Scene at the Missionary House—Annual Meeting at Rochester—Application of Personal Responsibility   299

IV. DETACHED SAYINGS AND WRITINGS   **305**

1. Behold How Great   *307*

2. Benevolence   *309*

3. One Beautiful Evening   *312*

4. The Bible   *315*

5. Motives for Engaging in Teaching   *317*

6. Will   *322*

7. From the Mary Lyon Yearbook   *324*

Acknowledgements

I am very grateful to the many people who helped bring this anthology together. Jennifer Hale (Class of 2010) was indispensable in scanning all of the documents gathered here into electronic format and editing them to be readable. Allison Brown did a truly excellent job converting text files into an aesthetically pleasing form and designing the cover and format of the book. Aimee (Tetreault) Gould (Class of 1995) proofread every document, and Monica Ballagh (Class of 2008) and Susan Pincus (Class of 2008) proofread large sections of this collection. Jennifer Gunter King in the Mount Holyoke Archives was quite helpful in enabling us to get access to the material there, and Wendy Watson, curator of the Mount Holyoke Art Museum, located the picture used on the cover. Dan Brown was a remarkably able and patient publisher. My greatest thanks, as always, go to Janet, a woman who would have impressed Mary Lyon, and Emma (Class of 2015), Lily (Class of 2017) and Clara (Class of 2021), who someday will reap the benefits of the work Mary Lyon did.

Foreword

> *The stone and brick and mortar speak a language, which vibrates through my very soul. How much thought, and how much feeling have I had on this general subject in years that are past. And I have indeed lived to see the time, when a body of gentlemen have ventured to lay the corner stone of an edifice which will cost about $15,000—and for an institution for the education of females. Surely the Lord hath remembered our low estate. This will be an era in female education. The work will not stop with this institution. The enterprize may have to struggle through embarrassments for years, but its influence will be felt.*
>
> Mary Lyon
Letter to Zilpah Grant, October 9, 1836

Before the 19th Amendment to the U.S. Constitution and the Seneca Falls Declaration; before Susan B. Anthony, Elizabeth Cady Stanton, Lucy Stone, Julia Ward Howe, Carrie Chapman and Alice Paul; before John Stuart Mill's *The Subjection of Women* and Virginia Woolf's *A Room of One's Own*; before all these came Mary Lyon. In 1837, by virtue of dogged determination and never removing her sight from her goal, Mary Lyon founded Mount Holyoke Female Seminary, the oldest continuing college for women in the world. Never seeking to draw attention to herself, she steadfastly fought to make sure that the school would outlive her and never become known as "Miss Lyon's School." Perhaps as a result, Mary Lyon has not drawn nearly the attention she deserves in histories of America, the women's movement or higher education.

This volume, for the first time, draws together the major documents and writings of Mary Lyon. In these writings, we can see the development of her ideas leading to the creation of a permanent institution of higher learning for women. The vision for Mount Holyoke Female Seminary was more than simply a college for women; it was to be an institution of a particular type marked by an academic education equivalent to that at comparable institutions for men and with costs low enough to be affordable to the middle class. Mary Lyon was hoping to train the teachers of the next generations, and indeed, the offspring of Mount Holyoke are scattered around the world.

Mary Lyon was born on February 28, 1797 in Buckland, Massachusetts. Her father died when she was five, and her mother raised Mary and her six siblings. At the age of seventeen, Mary began teaching, first in Buckland, and subsequently at a wide array of schools in western Massachusetts. Feeling the need to further educate herself, Mary enrolled at Byfield Academy in 1821, which was to be the first pivotal moment in her life.

Byfield Academy was run by Reverend Joseph Emerson. The education there required mastery of the selected texts, starting with creating an outline of the whole, and followed by learning and reciting all of the details. Religious instruction lay at the heart of all of the education. But, perhaps most importantly, Emerson demonstrated a belief that women could be held to a high academic standard. So influential was her time at Byfield, that Mary would later describe the academic curriculum she was using as "Emersonian."

At Byfield, Mary also met Zilpah Grant, Emerson's assistant. Mary became quite devoted to Miss Grant, and the two of them began a long association, beginning at Adams Female Academy, Grant's school in Londonderry, where Mary would teach in the summer before moving back to western Massachusetts in the winter to teach in her own school. In 1830 Mary finally ended her practice of changing locations throughout the year and moved to teach year round at Grant's new school, Ipswich Female Seminary. But, due to illness, Grant was absent from the school for long stretches, during which time Mary acted as headmistress, learning the skills of administration and perfecting her skills as a teacher. While working there, Mary made her first attempt to establish a permanent school for women, one which would not be tied to any particular teacher (as Byfield was to Joseph Emerson or as Ipswich was to Zilpah Grant), but one which would outlast its central figure. This initial attempt met with failure; there was simply not enough interest, and more importantly money, to create a permanent college devoted to educating women.

And so, with the foundering of her first attempt to put a school like Ipswich on a more permanent footing, Mary Lyon left Ipswich in 1834. She spent the next three years fully devoted to raising the money and support necessary to create Mount Holyoke Female Seminary. This was not an easy task. Since large financial donors were not forthcoming, Mary hatched the idea to raise money in smaller amounts, much of which would come from women who did not have access to family money. Mary literally began going door to door in towns throughout Massachusetts, pleading for funds for as little as the amount necessary to furnish just one bedroom at the seminary. These years mark the period when Mary Lyon did her greatest work. Bit by bit, weathering disappointment after disappointment, Mary raised the funds and support necessary to create a school, which opened on November 8, 1837.

The early years of the seminary were marked by increasing enthusiasm; applications to attend the college steadily rose, and the academic standards were increased year by year. The school had its most serious set back in 1840 when typhoid fever swept through the college, causing a third of the 120 students to fall ill and leaving nine students dead. But, the seminary persisted throughout this crisis, and while attendance fell the following year, over time it grew until there were over 200 students in the last year of Mary's life. To help her run the school, Mary surrounded herself with a set of dedicated teachers, working for very low pay as one of the ways to keep tuition low. Similarly, students did much of the domestic work to reduce the cost of hiring additional staff. Many students found Mount Holyoke to be too demanding, both physically and mentally, but those who endured emerged as teachers in great demand around the country and as missionaries around the world.

Mary Lyon died on March 5, 1849 after a long illness. In

what is undoubtedly a perfect illustration of the sort of women she was, the teachers at Mount Holyoke did not cancel classes on the day after she died, telling the students that they had no doubt that Miss Lyon would not want it any other way. On the monument marking her grave on the Mount Holyoke campus is an inscription from the last address she gave to the school: "There is nothing in the universe that I fear but that I shall not know all my duty, or shall fail to do it."

In the midst of all of her work running the Seminary, Mary made the time to write a book on the cause which was most dear to her heart. That book, *A Missionary Offering*, was an urgent plea to give liberally to foreign missions. The fact that Mary would write this book, and not the one we might have imagined she would write on the importance of women's education, is illustrative of the fact that for Mary, the founding of Mount Holyoke Female Seminary and the prospect of sending Christian missionaries throughout the world were not unrelated causes. Mary Lyon's devout Christian beliefs were the center of her every effort and cannot be simply dismissed as the conventional pieties of a more pious age. Mary saw herself as engaged in a life's work whose sole purpose was to bring glory to God.

> *I would desire such a frame of mind that I might be ever ready to say, not my will but thine be done. I would not desire anything that would not be for the glory of God and in accordance with the will of my Saviour. Sometimes I almost feel that I am not my own; but then again, I find my heart desiring those things from which I had hoped it was forever separated. Go where no one else will go, not seeking the praise of men, but the favor which comes from God only.*
>
> *Mary Lyon*
> *From The Mary Lyon Yearbook*

Editor's Note

Elizabeth Alden Green's, *Mary Lyon and Mount Holyoke: Opening the Gates* (Hanover, New Hampshire: University Press of New England, 1979) was indispensable in putting together this volume. Much of the information used in the brief biography of Mary Lyon found in the Foreword is from Green's highly readable and recommended biography.

Unless otherwise noted, the material in this volume is found in the Mount Holyoke College Library Archives and online at *http://clio.fivecolleges.edu/mhc/lyon/*.

With one exception, the letters are found in Edward Hitchcock, *The Power of Christian Benevolence Illustrated in the Life and Labors of Mary Lyon* (Northampton, Massachusetts: Hopkins, Bridgman, and Company, 1851). Edward Hitchcock was President of Amherst College and a longtime friend and supporter of Mary Lyon. After her death, he collected a large amount of her correspondence and edited the letters to be used as a biography. Unfortunately, most of the original letters have been lost, and thus we have only Hitchcock's edited versions of these letters. The letter to Zilpah Grant dated October 9, 1836 is not directly from Hitchcock's volume, but is found in the Mount Holyoke College Archives. [Hitchcock does include a portion of a letter discussing the laying of the corner stone, dated October 7 and addressed to Miss C. (Eunice Caldwell), which is nearly identical to the comparable portion of the letter to Grant. As Marion Lassing has noted, the context of this famous portion of the letter is interesting, and so the complete letter to Grant is included here.] Both Marion Lassing's book, *Mary Lyon Through Her Letters* (Boston: Books, Inc., 1937) and Elizabeth Alden Green's volume were very useful in identifying the addressees of some of the letters in the Hitchcock volume. Letters which were deemed to be of interest to the general reader are collected in the present volume; scholars seeking a more comprehensive collection should consult Hitchcock's volume and the Mount Holyoke Archives.

"New England Female Seminary for Teachers" is found in Edward Hitchcock, *The Power of Christian Benevolence Illustrated in the Life and Labors of Mary Lyon* (Northampton, Massachusetts: Hopkins, Bridgman, and Company, 1851, pp. 164-167).

The set of brief quotations in section 4 are all from *The Mary Lyon Yearbook*, edited by Helen Marshall North (Boston: Congregational Sunday-School and Publishing Society, 1895). That volume had a page for every day of the year, with each page having a passage from the Bible, a excerpt from a poem, and a quotation from Mary Lyon. The complete set of quotations from the Yearbook are reprinted in the order in which they appeared therein. Some of the quotations are from documents which also appear in this anthology.

A Missionary Offering, or, Christian Sympathy, Personal Responsibility, and the Present Crisis in Foreign Missions, was published in Boston by Crocker and Brewster in 1843.

I

LETTERS

1. The Seminary Concert
July 21, 1821

To Her Mother

Each passing day carries my heart home to you, my dear parent, and all my other friends, till I can no longer refrain from writing. Did you know how much my heart dwells on her who loves me with a mother's love, some of you, ere this, would have filled a sheet for my perusal. I long to see you; but I will suppress my tender emotions, while I have recourse to my slow, feeble pen, as a poor substitute for the rapid conversation at the meeting hour of a mother and daughter —conversation which stops not for thoughts. Recently I have thought more of you than ever, and there has been a *reason*. Dear mother, could you, in imagination, have visited Byfield this week, and have had presented to your view a true picture of the passing scene, methinks your heart would have risen in gratitude to Him who is able to soften the hardest heart, and arouse the most stupid mind. We have a female prayer meeting on Saturday evenings, termed "the seminary concert," for those members of the school who dare hope that they have an interest at the throne of grace; and these constitute about half our number. This has been regularly attended ever since the establishment of the seminary. Four or five weeks ago, it began to be an inquiry with many, what they should do for the salvation of their own souls and the souls of others. Even eight or nine weeks since, as I was conversing with Miss D., (a young lady whom I mentioned to you as designed for a mission to Jerusalem,) she expressed great anxiety for those who had no hope; observing that she thought Christians had much to do, and that their situation here as school associates gave them a peculiar advantage. Her observations made some impression on my mind, but on my heart I fear such impressions are mostly 'like the morning cloud and early dew.' With many other excellences, I believe she is eminently pious; and I hope she will be an instrument of much good in her anticipated situation. An increasing anxiety for a revival in the seminary began to prevail. I believe that in this respect Mr. Emerson has been highly blessed in his school. I cannot but think it has been owing, in a great measure, to his excellent instruction, together with the influence of his pupils, a great number of whom are pious. All, at this time, appeared to believe that it would be their fault if this stupidity and carelessness continued through the summer. Mr. Emerson's assistant expressed her feelings, at one of our meetings, in the most interesting and affecting manner. She feared that the Savior was here wounded in the house of his friends; that Christians in this school were grieving the Holy Spirit; that the state of their hearts presented obstacles to his special presence and work. The solemnity, affection, and tender solicitude with which she uttered these remarks, appeared to make a deep impression on every mind. Since that, a visible change has been in progress in the school. This week, especially, a deep solemnity has been depicted on every countenance. Sometimes, during devotional exercises, or while listening to Mr. E.'s instructions and solemn warnings, scarcely a heart has been able to refrain from sighs, or an eye from tears. Four express a faint hope that they have passed from death unto life; but they hope with trembling. They feel that there is great danger of being deceived; that they shall believe stupidity to be trust in God, and thus sink down in security, and finally plunge themselves in everlasting ruin. Such fears seem to me not unfavorable. Well may they fear, and well may we tremble for them, and for all those who are passing this critical period, this all-important moment of their lives. Should any cherish a false hope, should any lay their foundation in the sand, almost as easily might the dead be raised, as such be rescued from eternal destruction. May this not be the case with me?

This attention is entirely confined to the seminary. Imagine to yourself a little circle of about forty females, almost excluded from the rest of the human family, all appearing solemn as eternity.

Monday Eve. —We had a solemn time yesterday. Mr. E. is very solicitous for our spiritual, as well as temporal, welfare. This morning he made some remarks on the importance and manner of studying the Scriptures, and the importance of prayer. He daily gives us much good instruction. Friday morning was a solemn time. Mr. E. remarked upon the great importance of improving the present period to secure our salvation, observing that a little cloud had arisen, which was gently distilling a few drops on this favored spot. Though it was equally easy with God, yet it was not probable, when most of us should disperse and mingle with our friends and companions, that the cloud would follow us; but most likely that those who had not made their peace with God would gradually lose their impressions, and when they should return, the shower would be past. This school term closes tomorrow, and the vacation is two weeks. After earnestly and solemnly inviting, entreating, and warning us not to let the present moment pass, he closed by saying, "What you do, do quickly." There is great reason to fear that this cloud will pass by. It reminds me of the favorable appearance at Buckland last fall; but, alas! That passed away as the morning cloud and early dew. Will that be the case here? I cannot bear the thought. As we are about to separate, the members of the seminary concert met at our chamber after school for prayer. We had an impressive season. O my mother, will you not remember this meeting Saturday evening?

2. The Solemnity of Living
Byfield, August 11, 1821

To Freelove Lyon

I possess many facilities for improvement, but they only increase my obligation. I believe I have never before realized the solemnity of living, so much as I do this summer. I often think that, if possible, it is more solemn to live than to die. What important consequences may depend on a single word, or on the most trifling deed! With how much care and deliberation should we regulate all our conduct, and even our every thought! This requires the most vigorous exertion of all our faculties; nay, more, we need constant instruction from heaven, and the daily guidance of the Holy Spirit.

3. Trust in God
January 15, 1823

To Zilpah Grant

Pray for me, that I may habitually know and feel my dependence on God. How safe it is to trust in God! How easily can he give counsel and assistance in all things, the smallest as well as the greatest! And how ready and willing is he always to assist! It would seem that I have too frequently tried my own strength, that I have experienced too many instances of the particular guardian care and protection of God, to doubt in whom I should place my trust. Alas! I have a treacherous heart. But our God is faithful. The unfaithfulness of his rebellious creatures cannot exceed his mercy and long-suffering. His mercy endures forever, and his promises never fail.

4. The Influence of Example
Ashfield, December 30, 1823

To Zilpah Grant

By the last mail I received your letter. I am glad you have decided affirmatively respecting Derry. The new plan of that school will require some peculiar qualifications in those who are to take charge of it. I believe those qualifications, at least, are possessed by yourself in such a degree as will enable you, in the most important points, eminently to excel.

The more I think of your plan, the more I approve it. I cannot but hope that that academy will yet be the means of much good. Should the plan succeed, the influence of example would be something. Public opinion in favor of systematic female education needs support. Every proof that system is practicable, would add its weight in the scale.

Respecting myself, though the proposal did not strike my mind unfavorably at first, yet the more I think of it, the more I am inclined to decide affirmatively. The obstacles have seemed gradually to diminish, and the favorable circumstances rather to brighten by examination. In relation to my own *personal situation*, the prospect, since you first wrote me, has appeared sufficiently pleasant; indeed, I fear too pleasant. I tremble more than if the path appeared more rugged. The desire you have expressed that I should engage with you has been one means of inclining me to believe that my field of labor is with you. It did, however, lead me to much self-scrutiny. Expect not too much from me, I beseech you. I fear you will be disappointed. I have a strange, rebellious, wicked heart. When shall I be wholly devoted to God? I cannot trust myself. I find my best promises violated, my best resolutions broken. The half cannot be told.

5. Whispering
Londonderry, July 2, 1824

To Hannah White

The regulations of this school are such as to enable us to have much system and order. This regular system is calculated to give our pupils faithful, attentive habits. They feel that their course is marked out, and generally that whatever is assigned them must be accomplished. Composition, you know, is one of the most trying exercises. But even in this we have not had an instance yet in which any young lady has been in the least delinquent. In some respects, perhaps, this school meets our wishes more fully than any I have seen. I might mention particulars; but the beginning of all little evils in a school is whispering. Miss G. has adopted a plan to prevent this, which has been very successful. After leading her pupils to feel the importance of being truthful, and stating facts as they are, she requires each to bring in a weekly ticket with her name attached, stating whether she has, or has not, made any communication in school during the week, either by whispering, or by writing, or in any other way equally suited to divert the attention. We have some young ladies who have not made a communication of this kind since the commencement of our school; and probably none who have not passed some weeks without a failure on this point. Miss Grant, of course, would not adopt this plan unless the scholars evinced a conscience both enlightened and lively as to the distinction between truth and falsehood.

The prospects of this school at present are very promising. The trustees take a deep interest in its prosperity. They place great confidence in the principal, and are ready to do every thing she requests. The location here not being favorable for a winter school, our academy is open only thirty weeks in a year; Miss G. devoting the winter, however, as well as the summer, to the interests of the institution. I shall spend my vacation with Rev. Mr. C. He is at length united to his beloved P. She appears to be just such a wife as he needs; uniformly cheerful, polite, and attentive to all. They passed one night with me on their marriage tour; and when he led in prayer in the family, his voice and manner were just as formerly. You can imagine how much it recalled past scenes in Ashfield Academy.

6. Family Now Scattered
Londonderry, July 7, 1824

To Freelove Lyon

Three weeks from today our vacation commences, and then I shall probably think much of home. Although I am pleasantly situated, and have no more cares and little daily trials than I should expect, yet it would be pleasant to spend an hour with one of my dear sisters, to whom I could tell all my heart. The fact that no two of our family, unless it be our brother and our sister Rosina, are spending this summer together, awakens emotions peculiar and rather gloomy. Ever since I heard of brother Moore's death, but more particularly for two days past, I have thought much of my brother and sisters. I have seemed to review twenty years in relation to ourselves. Change and revolution, uncertainty and disappointment, decay and death, are stamped on every object. I see this family, that about twenty years ago were prattling children, united and happy in the arms of their fond parents, now scattered over four different states of the Union, and some of them seven hundred miles apart. I see the eldest, in whom we all placed confidence as a counsellor and friend, and to whom we are in some degree indebted, separated from her friends, carried by Providence into the lonely wilderness, there to pass her days almost alone and unpitied, where no one of us can give her a cheerful smile or a word of consolation. I well remember how much animation and energy she possessed, when she used to spend her days in teaching. But over her head age has crept apace; ill health has worn down her spirits; and, to use her own language, "sickness and trials have followed, till now this terrible blow is struck." Where now are her buoyant spirits? Where her resolution?

I see another sister, too, passing through different scenes, and now called to consign her oldest child to the silent tomb... You wrote in somewhat of a gloomy strain, but I hope it was only momentary. You will do well to endeavor to gain the confidence of your pupils, and to make them see the reasons of your requirements. Do not say too much to them at one time. I think it best to devote some attention to their behavior, even if they do not study so much. If your older pupils should be disposed to trouble you, perhaps it may be beneficial to converse with each one out of school, and entirely alone. By taking such a method occasionally, you may operate upon their feelings, and lead them to a right determination when you otherwise could not. The good influence of every well-behaved pupil in school is great. Endeavor to lead them *always* to speak the truth, and then let them know that you depend on their word. If they *are* truthful, and have enlightened consciences, so that you can depend on their stating facts as they are, I would recommend to you a plan to prevent whispering...

If you require it, you must see it faithfully performed; otherwise it will have a very bad influence on your school. If you adopt this plan, you would do well to begin at first individually with a few of the oldest.

Let me hear not only from yourself, but also from my other friends. Separation does not lessen the interest I take in their welfare. When I think of the older members of our family, I also involuntarily think of their children. I have the same kind of interest in their prosperity that I have ever had for that of their parents. Sometimes I feel that it would be a privilege to live, if I could only render myself useful to the children of my brother and sisters.

7. Our Course is Slower
Londonderry, September 26, 1824

To Amanda White

I am now engaged in teaching in the Adams Female Academy, Londonderry, N. H. This school commenced its operations in the spring. The plan may be called *Emersonian*, though considerably altered to meet our particular purpose. The care of the school is committed to Miss Grant. You know she is well fitted to guide, and I think she has improved very much since you knew her. She spent about six weeks here last winter, making arrangements with reference to the school. This was a very favorable circumstance. In every part of the plan I can see her design; consequently it is much more easily executed. Although, as you know, I have the highest opinion of the utility of Mr. Emerson's plan for young ladies of adult age, yet I never considered it fitted to carry a young lady through her whole course of school education; I mean, as conducted when we were at Byfield. It supposed too much previous improvement. The course was too rapid for ordinary minds, and also for such as were young, or but little improved. We have more classes, our course is slower, and the increased number of teachers will enable us to execute our plans thoroughly. We have three regular classes, denominated senior, middle, and junior. Certain defined qualifications are necessary to enter each of these classes. Members of the senior and middle classes can attend a course of drawing and painting if they choose. We have also as many preparatory classes as circumstances require. The young ladies are examined, and are placed where it is thought they will improve the most. They are classed, not at all according to the number of books they have studied, but according to the real knowledge they are found to possess. We have but very few under fifteen years of age who can enter the regular classes. We have this summer about sixty pupils, and we have sufficient employment. You know that Mr. E. attended to many little things in his school, which were not common in schools generally. Some, however, he was able only to recommend, and leave for the young ladies to accomplish, or not, as they thought proper. The design of Miss G. is to have every thing that is proposed for immediate attention pursued until it is accomplished; and the teachers see that it is done. This requires care and exertion. It is not a small task to instruct our young ladies in writing. Pen-making and the manner of holding the pen, I think, require one half the exertion in this department. Each is required to write with her own pen, and no one is allowed to request a pen to be made for her by any other young lady without permission. This we find not difficult. Though I should not enter into a particular detail, yet I believe you will think I have something to do. My friends, however, receive letters from me rather more frequently than when I was at Byfield; but I suppose they will even now complain.

In several branches we use a method in some degree new, commenced in Mr. Emerson's school two years since, and by him termed the *topic system*. Subjects are selected from the lesson, which are first to be simply defined; and then more or less, or all, that the book contains, is to be learned and recited.

Before coming to this place, Miss G. had tried the experiment, term after term, in her own private school, of having young ladies give daily attention to lessons from the Bible. She has great confidence in the study of this book for intellectual discipline, as well as for the guidance and control of the heart. Before she engaged to take charge of this academy, she gained the consent of the executive committee, that, in accordance with a deeply cherished purpose, she should feel at liberty to employ one seventh part of the intellectual energies of her pupils upon what is contained in this store-house of knowledge. While examining the classes at the commencement of the school, all were occupied in the daily study and recitation of Scripture history. Every week of the term, each pupil is expected to apply her mind closely, two hours or more, to the Scripture lesson given out early in the week, and recited the next Monday morning. This study has excited more deep and universal interest than any other. Some now feel the force of the truths they are learning; and many, I trust, will eventually be made wise unto salvation.

In gaining a knowledge of the Scriptures, a variety of methods is useful. While I was pursuing the study on the topic system, I thought it might be profitable to older members of Sabbath schools, and I will annex a few of the topics from Genesis. Creation; the Sabbath; garden of Eden; tree of knowledge of good and evil; tree of life; the serpent; disobedience of our first parents; expulsion of our first parents from the garden of Eden; Adam; Eve; sacrifices; Cain; Abel; Enoch; wickedness of man; the flood; Noah's ark; the rainbow; Noah; Babel.

8. Anxiety
Buckland, February 21, 1825

To Betsy Chickering

My school here consists of twenty-five young ladies. After so large a number had been admitted, I had some anxiety respecting it. I feared that I might attempt more uniformity about books, than, considering the circumstances, would be expedient. I expected, also, a cold winter, and my design was to have the scholars study in school. And as I possess not much natural dignity, I could foresee my scholars crowding around the fire, some whispering, some idle, &c. I remembered that, several years ago, I had a school of young ladies in this town, in which there was more whispering than in all the schools in which I have been engaged for the last three or four years. The fault then was mine, and I knew not but that the effects might be felt even now.

I kept my school occupied on general subjects at first, and now I have about as much uniformity in books as we had at L. In teaching, I am constantly wishing for your or Miss G.'s advice. Indeed, I sometimes need your assistance more than words can express.

At the commencement, I thought it best to assume as much artificial dignity as possible; so, to begin, I borrowed Miss Grant's plan to prevent whispering. All, with one exception, strictly complied; and that was one of the first young ladies in age and improvement. It appeared altogether probable that the termination of this affair would be a matter of considerable importance in relation to her, her father's family, and perhaps to the school generally. But after I had passed a few almost sleepless nights about it, a kind Providence directed the result in a manner which seemed the best calculated to promote the interests of the school; for at length she came cheerfully into the arrangement.

A circumstance, in relation to the first set of compositions, was somewhat trying. One pupil refused entirely to write; but I was assisted in leading her to comply with the requirement. Some other things I *could* mention. Suffice it to say, that I have had just enough of such things to give me continual anxiety; but God, in his providence, has been very kind to me. Many events have terminated as I desired, when it seemed not at all in my power to control them. Perhaps I have generally been able to accomplish about what I have undertaken. My school, in many respects, is very pleasant. I have but two or three pupils under sixteen years of age. With the exception of two or three, they are very studious. On the whole, I think it the best school I ever had; the best, because the most profitable to its members; I do not mean the best in which I have been engaged. I have an opportunity this winter to see the value of what I gained at Derry.

I hope, my dear sister, you live near your Savior, while I am far from him, and walk on in darkness. I hope you enjoy the light of his countenance, and rejoice in the God of your salvation. I do not think it favorable to piety to have so much anxiety as I have had this winter; but I would not attribute my coldness to any outward circumstances; I would rather fear that I have never known the love of the Lord Jesus Christ.

9. Chemistry
April 1, 1825

To Zilpah Grant

I wrote to Professor E., stating my general success and difficulties in experiments in chemistry, last summer. He returned an answer, generously inviting me to his house, and saying that I should do well to come to Troy, even if I could stay only two or three weeks, as he could tell me many things during that time which would be useful to me. At first, I thought it would be altogether impracticable. I had just closed my school, and wished to spend some time with my friends; but I remembered well the difficulties attending some of my experiments last summer, and thought it possible that further instruction might aid me sufficiently to compensate for the fatigue and the expense of the journey. I thought my personal gratification seemed to require that I should stay with my friends, but my duty to the school at Derry might require that I should leave them, not to see them again until next fall. At length, after suffering some trials in my feelings on this subject, I decided in the affirmative; and accordingly I packed up all, as soon as possible, and arrived here this morning.

I shall attend what lectures are given to the Rensselaer school, while I am here,—principally in chemistry and natural philosophy. I shall endeavor to review the most difficult and most important principles of chemistry, in order to avail myself of the opportunity to gain the information which I need. I do not intend to study hard.

10. When I Think of My Mother
September 25, 1825

To Her Mother

I have thought much more of you than usual, for a week or two past. Although my situation is necessarily rather different from what it was in childhood, yet you will not suppose that on this account I love my friends less. I sincerely desire that I may ever be saved from neglecting my early friends, especially my mother, to whom I am more indebted than to all others, except my Maker. When I think of my mother, I think of one who ardently and unceasingly desires my temporal and spiritual welfare; one to whom I owe much that I can never repay; one who never forgets me, and never forgets that I have an immortal soul; one the benefit of whose prayers I have long enjoyed, and whose desires, I trust, are now every day ascending to the throne of mercy in my behalf.

I have thought considerably this day of the importance of being prepared to do the will of my heavenly Parent. What is more desirable than to have the privilege of doing those things which are well pleasing to God; to have such a frame of mind, that the habitual and uniform desire of the heart shall be, 'Lord, what wilt thou have me to do?' But I find a strange propensity to desire ardently those things which would seem to be a peculiar gratification to myself. I *would* desire to have such a frame of mind that I might be ever ready to say, "Not my will, but thine, be done." I would not desire any thing that would not be for the glory of God, and in accordance with the will of my Savior. Sometimes I almost *feel* that I am not my own, but I find my heart repeatedly desiring those things from which I had almost supposed it was forever separated.

It seems as if you could not be so anxious to receive letters from me as I am to hear from my friends. Although my situation is far from being unpleasant, yet there is a kind of loneliness which is ever ready to oppress my spirits. You will remember, however, that we have now our cold, equinoctial storm. When this is over, much of the present gloom will be dispersed, and all our spirits will be more cheerful.

11. Unaccomplished Labor Accumulating on My Hands
Buckland, December 26, 1825

To Zilpah Grant

My school is larger than I expected, having about fifty scholars....

My heart is pained to see so much important unaccomplished labor accumulating on my hands, and I have engaged an assistant.

At present, there is a little more than usual religious attention in this town. The friends of Zion are hoping that the Lord is about to visit us. This circumstance produces in my mind some hopes and some fears. It adds, if possible, to my responsibility. The thought that some, who were beginning to think about their eternal interests, may here become so much absorbed in their studies, so much interested in the business of the school, as to exclude God from their hearts, is truly painful. I hope I may not be the instrument of hardening the hearts of those whom I tenderly love. My pupils appear very attentive to religious truth. Some are thoughtful, though I have no evidence that any are particularly serious, except those who profess to love the Savior. Two or three of the latter appear very well. That heart must be insensible, which could not feel on observing the general attention manifest when a sermon is reviewed, a Bible lesson recited, or any religious subject brought forward. Perhaps the Lord may visit us with his grace. In him is all our hope.

For a long time, I have at intervals been anxious about my own state of mind. I have felt that, if I were ardently attached to the Savior, my desires to honor him would be more uniform and uninterrupted. I have hoped that the Lord would direct to means which would effectually move my soul, so that I could no longer sleep when reflecting on the cause of our dear Redeemer. I have thought that possibly Providence had brought me to this place for good, that this season might be profitable to my soul. But let me not depend on any means; let me depend on nothing short of God. I know, my dear friend, that you will pray for me. Pray that I may be altogether devoted to the Savior, that I may ever do his will, ever honor his name.

Fourteen of my scholars board in the family with me. Before I came here, and for the first week after, I had much anxiety about the arrangements for these young ladies. We have finally become settled, so that every thing seems to go on well. The members of the school in the family have a table by themselves. As I was well aware that it would require more than an ordinary share of dignity to prevent too much, if not improper, conversation at meals, I thought it the safest to introduce some entertaining exercise. This requires an effort, on my part, which I had scarcely realized. But I find it pleasant indeed. I frequently think, How *could* Miss G. take care of so many last summer? But I recollect hearing you say that your first schools were as much your all, as your one hundred pupils at Derry.

My spirits have been unusually uniform for four weeks. I do no recollect an hour of depression. I consider this a blessing for which I ought to be thankful.

12. Special Influence of the Holy Spirit
Buckland, February 20, 1826

To Amanda White Ferry

I can scarcely believe I have written you so seldom since you have been away. The truth is, for two years past, my time has been so constantly occupied that I now understand what you mean, when you say that it is almost necessary to blind the eyes and harden the feelings against present and urgent calls, and calmly sit down to write letters of friendship. Besides, every thing which I could write, you will receive from other sources.

Your sister H. assists me, and we have a pleasant school of about fifty members. I enjoy so much that I sometimes almost fear lest I may have all my good things in this life. We have eleven in our school professedly pious, and some of them appear very well. Some others are particularly attentive to religious truth.

There is more religious attention in this town at present than usual. I have had a faint hope, through the winter, that this town and my school might be visited by the special influence of the Holy Spirit.

13. Independence
Londonderry, July 4, 1826

To Freelove Lyon

This day, you will recollect, completes half a century since the Declaration of our Independence. How interesting must be the reflections of those few who can remember that eventful day! And to every one, the events in our history must be an exciting theme. Who, on the face of the earth, fifty years ago, could have anticipated such results? It is true that Washington, and almost all Americans who lived in the days of Washington, hoped for independence. But did they look forward to this time, and anticipate such a nation as this? Must not all believe that promotion cometh neither from the east, nor from the west, nor from the south; but God is the judge; he putteth down one, and setteth up another? Must not all exclaim, this is the finger of God? We wonder why we are made to differ from others. Perhaps that same Being, that could with a glance look through the course of the Israelitish nation, from the selling of Joseph to the coming of the Messiah, has designs of mercy on all the nations of the earth, through the unparalleled blessings which he has bestowed on this great people. And have not his dealings with our beloved country some connection with the causes which will bring forward that happy day, to which all who love the Lord Jesus Christ are looking with earnest prayer?

Considerable attention has been devoted to the celebration of the anniversary in this place; consequently we have not been able to continue the usual exercises of the school. We have had some anxiety for our young ladies, as the scenes of the day would, of course, be rather exhilarating. Perhaps you will wonder why there should be this anxiety. I will tell you, my sister. We believe the Holy Spirit is now with us by his special operations. It is now a very critical period. I think the school is in such a state as ours was last winter, about three weeks before its close. Seven or eight give more or less evidence of a change of heart. A few at the present time are deeply affected. Several others are in some degree solicitous, and perhaps nearly half the school occasionally inquire with interest what these things mean. This school is very different from our school last winter. We have about ninety pupils, of a great variety of character. A large number, we have no doubt, are yet thoughtless. Throughout the school, however, there is a propriety of conduct, and an interest in Scripture recitations; and when I look on their state, it seems as if the fields were white already to the harvest.

14. We May Love our Friends Very Ardently
Derry, August 22, 1827

To Freelove Lyon

I love Miss G.'s society more than ever, and I believe we may love our friends very ardently. And love them according to the principles and spirit of the gospel. I also think we may love them in a manner displeasing in the sight of God. May I love in that manner which God will approve. I have been interested in the lovely and perfect example of Jesus Christ. Though he loved all his own, as the world loveth not, and though he laid down his life for his enemies, yet, as a man, we have reason to think he acknowledged some as his particular friends. It is said, emphatically, that Jesus loved Martha, and her sister, and Lazarus; and among the twelve was found that disciple whom Jesus loved.

My health is very good. I believe I have had more vigor of body and mind than usual, this summer.

15. Sympathize With You in Your Trials
Ashfield, December 10, 1827

To Zilpah Grant

I ought to be humbled in view of my own ignorance, and to be led to depend more entirely on God. I know that I have been earthly and grovelling in my desires, that I have been far from the fountain of life, and that I have been inclined to trust the creature more than the Creator. Since I received your letter, I have deeply felt that I needed a heart conformed to the will of God, that I should place my affections on things above, and not on things on the earth; and I believe that my distance from the fountain of all consolation does not seem quite so great.

If I should try to tell you how much I sympathize with you in your trials, how my heart bleeds when I think of you, and how I want to be with you, and share in your daily sorrows and joys, the attempt would be altogether in vain. I know I can do nothing but commit you to God. May I have a heart to do this daily. May I remember you as Paul did the Romans, (Rom. i. 9.)

It is a sweet relief to my mind that you have a Father in heaven, and I do believe that all things will work together for your good, though the way in which this is to be effected may seem to us very undesirable. You may not be saved from trials, but I do believe you will be supported under them; and, after all, I trust you will find more enjoyment even in the present life than the worldling, who has no such support…

When you supplicate the throne of mercy in my behalf, pray that I may love my dearest friends according to the spirit and precepts of the gospel; that I may so regard and improve my most precious blessings, that it shall not be necessary to take them from me, and that I may be like Him who, when on earth, was holy, harmless, and undefiled. You know I am prone to be earthly, and that I need the grace of God.

16. Examine My Past Life
Ashfield, January 6, 1828

To Zilpah Grant

For some time I have been endeavoring to examine my past life. The review is sad and mournful. It is now the twelfth year since the thought first entered my mind—Can these be the feelings of an unregenerate heart? I remember the moment as well as if it were but yesterday; but since then there has been a period of clouds and thick darkness. What an immense loss I must suffer through life, on account of the misimprovement of so long a period of my existence! I humbly hope I shall finally be saved, although as by fire; but I have no reason to expect ever in this world all that spiritual enjoyment with which I might have been favored, if all these years had witnessed a regular advance in a life of faith and piety. Neither can I expect that satisfaction and success in laboring in the cause of the Savior which I might enjoy, if I had received that preparation which can be gained by no means but by a long course of active, faithful obedience. May I be enabled to improve the precious moments as they fly, realizing that when they are gone they can never be redeemed.

It seems to me more and more important that the professed followers of the Lamb should commence their Christian course, guided by the pure and perfect standard of truth. Is it not too true that many take their standard from those around them, and on that account live a life which leads others justly to inquire, "What do ye more than others?" During all these years, I know not how many, just commencing a life of godliness, may have received an impression from me which will be felt all their lives. May I, in this, be saved from blood-guiltiness. But I tremble lest even this winter should bear witness against me. You know that I frequently feel that I can do little or nothing to aid Christians in a life of holiness. In this respect, my responsibility is greater than ever before; indeed, it is so great, that I know not what to do. Almost half of my pupils have more or less hope that they are the friends of the Redeemer. Several have indulged this hope but a few months; in some it is like the faint glimmering of a distant taper. But few can be considered established Christians; and of scarcely any have I much evidence that they possess deep feeling and a lively faith. Here we are; what shall we do? What can we do? The influence of these on each other, the influence from absorbing studies, and that which I may exert, may produce an impression which shall affect their whole lives. These precious souls have been sent here by the providence of God; but what to do I know not. I am weaker than weakness itself, and my wisdom is altogether folly. May I be more and more sensible of the preciousness of the direction, "If any of you lack wisdom, let him ask of God."

17. The Privilege of Laboring
Ashfield, February 12, 1828

To Zilpah Grant

I feel that there is one way, and only one, in which I can guard against this easily besetting sin, and that is, to seek daily the presence of Him who can turn the hearts of all as the rivers of water are turned. I have been too much inclined to seek to direct my own path. May I be saved from this. The Lord in great mercy has given me a field of labor; so that for several years I have not doubted about the path of duty. The privilege of laboring is to me more and more precious. I would not choose the spot. I would not choose the circumstances. To be able to do something, is a privilege of which I am altogether unworthy. Should I be laid aside, as a useless servant, it would be just. I would humbly seek that I may be permitted to labor faithfully and successfully, that I may be saved from those temptations which my feeble heart cannot withstand, and that I may be blessed with whatever may be desirable for health of body and health of mind, and for general usefulness. For little else of this world do I feel at present that I ought to ask. May I be the Lord's, spirit, and soul, and body.

18.
I am not Indifferent to Enjoyments
Ashfield, April 3, 1828

To Zilpah Grant

I am not indifferent to enjoyments. Your society seems to me a greater blessing than ever before. If I should enjoy it, may my heart be filled with gratitude to God; if, in his providence, he should deprive me of this, in a greater or less degree, may I never complain *in my heart* of Him who does all things well. The will of the Lord be done. My own strength is weakness. I am a sinner, a great sinner. I can have no hope but in the infinite mercy of God. Sometimes I do hope I depend on him. But O, my wicked heart! I dare not trust it. Still the Lord can give me pardoning mercy; he can give me strength; he can give me submission to his will, and a faithful, obedient heart. It may be he will do it. My daily desire for myself is, that I may know and do the will of God; that I may live by faith; that I may have a calm and quiet mind; that I may be a help to you; that I may be useful in your school; and that, in some way or other, I may be permitted to do something for the salvation of souls. I know I am remembered in your prayers.

19. Afflictions in this World
November 28, 1828

To Zilpah Grant

It seems to me more and more that we must expect afflictions in this world; but I think it appears to me more and more, too, that they are no cause for despondency. I feel that it is safe trusting in God, that he is a sure rock, which can never be removed. I believe that the blessings of this life are very great, and will continue to be so; and that trials are trials under all circumstances. But I think I can faintly see that there is a foundation for support, when this world is not made all in all.

With the exception of sister Putnam's family, I find my friends well. The hand of affliction is now pressing sorely on that family. May I, and my family friends, be enabled to place our confidence in God, and cheerfully acquiesce in his government. I believe I mentioned to you that my sister and her husband were both sick. At first, her sickness appeared to be principally debility, produced by care and anxiety for her husband. But it resulted in a complication of diseases, which were baffled by the skill of physicians. About the time I first heard she was sick, she had so far recovered as to leave her room. It was not long, however, before she became worse again. Her head was very much diseased, and at times her suffering was great. Soon her mind, at intervals, appeared to be affected; still it was hoped it would be nothing permanent. But all hope has failed; the result has been evident derangement, and by the advice of physicians and friends, she has been separated from her husband and children, and removed to the Insane Hospital at Hartford. She knew she was deranged, and was very urgent indeed to go to the hospital. Brother Putnam was not able to accompany his wife. Since she left, he has been much more unwell, and is at this time in a critical state. His physician tells me, that he fears more the loss of his limbs, than an *immediate* loss of life. Thus five little children, the oldest only in the eighth year of her age, are left, like orphans, while their father and mother are living.

My sickness, and all its attendant consequences, seem to me a small trial, compared with what I am now called to experience on account of my sister's family.

20. Care of the Family
Buckland, February 2, 1829

To Zilpah Grant

Among other cares, I am devoting many thoughts and some attention to sister Putnam's family. They are a little more than a mile from me. The whole care of the family, for several months, has rested on my youngest sister. I have been to see them often, and have known so much of their general concerns as to be able to consult with and advise sister F. I have felt it to be a great privilege that it was in my power to administer to the comfort of that afflicted, and to me very dear, family. Besides this, I have written to Hartford, almost or quite every week since my arrival in B.; but I shall have no more of this to do now, as my sister returned last week. She wishes very much to see me often, and says she does not mean to place much confidence in her own judgment at present. I have been to see her twice, and shall probably visit her at least once a week through the winter. Her mind is still weak, and in some respects she appears not quite the same as formerly; but, on the whole, she is to me exceedingly interesting. Her calmness, self-government, and settled resolution to go forward in the path of duty, under her present weakness of body and mind, and under all her complicated trials, considering her natural ardor of feeling, give me a very important lesson. It is a question yet to be settled whether sister, with her health, and under her circumstances, can keep her children together. I am exceedingly anxious that they should not be separated. There is no probability that they could be placed where their discipline, the formation of their minds and habits, and the regulation of their dispositions, could be nearly so favorable as under her care, if she regains the use of her mind. Now, my dear friend, I want your advice. If I should see that, by furnishing them yearly with what I am able to spare from my earnings, it would enable sister to keep her family together, would it not be a good time to cast my bread upon the waters?...

You remember that, after my sickness last summer, my hair came off by handfuls. For several weeks past, I have not lost any, so that I hope I shall continue to have enough to support my combs. For a while my head was very cold; but since I began to wear a turban, it has been quite comfortable...

I hope you will be enabled to do as much this winter to correct the erroneous opinions of your teachers about schools, if they have any, as you have done to correct mine from year to year...

Notwithstanding these sober hours, life seems to me more and more a blessing, on account of its labors, and not as a period of rest...

For two or three weeks, I have been rather encouraged about the spiritual state of our school; but appearances this week are less favorable. Thus we go on between hope and fear. Do pray for us...

I have seventy-four pupils, and Miss L. B. assists me this winter.

21. I Would Have All Contented
Ipswich, September 21, 1829

To Her Mother

I have been considering, or rather reconsidering, the subject of my winter labors. I am more inclined to think that I ought to continue them here through the winter. My dear mother, what do you think about it? At first, it seems more like parting with my family friends, than the present arrangement. But, at second view, the subject appears rather differently. It is true that I have not generally favored visiting so much as to approve of the feelings and conduct of some, who seem to think that every thing *must* bend to this one object; that, however much self-denial they might practise in relation to others, if it is a mother or sister, every other object must yield. I would have all contented, wherever Providence may place them, whether or not they may be favored with the society of father or mother, brother or sister. And if duty should call, I would endeavor to be contented, though years should pass without my beholding the face of one near relative. With my present prospects, I have no need to anticipate this trial. By visiting my native place once a year, disencumbered of school affairs, I might in a few weeks enjoy quite as much of my friends as I now can....

The religious state of our school is interesting, and has been so for several weeks. The Spirit of God is evidently among us, operating on the hearts of our dear pupils. The work is silent and gradual, but the effects are certain; and that it is the work of God there can be no doubt. Eight or nine have indulged hope that they have found the Savior, and the state of many others is very encouraging. So far the work has been slow; but the way seems all prepared by the Holy Spirit for richer and more abundant displays of mercy. It does appear that the fields are white already to the harvest. The blessing seems just ready to descend upon us. If there is no Achan in the camp, if there is no stumbling block in the way, if there is not a manifest and decided fault on the part of Christians, we shall probably see greater things than these...Perhaps the Lord may put it into the heart of my dear mother to pray for these souls that prayer of faith, which God will hear in heaven, his holy dwelling-place, and answer on earth. The school is very attentive to general instruction on the subject of religion, but still there are many who think little or nothing on these things, and care as little as they think. Give my love to your family, especially to Mary. When I last parted with her, I supposed ere this she would probably be called to know the realities of eternity. May the Lord bless her.

22. My Labors are Indeed Abundant
Buckland, January 1, 1830
To Zilpah Grant

In dwelling on Matt. vi. 25, 26, "Take no thought," &c., in school, yesterday morning, I endeavored to point out that anxiety which is there prohibited. While I was speaking, I felt that I was condemning myself. I endeavor daily to avoid excessive emotions on any subject, but in no case do I find so much difficulty as in this.

Our young ladies are deeply engaged in study; but I fear about our spiritual state. With the exception of two or three cases, we have remained just about the same for three weeks.

My labors are indeed abundant, my cares almost overwhelming, and they continue to increase. I devote more attention to individuals than formerly. My pupils come to me with more freedom and more frequency. This I encourage. I consider it an important way of doing good, especially as this is my last winter with them. It is necessary to make such arrangements, that the school is never all together except when I am with them. It is always convenient to find some one whom I want to see, or some one who wants to see me; so that I have not a single half hour on which I can depend, from eight in the morning till nine in the evening. You will say that I need more aid, and I am happy to relieve your mind by informing you that the health of Miss W. is so far restored that I have engaged her for the remainder of the winter.

It is late, and I have written this while half asleep in body; but my heart has been awake.

23. The Word 'Thinking'
Buckland, January 20, 1830

To Zilpah Grant

I want a few of your ideas on the fifth and sixth chapters of Upham's Philosophy very much, especially on the distinction between ideas of sensation and reflection, or those of internal and external origin. How much is to be included in the word *thinking*? (Page 85, sect. 62.) Is it not used in a vague sense? What is your opinion about our having two ideas in the mind at the same time?

24. That Blessed Home
Ipswich, October 24, 1831

To Zilpah Grant

Rev. Joseph Emerson was in school this morning...I rejoice to have him take up the business of lecturing to popular assemblies. His spirit is so pure and so exalted, that, whatever may be his subject, I think he cannot fail to do something to purify the hearts of others, to raise the grovelling mind, and expand the contracted soul, though he may say some things which may be considered extravagant. O for a multitude of such souls as his! Could they be scattered all over the earth, this polluted and wretched world must soon become changed. The more I see of the rest of the world, the more I admire, the more I love such a spirit as his. What a delightful place will heaven be! Thanks be to God, that "nothing shall enter there that defileth or maketh a lie"! Shall we, my dear sister, after passing through this wicked world, and having been so severely tried with our own evil hearts,—shall we, being washed and made white in the blood of the Lamb, be permitted, through rich, free, and wonderful grace, to sit down in that holy place, where there shall be no more pollution, no more pride, no more selfishness, no more disobedience to God; where we shall be no more distressed with our own sin, no more pained with the sins of others? May you, my dearest friend, be ripening more and more, continually, for that blessed home.

25. State of Calm
Ashfield, November 22, 1831

To Zilpah Grant

It is wonderful to me how the mind, after a state of doubt and difficulty, from which it seemed impossible to be extricated, can, without any new light, or new evidence, settle down into a state of calm and quiet decision.

26. Vocal Music
Ipswich, January 29, 1832

To Zilpah Grant

I am almost a stranger to lively faith and sensible communion with spiritual things. Subjects of great anxiety, I believe, I generally delight to commit to God; and I seem to have a reliance on him which casteth out fear. But most of these subjects are more or less connected with the world. In view of invisible and divine realities, my mind is darkened, my perceptions feeble, my heart cold and stupid. It seems as if such a low, grovelling worm of the dust could never be fitted for heaven. With men it is impossible, but with God all things are possible.

Ever since vocal music was introduced into our seminary, I have had an increasing sense of its great practical importance. By our influence, and the influence of our pupils on this subject, probably hundreds may be benefited for a succession of generations. Those who have been able to sing from childhood, do not know by experience the feelings which *some* have who cannot sing. When passing near the music-room last summer, and thinking that a large part of the choir, probably, had no more of a natural voice than myself, I found it necessary to restrain, with firm determination, a rising murmur. I have sometimes felt, that I would have given six months of my time, when I was under twenty, and defrayed my expenses, difficult as it was to find time or money, could I have enjoyed the privileges for learning vocal music that some of our pupils enjoy.

27. The Most Suitable Location
Ipswich, February 4, 1832

To Edward Hitchcock

Knowing that you are interested to learn any thing about the proposed plan for a permanent female seminary, which has been agitated by some of its friends for more than a year, I make no apology for this communication. The friends of this object, I think, are beginning to look upon it in a more extended view, and are beginning to consider it an important object, as connected with the prosperity and advancement of female education in general, and not simply as a *very good* thing to promote Miss Grant's and Miss Lyon's school, and facilitate their usefulness. These local, private, and personal views, I think, should be far removed from this object. Could I but be permitted to labor in the portico, and spend my days in clearing the ground for that which is destined to continue, and to exert an extensive and salutary influence on female education, and on religion, from generation to generation, it would be the height of my ambition. What permanent female seminaries are now in existence? What one in New England, of a high character, is necessarily, from its plan, destined to outlive its present teachers? Ought this so to be? Are not a few permanent female seminaries needed? —say one or two in a state? Could there be a few of this character, designed exclusively for older young ladies preparing to teach, and soon to go forth and exert an influence in a variety of ways on the cause of education and religion, —a place of resort, where those from different parts of the country, designing to spend their lives in doing good, might come together, together receive instruction, form and mature their plans, and exert over each other's views and feelings an extensive and powerful influence,—would not great good result? Might not such seminaries have an extensive influence in removing that false mantle of charity, which has been thrown over a great many *little* schools, and great ones, too, which have, to a great extent, had the moulding of the female character, but which have not been what they should be?

The prospect now is, that this subject will be presented to the public in some form or other. The attempt may be fruitless. The institution is to be entirely new, not having any connection with that which is the present field of our labors. To give the public confidence, it has been considered very important to obtain an able board of trustees. This business has been on hand several months. It is now settled. Seven have been appointed as trustees elect, and have accepted, and, if the plan should go forward, will obtain an act of incorporation, and will become the trustees. They are the following: Hon. William Reed, Marblehead; Rev. Dr. Fay, Charlestown; Professor Emerson, Andover; Hon. Rufus Choate, Salem; George W. Heard, Esq., and William Heard, of this town. They have had one meeting, and have appointed a committee of inquiry.

It is generally understood that the location should be in Ipswich, but it is not absolutely necessary. Some of the trustees, I believe, consider it somewhat doubtful whether this is the best location, and, if it is not, will be disposed to make inquiry about other places. Not much has been said about it, however. Feeling that a genial soil would be of vast importance in this first attempt, I have been exceedingly desirous that the locations on Connecticut River should receive at least a little attention, before it is finally settled in Essex county. It is not best that I should say much about it; but these trustees are capable of looking at facts as they are, if their attention should be directed to the subject. The location is to be decided before the object is presented to the public, probably at the next meeting of the trustees. My only desire is, that the state of feeling in your vicinity should be tested, and the facts laid before the trustees. I do not know that there is any way by which it could be done, but I thought it barely possible that some benevolent individuals might devise some plan. I write these things to you merely because I can do nothing more than to mention it to some of my friends in that vicinity. It would not be well that the subject of this communication should be known generally. There is no objection to your mentioning it to individuals, if you should think it desirable. One reason why I feel desirous that your part of the state should be the proposed location is, that I think it might affect the public in general more favorably, and there would be a greater prospect of success. If you think it a vain thought, a foolish and impracticable scheme, my only request is, that you would commit this sheet to the flames, and bury the whole in oblivion.

It is true that this plan was started in view of Ipswich, and, of course, the trustees were chosen from this vicinity, and there is no hope that it could be transferred, unless it should be obvious that it will meet with more success and more encouragement from the public by being located in that part of the state. It is rather probable that an attempt will be made in Ipswich, and perhaps in the vicinity, to ascertain what amount can be raised for the object. If an attempt could be made at the same time in the valley of the Connecticut, the object being fully understood, it seems to me somewhat probable that the west would so far exceed the east, that it would be very manifest that that was the most suitable location. In such a case, it would be very important that a part of the trustees should be from that vicinity. This board can make changes in their own body, such as they shall deem expedient; and if they shall decide that the public will not accept of Essex county as a location, such a course will probably be taken. Besides, twenty-five gentlemen, in different parts of New England, are appointed as a board of visitors, if the plan should go into operation.

If any thing should be attempted on this subject in your part of the state, would it not be inexpedient to name any definite location, nearer than to say, a location in Massachusetts, on or near the Connecticut River? Doubtless Amherst or Northampton would be the place. Each would have its peculiar advantages, and I am by no means sure which would be the most favorable.

Nothing can be done on a subject like this, without the attention of a few benevolent individuals, whose time and talents are exceedingly precious, and whose hands are already full of other great and important concerns. None but such men could do the work. None but such could excite an interest on this hitherto neglected subject. None but such could carry it forward. None but such could give any hope of success.

If any thing should hereafter be done on this subject, would it not be well that the *leading friends* should not all be from Amherst or Northampton? If it should be thought best to make any inquiries on the subject, perhaps you would think it well that some benevolent gentleman, yourself or some other one, should correspond with some gentleman of this board. Some members have devoted considerable attention to the subject, others have but just glanced at it yet. I could mention with what individuals it would be most favorable to correspond.

I must now, my dear sir, beg that you will not look on this subject in the view of personal friendship, and feel under a kind of obligation to treat it with some little respect. Unless it commends itself to your judgment as one which has a high claim on our benevolence, I could not ask you to devote to it a single moment of your very precious time. But if it has such claims, I would most gladly raise my feeble voice, entreating all who would befriend such an object to lend a helping hand.

28. Etymology
Ipswich, March 18, 1832

To Zilpah Grant

We are trying an exercise in connection with Grimshaw's Etymology. I wish some way could be contrived to have the English language studied with as much intensity as the Latin is. I have a few floating ideas upon this subject. I hope I shall do more next summer than ever before to enrich the minds of our pupils with a store of English words, associated with the ideas which they were designed to communicate. I do think that there is a deficiency on this point; but how to remedy it is the great question.

29. Perceive the Truths
Ipswich, August 17, 1832

To Zilpah Grant

O that my soul were in health as my body is! When my obtuse intellect and more obtuse heart can perceive the truths of the Bible, they seem exceedingly precious. The vagueness of my own mind is most trying, as connected with religious things. I often enjoy the anticipation of its not being thus in heaven. What a wonder of mercy, if I shall at last find a seat in that glorious world, where the will of God shall be known, and loved, and obeyed! If, amid so many deviations, so much lack in our services, the little seasons of conscious sincerity, when we desire for ourselves and others that we may do just what God sees to be exactly according to his will, are so precious, how glorious must heaven be! Did we know nothing more than that God is there, and that his will is done continually by all, it would be enough. Do you think it any proof of great holiness in those who shall live in the days of the millennium, that we are taught to pray that the will of God may be done on earth, as it is in heaven?

30. The Death of My Dear Sister
Ipswich, September 15, 1832

To Zilpah Grant

A letter arrived this morning, stating the death of my dear sister Ellsworth, —Rosina, you have heard me call her. She was a very dear sister to me.

This event of Providence is peculiarly suited to touch the tender cords of my heart. She was a kind of darling among us all, and among others beside our family friends. She has left four little sons. Sister Moore, in writing of her, says, 'Another such blow cannot be struck in our family. Among all her numerous relatives, none can fill her place. Heartfelt kindness marked her whole manner. It seemed to reverberate from heart to heart the moment she was announced. The sound of her voice, like some charm, infused a thrill of joy, animating every countenance. Even now, I seem to hear her sweet voice, and see her animated smile, and the welcome of her fine eyes, when lighted with Joy on seeing her friends.'

There is very little prospect that my sister at Hartford will ever be any better. Her bodily health begins to be impaired. She has attacks that are rather epileptic in their character; and these, to some extent, endanger her life.

I went to school this forenoon as usual. About half past eleven, I was sent for to see Miss Kingsley. I sat by her dying bed most of the time till four o'clock, when she fell asleep in Jesus. Some of her dying words and her dying prayers we will send you. It has been one of the most precious seasons I have ever enjoyed. M. G. endeavored to write some of her words, to preserve for her friends, and she remarked this evening that it was the happiest day of her life.

31. My Mother has Buried Two Children in One Month
Ipswich, October 6, 1832

To Zilpah Grant

My dear afflicted sister has finished her work and her sufferings. If you made any inquiries at Hartford, you found that she needed none of your sympathies. It is a great comfort to me, that she was so favorably situated during the last months of her life. The care I have had for her, ever since the death of her husband, has been so great that it now seems as if one of the strong cords, which bound me to earth, was broken asunder. The dispensations of Providence towards her have been very gracious. She was comfortably situated; there was nothing peculiarly trying in her last sickness and death; and now, I trust, she is sitting at the feet of Jesus, clothed and in her right mind. My mother has buried two children in one month, five hundred miles from each other.

32. I Know Not What I Ask
Ipswich, November 3, 1832

To Zilpah Grant

In observing how ignorant the disciples were on some points, after they had been with Jesus three years, I was reminded of our inability to determine the way by which Christ will be most glorified. How easy it would have been for Christ to make them understand that he should rise from the dead! But he knew it was not then best that they should understand this clearly. How little do I know what is best! I can pray, without reserve, that the will of God may be done; that the kingdom of Christ may speedily come; that the events which Christ sees to be best may take place, and that we may have hearts to do the whole will of God. But when I pray for particular blessings, I often feel that perhaps I know not what I ask; and it is a delightful privilege to refer the whole to God. I hope that Christians in this school may be fitted to labor in the field of Christ. May the regenerating influence of the Spirit be given, and may many be born of God. How few have been the hopeful conversions the present year! I was forcibly reminded of this today, when I inquired who had made a public profession of religion. Almost all, who hope they are Christians. O, may the Lord again return, and may the showers of divine grace descend as in former days.

33. How Sweet is Life
Ipswich, November 9, 1832

To Zilpah Grant

A week ago today, I mailed a letter for you, which was a little later than I designed, on account of a severe cold. I have now quite recovered. Goodness and mercy follow me continually. I feel so well every morning, when I rise, that I do emphatically *enjoy* health. I never was more sensible of enjoyment from this source. My daily business, connected with school, is peculiarly sweet and delightful. I do not think I ever did love a school so much in so short a time. I do not know how it is, but every thing is so pleasant. From duties in prospect I have none of that shrinking which I often have. There is an unusual evenness and uniformity in my feelings, freedom from excitement, or any rising above the common level. My cup is full and running over, and every future labor, or future scene, seems all that I could desire. I often say to myself, "How sweet are all my labors! How sweet is life!" In what I have said, I have not referred to religious enjoyment. I find great cause for daily repentance in the sight of God. Though I often walk in darkness, and see no light, I am not left to wander long without any light. In my own experience I have abundant evidence that the Savior is ready, not only to forgive seven times, but until seventy times seven. I have been very much interested, within a few days, in some parts of Scripture which treat of the forgiveness of sin. How boundless is the love of Christ in the way of pardon! How inexpressibly great and glorious is this subject! During a few months past, I have learned a little of the Minor Prophets. I have just commenced reading these books. I am now reading Hosea. The figurative language in the second chapter is exceedingly forcible. How strikingly are described the treachery, ingratitude, unreasonableness, and wickedness of spiritual departures from God! How exceedingly sinful is sin! How deserving of all the judgments denounced against it! But the boundless love and mercy of God, as exhibited in the promises contained in this chapter, I think most wonderful; and so of all the promises to guilty sinners. How very interesting that Peter should receive an assurance that, though Satan had desired to sift him as wheat, Jesus had prayed for him, that his faith might not fail! Our Mediator will never leave the weakest nor the most unworthy of his followers. He has undertaken in their behalf. He has begun their salvation, and he will complete it. How safe it is to trust in him! Here is all our confidence, all our hope. Here is an unfailing fountain. May we, my dear friend, both of us be permitted to rest under the shadow of his wings. May we walk with the Savior day by day, hear his voice, and listen to his words. May we feel as he would have us feel, think as he would have us think, speak as he would have us speak, and do what he would have us do. It is, indeed, a precious privilege to live, if we can have a single eye to the glory of God. I want you should pray for me daily, that I may have a heart filled with love to Christ, that I may have a zeal according to knowledge in laboring in his service, and that I may have wisdom from above to direct me in the right path. Pray that our teachers may be holy, devoted to God, and faithful in his service; that we may none of us be entangled in the things of this world; that we may all be able so to connect our temporal duties with the great business of eternity that they shall not prove a snare.

34. Come Here to School
Ipswich, 1832

To Abigail Moore

In advising you what course to take in future, I should be guided very much by your own views and feelings about giving up yourself to do good—to do all you can to render those with whom you may be connected better and happier. I used to think much about leading my friends to endeavor to educate themselves, that they might take a more respectable position in society. This is comparatively of little importance. There is a great work to be performed before that time shall come which is foretold, and many hands are needed to be employed in this work; not only those of ministers and missionaries, but also of females. The labor to be done seems greater and greater every year; perhaps I may say every month and every week. How much is to be done by influence, in a variety of ways! How much prejudice to be removed! What an almost endless catalogue of evils exists among the middle-aged and youth of the present generation! And the children will follow on in their steps, unless some greater and more powerful influence is used. I do most ardently desire that laborers may be raised up, possessing willing hearts and a self-denying spirit. Teachers of the right character can do much.

Now, my dear niece, will you not, in a measure, forget self, and decide to give yourself wholly to the service of the Lord, to labor in his vineyard, wherever he shall call, and "whatsoever you do, to do it heartily as unto the Lord, and not unto men?" If this is your decision, and you have evidence that you possess a tolerable aptness for teaching, and can obtain your mother's consent, (do nothing without your mother's consent,) I should think it might be your duty to make even a great pecuniary sacrifice, in order by that means to be prepared to do the greater good. You need that skill in exercising moral power over others which you cannot possess without a thoroughly cultivated mind, and cultivated on the best principles. If your object is to devote yourself wholly to the service of God, and to labor to promote his glory by increasing human excellence and human happiness, I advise you, by all means, to bear the expenses of the journey, and come here to school...

Your tuition will be twenty-five dollars a year. I will give you enough to pay your tuition bills while here, without any charge, except the charge in Heb. xiii. 16. I should be glad to do more for you in this way, but, consistently with prior obligations, I cannot. I will endeavor to help you plan and economize, and if it should be best that I should *furnish* you with more funds, I should expect that you would pay me interest and principal when able.

May you be guided in the path of duty, which is the path of peace.

35. I Should Labor Elsewhere
December 9, 1832

To Zilpah Grant

I take my pen to introduce a subject, which has agitated my mind for several months. Is it not your solemn duty and mine to review the question, whether my services are needed as much in our beloved seminary as in some other portion of the Lord's vineyard? This is a question of deep solicitude with me. For a long time, *previous* to the present year, I felt that the question was settled. I had made a kind of decision, that I should not mention the subject to you again. For some time after the above query arose in my mind, the trial of mentioning it to you seemed greater than I could bear. Often, when alone, I have found relief in tears. The burden of my prayer has been, that if it were most for the glory of God that I should continue to labor with you, the path of duty might be made plain, and if it were his will that I should labor elsewhere, the way might be laid open, that you might see it, and both of us be prepared for the separation.

In taking the superintendence the past year, I have seen that very many of the things which you and I do, when we are together, can be as well done by our experienced teachers. In the present improved state of the institution; there is really no more business that would come under the head of superintending than can be done by one of us. Of the labor which needs our experience, and even *mind*, some could be done nearly as well by one as by two; some just as well, and some could be done better. I have been led to make a little calculation how much might be done by the assistant teachers, and what is the least amount of labor which it is indispensable that the principal should accomplish, in order that the institution may flourish. After a while, the query involuntarily arose in my mind, whether my services were really needed here, whether the experience I had gained was not more needed somewhere else, in this needy, impoverished state of the world. I did not intend to mention the subject till you returned; and in the event of my leaving, I supposed it would probably be best for us to take a year to plan for it.

But since your proposal that I should journey next summer, a new query has arisen, whether my leaving *then*, and not returning, might not be a less injury to the school than my leaving at any more distant period; whether it might not cause less excitement, and be less the means of increasing your labor. I should very much need more time to collect and arrange the fragments of improvement which we have been enabled to make, which are now more in my possession than in yours, in order that I might transmit them to you in the best order. But it would undoubtedly be my duty to take some time to become refreshed, and during that time I could collect these items from memory, notes, &c., and arrange them for your use about as well as if I were on the spot. I could have no object so important, and surely I could have none *so very dear* to my heart, as that of leaving this dearly beloved seminary, this darling of my heart, under the most favorable circumstances. Now, my dearest sister, the subject is before you. Will you commend it to our heavenly Father every morning with me? My faltering pen has obeyed my will; I have succeeded in telling what I would. And now I beg, that while this question is under consideration, you will never allude to personal considerations on either side, for they are not the data by which this interesting question must be decided. It would be to us both a needless trial of our feelings. You will ask about our great plan. I do not think there is one chance in twenty for it to succeed. If it should, a different course might be taken.

36. Gone Home to Glory
Ipswich, January 15, 1833

To Zilpah Grant

Is it indeed so, that your dear sister has gone, to dwell forever with the Savior? It is pleasant to think how many, whom we have tenderly loved, have, during the last year, gone home to glory, and are now enjoying that which eye hath not seen, nor ear heard. It brings the heavenly world very near. May we both be preparing for that everlasting rest. But it is a great privilege to live and labor in the cause of Christ.

37. Benevolent Gentlemen
Boston, February 4, 1833

To Zilpah Grant

I have seen Rev. Daniel Crosby, of Conway, this forenoon. He is an energetic man, and his talents are much respected abroad. He is a young man, and not worn out. Perhaps Providence will make use of him to accomplish this object. He says, it needs to be taken hold of by those who have not every thing else in their hands, and by those who will not be crushed by difficulties. He seems to grasp the whole subject at once, and to see its importance. He says, if all the attempts shall fail now, the effort will prepare the way to raise the forty or fifty thousand dollars some twenty years hence.

I feel more and more that the whole business must, in name, devolve on benevolent gentlemen, and not on yourself or on myself. I do not feel so much afraid as I did that they will not take the right steps, but I feel much more afraid that they will not act at all. If the institution is ever founded, it will be safe only in the hands of God, and under God, in the arms of the whole benevolent community, including not only the rich, but the poor. If any thing at all *should* be done, the less you and I have to do with the business part of the affair the better. Fewer needless, unkind remarks will be thrown out, less jealousy will be excited, and our private influence will be more extensive and useful in directing matters for the good of the institution. It is desirable that the plans relating to the subject should not seem to originate with *us*, but with benevolent *gentlemen*. If the object should excite attention, there is danger that many good men will fear the effect on society of so much female influence, and what they will call female greatness. They will think and say, "Miss Grant and Miss Lyon want to do some great thing, to have a large sum of money raised, and a great institution established, and to see themselves at the head of the whole, and then they will be satisfied." I imagine I have seen a little of this already, and if more interest were to be felt in the cause, more jealousy might be excited.

38. From Generation to Generation
1833

To Daniel Crosby

I received yours of yesterday. I have most ardently desired that this meeting might take place, hoping that it might be the first link in a chain of means to draw the interest of the Christian community to this object. If such an interest can be secured, the time will ere long come, when friends will be raised up to sustain the labor, and even bear the reproach of being chimerical, if need be, as all who lead in any great and good cause must expect to be called.

The gentlemen of this region, that I think it most important should go to Amherst, are, Mr. G. W. Heard and Rev. Mr. Felt. I expect to be there as you suggest. The most important thing now is, to lay the subject before those who are capable of becoming enlisted in its favor. He that can now awaken an interest, will do more than he, who, at some future time, shall be willing to bestow largely of his abundance.

I hope, dear sir, that all who are ready to devote some of their precious time to looking at this cause, in its feeble and forlorn state, and to inviting their brethren in the Lord to look at it, will hereafter receive an abundant reward.

If the proposed institution should ever be founded, I hope and pray, that from generation to generation it may assist the church in fulfilling her covenant obligations to her own children, and in grafting many a wild olive branch upon the true vine. Unless the building can be the Lord's, let it never be built; unless the Lord go with us, let us not go up.

39.
Liberal Christians in Common Life
Ipswich, February 24, 1833

To Zilpah Grant

I begin to doubt whether you will consider it expedient to go to Amherst on the best terms on which there is any hope that we can go. The highest of my hopes is only that by some means, the rent can be collected by dollars and cents from the farmers and mechanics all over Franklin and Hampshire counties, in order to make an experiment of three years. The greater prospect is, that, at the close of that period, the school will be thrown on the public without a home. But I am inclined to hazard, for nothing will ever be done without it on this subject. I cannot see one important step toward the "New England Female Seminary," which can safely be taken at present, and perhaps not for many years to come, unless this experiment at Amherst can be tried. If an agent for raising funds should now be sent out, in towns where he would need to raise one or two thousand dollars, he might not raise more than twenty or fifty. As the subject has gone forward for three years past, the public will not be prepared to be called on for money for twenty years to come. The plan of finding a location where they will do something handsome seems equally fruitless. It is known at Northampton how the matter stands; but the people there manifest no wish to do any thing about it. At Worcester, nothing can be done. There is no inducement to go to Brookfield. If Mr. Felt were now to visit every town suitable for a location in the state, to ascertain what amount could be pledged, if the school should go there, I believe that Ipswich would bear the palm.

Interest and zeal, I think, are what we now need. This is not the time to inquire how the money can be raised; but it is needful now to put forth every nerve and sinew to awaken an interest among ministers and other good men, till they shall feel that the object is good, and that it is feasible. But this interest cannot be awakened so much by writing, preaching, and the like, as by putting certain secret springs into action. Now, if any thing is done at Amherst, I think it should aim only at an experiment for three years, with the express design of preparing the way for a permanent seminary. If this experiment can be made, borne on the broad shoulders of an associate body of gentlemen from different parts of the state, as their plan, I have a hope that these gentlemen would so bring the subject before the public, that it would be safe, before the close of the three years, to solicit of the community the sum of forty thousand dollars....

One point more. The funds for Amherst College have been collected, not from the rich, but from liberal Christians in common life. At the commencement of that enterprise, the prospect was held out that it would be a college of high standing, where the expenses would be low, and that it would be accessible to all. This was like a mainspring, without which it is doubtful whether it would have been possible to raise the funds. I am inclined to think that something of this kind may be indispensable to our success. The great and honorable among the good will not listen to our cause; but perhaps the more humble in life, led forward by their own ministers, may befriend this important but forsaken object. If so, if there is any class of Christians that we should seek to gratify, it must surely be the benefactors, whether high or low. If the same class of Christians who support our missionaries should contribute principally to the raising of the funds, is it not important that the style of the whole establishment should professedly be plain, though very neat? If it were *really* plain, would it not be more respectable to have it professedly so?

40. A Few Words About My Feelings
Ipswich, March 1, 1833

To Zilpah Grant

Yesterday was my birthday. Thirty-six years of my life are gone, and now I am one year more than middle aged. To look back step by step, it seems a long life, and the remaining years in prospect seem few and short. But my life and strength may be prolonged for many years to come. I would that it might be so, if it is the will of the Lord. But in one thing I can rejoice, —that, as long as the Lord of the vineyard hath any need of my feeble service, he will allow me the unspeakable privilege of living and laboring; and when he sees it to be best that I should labor no longer in this dark, wicked world, which has been promised to the Savior as his inheritance, then may I be prepared to lay down this tabernacle with joy and rejoicing, and go to dwell with Christ, which is far better. Daily, my dear sister, do I endeavor to ask for you the same blessings which I ask for myself. O, this vast field, which is white already to the harvest! May laborers be raised up in great numbers, to gather in the harvest, which is continually wasting away. May those who are in the field labor while the day lasts. May you and I be so directed, that we shall spend the remainder of our days in that manner which shall be the means of the greatest possible results.

One thing I have, for several weeks, wanted to propose to you. It is this: if Providence should ever make it plainly our duty to occupy different fields of labor, and to dissolve our legal connection, I should deem it one of the greatest earthly blessings which I could possibly enjoy, to keep as many of the cords which now bind us together unbroken as could be done under existing circumstances; that we should assist each other in forming plans; that we should visit each other often, write to each other often; that we should each feel that, next to our own field of labor, that of the other is the most endearing—the field to which we have pledged our services, our influence, our hearts. A union somewhat like this would be to me an unspeakable satisfaction; it would seem to save my bleeding heart from sinking under the stroke of a separation; and my judgment says, that such a union would be suited to advance the great cause to which we have consecrated our lives.

Two days ago, I received yours, written January 10, replying to mine of December 10. After sending mine, I felt that I could leave it all with God. After that, however, there was a solemn weight resting on my soul; a feeling that one step had been taken toward accomplishing the greatest change that has ever taken place in my situation and labors, and probably the greatest that ever will take place in my life. But after receiving a few lines in Miss C.'s, acknowledging the receipt of mine of December 10, I felt that all, for the present, was done, —that God, in his own time and manner, would by his providence point out the path of duty, and I could most cheerfully and quietly wait. The peace and freedom from solicitude which I have been permitted to enjoy, with regard to the final issue, have been uncommon. When I have opened your letters, I have had no painful solicitude to find a line indicating your opinion on the question. But since the reception of yours two days ago, my mind has been most intensely occupied, and I can now give you only a few of my general, scattered thoughts.

A few words about my feelings. If it should be plain, or equally probable, that you and I could both of us accomplish as great an amount of good to spend our remaining days together as we could to occupy different fields, it would be a blessing which would be most grateful to my heart; or, if it should be equally probable that we could accomplish as much good during our lives, to continue together three years more, and then separate, I should be grateful for the privilege of being with you so much longer.

Now I will endeavor to write according to my judgment, though my opinion is not made up on any point. The reasons why it seemed to me, that were we ever to occupy different fields of labor it might be better that we should commence soon, were two, —one relating to my own usefulness, the other to yours.

If I should separate from you, I have no definite plan. But my thoughts, feelings, and judgment are turned toward the middle classes of society. For this class I want to labor, and for this class I consider myself rather peculiarly fitted to labor. To this class in society would I devote, directly, all the remainder of my strength, (God permitting,) —not to the higher classes, not to the poorer classes. This middle class contains the main springs, and main wheels, which are to move the world. Whatever field I may occupy, it must be an humble, laborious work. How I can get a footing sufficiently firm for my feet to rest upon for the remainder of my days, and where my hands can work, I know not. But by wandering around, and by resting from my labors a year or two, perhaps Providence might open the door. I should seek for nothing permanent, to continue after my death, as to the location of my labors; but I should consider it very desirable that I should occupy but one more field, that I should make but one more remove, till I remove into my grave. I shall soon be literally forty years old; and if I am ever to leave my present field of labor, and begin entirely anew, it seems desirable, for my future usefulness, that I should begin soon, before many more of my remaining days are gone, or much more of my remaining strength exhausted.

If I should journey next summer, it might be better, for you and for the school, that I should not return at all, than that I should return to spend merely a year or two. It might be less hazardous to your strength to go right forward alone, than to have these changes. You want I should write how I judge, and feel inclined to decide. I wish I could tell you more definitely than I can now. My mind seems exceedingly reluctant even to incline to one side or the other. One thing, however, is clear. Considering your views and feelings, I do not think it best that we should separate so soon as this spring, at any rate. How long it is best that we should continue together, I do not know. As your letter has been so long delayed, perhaps it will not be best to attempt to settle these questions till we meet face to face.

Your arguments against a separation *now* are weighty. I have considered most of them in some form, though, perhaps, not with the distinctness with which you have expressed them. My query of December 10 I designed not specifically to be, whether we ought to separate this spring, or in one, two, or three years from this time; but generally, whether it was best that we should continue together permanently, or that we should separate as soon as it could be effected to good advantage; say, at the most suitable time in the course of two or three years. I do not think I expressed this clearly. Looking at the subject in the form of this last query, I will dwell a moment on the main arguments. The hope of founding a permanent seminary. This is so great an object, that it would be right to sacrifice considerable good for the sake of a small probability of success. But we must guide our steps by probabilities. My feelings are most deeply interested in this cause, and so strong is my belief in its utility, that I do believe that such a work will be effected at some future day, perhaps some twenty or fifty years from this time. But if it must be delayed entirely for several years, I have thought that there was nothing that we could do together which we could not do separately. And as the probability in my own mind, founded, I think, on evidence, was altogether on this side, it seemed my duty to decide according to this probability, knowing, that if any indication of Providence should appear in favor of the great object, either before it should be time to act, or before I should take fast hold of any other, (which time must be considerable), we could again unite our labors as before. My candid judgment has been, that the probability that such a seminary would be founded during our day has been constantly diminishing; but I have felt it my duty not to say much about it, but to put forth every possible effort, till we should professedly give up the subject for the present. If, in my own mind, the chance two years ago was equal to one in five, it is now reduced to not more than one in fifty; I would say to one in one hundred, or five hundred, if we except the ray of hope which beams from the possibility that an experiment may be made at Amherst, and the possibility that something favorable may grow out of such an experiment, if it should be made. My belief has been, that unless something unexpected should be brought forward by the wheels of Providence, the time has nearly come, when it will be your duty and mine professedly to relinquish the object, —not our interest in the plan, but our attempts for its execution. This I have not expressed before, and now it pains me to acknowledge my conviction. My conviction arose from the manner in which the scheme is regarded by various individuals, who, I think, are a fair index of the public. The public, as such, know nothing of any consequence about the object, and care less than they know. The public, as such, know not, and care not, how Miss Grant and Miss Lyon are united, or when they separate, or how, if the school at Ipswich can go on well.

A few words about the importance of the prosperity of Miss Grant's school. I consider it more important that it should continue to flourish during her life, or during her ability to labor, than any other school in the land, which is the property of a private individual. But, after all, it is short-lived. I view it as just like Mr. Emerson's school. It was very important that Mr. Emerson should prosper during his days of labor, and that he should have a place where he might put forth his strength to peculiar advantage. But where is his school now? If we ask, "Where are his labors?" I would say, "All over the earth, and their record is on high."

If the plan for the permanent seminary does not succeed, I have long felt that you and I must continue to labor, and make no more attempts for any thing permanent to result, except what is planted permanently in the hearts and in the lives of those over whom God may give us a direct or indirect influence. I consider it so important that your school should continue to flourish during your remaining days of labor, that I ought to take a course which would diminish my present usefulness, and hazard my future usefulness, rather than greatly to hazard the prosperity of Miss Grant's school, and her usefulness thereby. A small hazard may be justifiable.

This letter has cost me more hours than any letter I have written you this winter, and I fear it will cost you more to read it; and how little it contains! If the experiment is made at Amherst, the hand of Providence would, undoubtedly, make it plain duty for us to continue together.

41. A New Beginning
March 14, 1833
To Zilpah Grant (implied, but not certain)

I consider the friends of the original plan as having all failed, except Messrs. Felt and Heard. The subject is now about to assume a new aspect, and to have a new beginning. Will it not be best to endeavor to operate on a new circle of friends, who have hitherto known but little on the subject, rather than on those who have known *something*, and cared *less*? Is it not also very desirable to exert an influence through *gentlemen*, rather than directly by ourselves? Without a strict adherence to this purpose, in the preparatory steps, I think the plan will utterly fail. This purpose, adhered to, will increase our labor, but it may turn to much more account in the end.

42.
Door of Providence Will be Closed
April 6, 1833
To Zilpah Grant

I think there are more than nine chances out of ten that the door of Providence will be closed against all future operations towards founding a permanent institution.

43. If This Effort Should Fail
1833

To Zilpah Grant (probable, but not certain)

If this effort should fail, it seems to me evident that it will be the duty of Messrs. Heard and Felt, and of ourselves, to take a different attitude; to give up all thought and expectation of doing any thing directly for the object, but only to disseminate knowledge which may operate on the next generation. If the effort now commencing should fail, I think that we should select a favorable location for usefulness, and settle down for life, disclaiming all expectation that any plan for a permanent seminary will ever succeed in our day. We may describe the advantages of such an institution, what the public ought to do, and what they probably will do in the next generation. We might always speak as if the public were not now prepared for such an undertaking, and would not be prepared for many years. When it is evident that all has been done that can be on our part, would there not be essential advantages in our taking this attitude? It would be more according to the common leadings of Providence that we should in this way collect the materials, and that the temple should be built by our successors.

44. An Institution in the West
Ipswich, April 16, 1833

To Zilpah Grant

I believe I once said something to you about having an institution at the west, with the style plain, the food simple, almost all the labor done by the teachers and scholars, and the expenses very low. Involuntarily my spirit has been stirred within me to try such a plan on a small scale, but I have heretofore subdued these emotions.

45. Learn This Lesson Fully
May 2, 1833

To Zilpah Grant

I am very glad, my dearest friend, that you propose to endeavor to learn that you *can* do without me. I should rejoice to have you learn this lesson fully, even if we should hereafter decide that it is our duty to continue through life to labor together.

46. Missions in Ceylon
New York, July 8, 1833

To Zilpah Grant

On my way I was introduced to Mrs. L., who had been to Boston to bid a second daughter farewell, to go and labor in Ceylon. I was exceedingly gratified with her spirit. She appears like a mother who would strengthen the hands and encourage the hearts of her children in the path of duty. Fourteen years ago she went to Boston to bid an older daughter farewell. The daughter now gone was then about six years of age, and remembers but little of her sister. Mrs. L. feels that she is sending this daughter to a mother, and hopes that they will be assigned to the same field of labor. She remarked, that when she viewed the subject of giving up her daughter as a *whole*, she could rejoice and be thankful; but that when she directed her mind to the particulars, nature sometimes recoiled.

Sabbath evening, the missionaries received their instruction from the prudential committee, and sailed on Monday. I enjoyed the privilege of being present on both occasions. The scene on board the vessel, on Monday, was calm and lovely. Every countenance seemed softened with tenderness, and yet almost every one reflected, in some degree, the elevated joy, so strikingly manifested by the departing missionaries.

The monthly concert, on Monday evening, was interesting, as it always is in Boston. Dr. Wisner drew some comparisons between the missions in Ceylon and in certain other places. He remarked that, at some stations under the board, the work had gone on so rapidly that, as might be expected, there is more appearance of religion than reality; and, therefore, there probably will be reaction. Not so in Ceylon. Every inch that is gained seems secure.

I should like to know more than I do about the Ceylon missions, and, indeed, about all the other missionary operations.

47. Philadelphia
Philadelphia, July 22, 1833

To Zilpah Grant

On Friday morning, I went with Dr. B. to the United States mint, and to the porcelain manufactory. I value these two visits highly. In the afternoon, I went with Miss E. to the House of Refuge. The girls were assembled, and one, who was of age, was that day to leave. They sang a parting hymn, and many of the girls were affected to tears. The neat, whitewashed little rooms and clean beds, the orderly circle of cleanly and decently-clad girls, and the general air of neatness, order, and system came up in my mind, in striking contrast with the many dirty hovels which I have often passed, and the filthy children, the confusion, disorder, and misrule generally attendant on such habitations. That heart must be very hard which cannot rise in gratitude to a kind and good Providence for making such provision for poor, outcast children of wicked, degraded parents. "O that men would praise the Lord for his goodness, and for his wonderful works to the children of men!" We were late, and our time limited. On that account, we did not visit the boys' department.

From the House of Refuge we went to the Penitentiary. What abundant evidence have we every where of the wickedness and guilt of man! Man is emphatically the enemy of man. How little, comparatively, have we to fear from the fiercest of the brute creation! As it is only man that we fear, and he only is our enemy, what cause have we for gratitude that the ingenuity and skill of man are combined for our defence!

Saturday we visited the Old State House, Independence Hall, &c. It was a clear day, and we had a fine view of the city, though, after the business of Friday, we found it rather fatiguing to ascend the many steps. President Jackson was received in Independence Hall, which was richly furnished for the occasion.

Our course led us next to the navy yard, to see the wonderful ship, (the Pennsylvania,) which truly exceeded all my ideas of its magnitude. I expected to see a great vessel, but not such a mighty fabric. We ascended the many flights of steps to overlook the deck, and felt ourselves richly rewarded for our efforts.

A visit to the New Marine Hospital completed the business of the forenoon. The architecture of this edifice exceeds that of any other I have visited. If you have seen it, you doubtless observed the plan for ventilation. The walls of the chambers adjoining the passage do not extend entirely up, and yet the beautiful, white, polished arching overhead is such as to give an appearance slightly deceptive, so that, at first view, this aperture for ventilation would not be observed. I would that it abounded in as rich provision for the soul as for the body.

In the afternoon, we visited the Academy of Natural Science. I closed the week, greatly interested during the last three days, in fine health, except some little suffering in muscles and sinews.

48. The Catskill Mountains
Catskill Mountain, August 8, 1833

To Zilpah Grant

I remember that, for my own sake, you are more desirous I should dwell on what I see and hear than on the seminary at home, in which my heart is so much interested, but about which I have not indulged one moment's anxiety since I left you. I see enough to make my letters interesting; but these fragments of time, so few and so short, are worth but little in trying to recall and describe what I have seen and heard. And even if I had sufficient time, I have so little tact, that it seems to me my letters, of all things, must be the most insipid.

I am now twenty-two hundred feet above the Hudson, on one of the peaks of the Catskill Mountains, termed Pine Orchard, snugly settled in a pleasant chamber in the "Mountain House."

The Catskill is indeed a delightful chain of mountains. I have been favored with fine prospects of it at various points. This afternoon, we have taken a drive to see one of the mighty wonders of nature. As from different situations we behold the broad sides, the various summits, and numerous peaks of the mountain, the whole seems like a vast ocean of luxuriant green; at one time, waving gently with the undulating breeze; at another, rolled and tossed by the mighty tempest into lofty billows and deep gulfs.

The highest peaks of the Catskills are from eight to twelve miles distant from the Hudson. The two highest are Round Top, three thousand eight hundred and four feet above the river; and High Peak, three thousand seven hundred and eighteen feet. Pine Orchard, on which we are situated, furnishes a most extensive prospect. The "Mountain House" stands near the brink of a precipice, with a bold, commanding front. It is indeed a delightful spot.

The nearer scenery is composed of the neighboring peaks of the same grand chain. On one hand, they rise with a familiar nearness; on the other, they recede to a more respectful distance. On one side, we behold neighboring summits, rising high above our heads; on another, we cast our eye downwards on the waving tops of the thick trees, with their rolling surface; while in a third direction, rival mountains seem to unite, tipped with the blue summits of more distant and higher peaks.

The more distant scenery embraces the rich and extensive valley of the Hudson. The view is said to extend about one hundred miles in length and fifty in breadth. But I will not attempt to tell you of the finely-cultivated fields, enclosed by neat, regular fences; nor of the towns, villages, and cottages scattered over the whole prospect; nor of the beautiful groves, whose rich foliage at this season finely contrasts with the sterile appearance of the neighboring fields, just disrobed by the hand of the reaper; nor of the long and winding course of the Hudson, whitened with sails, ornamented with islands, and lined with villages, trees, and wooded embankments.

I noticed the first impression on my fellow-passengers, as we ascended a very long flight of steps into an elevated piazza, fronting the valley of the Hudson. Scarcely looking after their baggage, almost all, with one consent, stopped to admire and wonder. In the spacious drawing-room within, the numerous visitors seemed full of glee; but without, in the piazza, and on the broad, flat, projecting rocks around the house, the low voice and sweet stillness reminded me of a company in a gallery of paintings.

49. Niagara
Buffalo, August 31, 1833

To Zilpah Grant

I hastened away from the Falls yesterday, without being half satisfied; with the hope that, by leaving then, I should be able, either by stage or by steamboat, to reach my sister in Fredonia before the Sabbath. The stage, instead of going this morning, as I expected, will not leave until four this afternoon, and, of course, will travel most of the night. As it is rainy, the boat will not touch at Dunkirk at all. My conscience will not allow me to take the stage and travel all Saturday night, if I abide by the rule, "not to do any thing of which I doubt the propriety, unless I equally doubt the propriety of not doing it." So here I am, and must stay here, for aught I see, until Monday.

I have many things on hand, with which I should be glad to fill this sheet. Perhaps you may expect that I should tell you something of the great Niagara, or, rather, that I should tell you how this exhibition of the power of God affected my mind. I cannot tell you any thing about it. I have heard so many things said by one and another who visited the Falls; one saying, "You will be disappointed;" another, "You will not be disappointed, if you stay long enough;" a third, "I do not think it exceeds this object, or that;" and a fourth, "You never will wish to see any thing more; every grand object will lose its charms after your visit to Niagara." I have heard many compare it to fleeces of cotton, to banks of falling snow, to the dashing of ocean waves, to the roaring of thunder, &c. I feared that I should be unable to feel the soul-moving power, and I had an ardent desire that I might not acknowledge, even to myself, any second-hand emotions, any influence which did not affect my own heart. But I have been to see for myself, and I am glad I have been. I want to go again; I shall love to dwell on the most distant remembrance. I spent a day and a half, and my time was most fully occupied. I would give you a description of my ramble, but I could not tell you what I saw, what I heard. O, the voice of many waters! I had formed no conception of the scene, or, rather, of the many scenes. Perhaps it is because my powers of conception are so feeble. It does, indeed, mock all attempts at description; it is a stain upon human pride and greatness; it laughs to scorn all the trickeries of art.

Very much depends, I believe, on the order in which the various parts are viewed. The smaller should be viewed first, and then the greater; and in going from step to step, the soul continually expands to take in the larger views, until we reach the climax. The last step should be to cross over to the Canada side, and there take a view of the whole. This is merely my opinion. I have heard no statement about it; but I am almost confident that it is so.

50. Mental Discipline
Detroit, September 18, 1833

To Zilpah Grant

Every date carries me farther from you. When I left Chatauque county, New York, I hoped to be able to return there this week; but finding it inexpedient, I decided to spend the Sabbath here, and take the earliest boat next week. But one says to me, "Do not, on any account, take the Ohio, which leaves on Monday. I would not have a friend of mine go in her, for she is always meeting with accidents. On one voyage she caught fire three times; but the New York, which goes on Tuesday, is a good boat." Another says, "The New York is very easy to capsize, but the Superior, leaving the same day, is a large, safe boat." Another says, "I should not feel so safe on board the Superior, for she is a very old boat. Besides, it will be just about the time for the equinoctial storm."

I agree with you that "the manner in which recitations are heard has a great effect on the mental discipline of the scholar; and in this point our teachers should excel." Can we not do much to promote this object the coming winter?

I am in doubt as to what grammar it is best to use in our lower classes.

Besides requiring a thorough knowledge of good old Murray, embracing a clear understanding of all his notes and remarks, I have a query whether we ought not to include, as essential to completing our course, an ability to criticize in a philosophical manner his erroneous Latinisms; a knowledge of the particular resemblances and differences between Murray and our preparatory book; and an ability to arrange the differences under two heads, essential and non-essential. Finishing with a book of such an elevated style as that of Murray's Grammar, it would not be so great an evil to have the style of our preparatory book ordinary. What a pity that in our late primary school books there is not more of *elevated* simplicity!

51. Revival at Andover
Ipswich, December 3, 1833

To Her Mother

Perhaps you may have heard that there is at this time in progress a very powerful revival at Andover. It is said to be one of the most glorious displays of divine grace in modern times. Some Christians in this region are hoping that another such visitation is about to return, as the American churches enjoyed two or three years ago. Some gentle dews have descended around us; but there has been in no place, for a long time, so copious a shower as is now witnessed at Andover. In Park Street Church, Boston, there has been, for a few weeks, increasing interest; and in several places around, there are favorable indications. I mention these encouraging things to enlist your prayers, that all this region may again be visited with a refreshing from the presence of the Lord; that his name may be honored in the salvation of souls. This beloved institution you will also remember, as you have delighted to do from year to year. Our present number is one hundred and sixty. Nearly half are hopefully pious. Some appear to be established Christians; some are like many whom we find in all places, who have only a name to live, while we fear they are dead.

My dear mother, *I* very much need your prayers, that I may be revived; that I may have clearer views of salvation by Jesus Christ, and of the wonderful manifestations of God's love in giving his only beloved Son to save a lost world.

52. The Presence of God
Boston, December 16, 1833

To Her Mother

During the past week, I have been attending a very interesting course of meetings in Park Street Church. We hope there is a good work begun in Boston, which will be carried on in this great city, and extend into the country, till the whole region shall be watered. I want you should pray for this city, for this region, and for our school. Pray that sinners, who are out of the ark of safety, may be turned unto the Lord. My dear mother, I want you should pray for me in particular, that I may, from day to day, do my whole duty; that I may know what I should do, and how I should do it; that I may be so faithful to souls, as to free the skirts of my garments from their blood.

Whether I eat or drink, or whatever I do, may I do all to the glory of God; may all my labors be subservient to the advancement of the cause of our ever-glorious Savior.

During the past week, I have, as I trust, enjoyed much of the presence of God. The heavenly world has seemed very near, and it has appeared an unspeakable privilege to dwell forever in the presence of the Lord. It is a wonderful mercy that I should be permitted, so guilty and unworthy as I am, to enjoy so much of the presence and glory of my Savior.

53. Lord, What Will Thou Have Me To Do?
Boston, December 18, 1833

To Zilpah Grant

The seasons which I have recently enjoyed have, I hope, through infinite mercy, been profitable. I think I have had a deeper impression than ever before of my inexpressible vileness in the sight of God, and of the infinite and glorious fullness in Christ; a deeper sense of the divine presence and glory; of the real object for which we should live, of the worth of souls, of the duty and privilege of cooperating with Christ in his great work, of the *efficacy* of prayer, and of the infinite power of the Holy Spirit. When my thoughts go back to Ipswich, my heart rises, crying, "Lord, what wilt thou have me to do?" I cannot atone for any past neglect, neither would I desire to do it; the blood of Christ is sufficient to atone for all sin. *Pray* for me, that I may have strong faith in the promises of God, and that I may constantly have the teachings of the Spirit. The same blessings which I seek for myself, I ask for you. May the Lord bless you, and keep you.

54. Our Farmers
Ipswich, March 5, 1834

To Thomas White

I have long felt a great desire that the advantages of a seminary like this should be brought within the reach of the common people generally, and that by some means the expenses should be reduced to a level with their ability. I do wish our farmers would look at this, and see what can be done. If they would take hold of it vigorously, I do think something could be done, perhaps something which would secure the interests of thousands of their posterity. While it is desirable that every benevolent man should be able to grasp all the benevolent objects of the day, and do something for all, I doubt not but the best interests of the whole are promoted by having one mind directed to one object, and another to another. I have been thinking that if this object should be brought up, and viewed in its true light, some of our fathers in the cause of benevolence might select it as the child of their prayers and of their charities. Who would be more likely to begin upon it than our wealthy farmers?

And now, my dear sir, in your old age, would you not be glad, with a few other kindred souls, to be the means of commencing a great work, which, in importance to the welfare of our country, of the church, and of the world, shall not fall behind the home missionary, or any other of our leading benevolent societies? Would you not gladly see such a work begun, and advancing? And how would your heart rejoice, if, before you sleep in the dust, you could see it rise and spread as our foreign missionary operations have done? This, I believe, may be accomplished, and he who, first putting his hand to the work, shall say to others, "Come, and do likewise," will deserve a place with Mills, with Robert Raikes, and others of like eminence. I do long to have some one or more gentlemen look at this object, till they are ready to do something for it. I would gladly do as much of the work as I can, and I find other ladies ready to join in it.

I have long had a secret hope that the time would arrive,

when I could consistently give up my present sphere of labor, and in some way devote my life, my strength, and all my powers to this object. That time has now arrived; and, after laboring half a year longer for this seminary, I expect to close my connection with it.

55. Proper Educators for the Children of the Church
Ipswich, May 6, 1834

To Zilpah Grant

Is it not true, that, on extraordinary occasions, it may be the duty of benevolent individuals to labor without expecting to receive that which is their just due? Does not any good object, which has not yet gained the public confidence, often furnish such an occasion? In such emergencies, has not the church always been able to furnish some who are ready to turn a deaf ear to louder calls, and continue to do so, while the necessity lasts! Was not the apostle Paul one who acted preeminently on this principle? How plainly does he teach, that the laborer is worthy of his reward, and that the Lord hath so ordained, that those who preach the gospel should live of the gospel. Yet he used not this power, lest he should hinder the gospel, and lest his good should be evil spoken of. That necessity has passed away, and it is no longer desirable that in Christian lands the gospel should be without charge. But do not some of our missionaries adopt a similar principle? How great are their sacrifices, compared with those of ministers at home! What minister in a Christian land would not sooner relinquish one half of his salary, and even one half of the remainder, than subject his children to the evils to which the children of missionaries are exposed? What reward is given to missionaries for all this sacrifice? Does it not appear, that even justice, to say nothing of mercy, would compel those who send them forth to pledge at least the education of their children? This would be but a small return for the debt of gratitude due to some of our missionaries from the churches. But this return, the most precious of a pecuniary kind that can be made, the Christian public are not sufficiently enlightened to render. But the missionary cause has not been forsaken on this account. Louder calls do not turn the devoted missionary from his purpose. Is not this the condition of the object under consideration? Is it not very important that mothers should be so trained, that they will be proper educators for the children of the church? To effect this, is there not great need of female seminaries, cheap but good schools? And is there any hope of establishing such schools without the aid of the benevolent Christian public? And while the public are so little prepared to contribute liberally to an object like this, may it not be expedient that those who first enter the field as laborers should receive as a reward so little of 'filthy lucre,' that they may be able to commend themselves to every man's conscience, even to those whose minds are narrow, and whose hearts are not much enlarged by Christian philanthropy? If such a course should be desirable at the commencement, how many years, or how many scores of years, must elapse before it would be no longer needful, time and experience alone can decide.

56. Good Mothers
Ipswich, May 12, 1834

To Her Mother

I do not expect to continue my connection with Miss G. after this summer. I have for a great while been thinking about those young ladies who find it necessary to make such an effort for their education as I made, when I was obtaining mine. In one respect, from year to year, I have not felt quite satisfied with my present field of labor. I have desired to be in a school, the expenses of which would be so small, that many who are now discouraged from endeavoring to enjoy the privileges of this, might be favored with those which are similar at less expense.

The course of instruction adopted in this institution, and the course which I have endeavored to adopt when I have instructed among my native hills, I believe is eminently suited to make good mothers as well as teachers. I have had the pleasure of seeing many, who have enjoyed these privileges, occupying the place of mothers. I have noticed with peculiar interest the cultivated and good common sense, the correct reasoning, the industry and perseverance, the patience, meekness, and gentleness of many of them. I have felt, that if all our common farmers, men of plain, good common sense, could go through the country and witness these mothers in their own families, and compare them with others in similar circumstances, they would no longer consider the money expended on these mothers as thrown away.

Since I have lived to see so many of these ladies in their own families, I have felt more than ever before, that my field of labor was among the most desirable. I have felt that I could thank Him who has given me my work to do. O how immensely important is this work of preparing the daughters of the land to be good mothers! If they are prepared for this situation, they will have the most important preparation which they can have for any other; they can soon and easily become good teachers, and they will become, at all events, good members of society. The false delicacy, which some young ladies indulge, will vanish away as they see most of the companions of their childhood and youth occupying the solemn and responsible situation of mothers. It will no longer appear like a subject for which no care should be taken in the training of daughters.

While, in the good providence of God, I have been permitted to occupy a field of labor where I could aid in preparing some who must mould the character of future generations for their great work, and while I have enjoyed much in my labor, I have not been quite satisfied. I have looked out from my quiet scene of labor on the wide world, and my heart has longed to see many enjoying these privileges, who cannot for the want of means. I have longed to be permitted to labor where the expenses would be less than they are here, so that more of our daughters could reap the fruits. Sometimes my heart has burned within me; and again I have bid it be quiet. I have sometimes speculated, and built airy castles, and again I have bid my mind dwell on sober realities. I have thought that there might be a plan devised by which something could be done. I have further thought, that if I could be entirely released from all engagements and all encumbrances, perhaps I might in time find some way opened before me for promoting this good object. With this view, I decided some time since, if Miss Grant's health should be sufficiently restored, to propose a separation. That time has now come, and we have agreed to close our joint labors next fall. Miss Grant is to be absent through the summer term, to improve her strength, and we shall spend most of the vacation here together, in getting ready for the winter, and then I expect to leave this scene of labor forever.

I do not expect immediately to commence in any other field. I very much want six months or a year to read, write, plan, and do a thousand other things. I do not expect to be idle. This may seem like a wild scheme; but I cannot plead that it is a hasty one. I have had it under careful consideration two years or more, and for one whole year the question has been weighed by Miss Grant and myself.

I hope and trust that this is of the Lord, and that he will prosper it. In this movement, I have thought much more constantly, and have felt much more deeply, about doing that which shall be for the honor of Christ, and for the good of souls, than I ever did in any step in my life. I want that you should pray for me, my dear mother, that I may in this thing be guided by wisdom from above, and that the Lord would bless me, and make me a blessing. My daily prayer to God is, Lord, what wilt thou have me to do? If the Lord go not with me, let me not go up hence.

Perhaps you may inquire, what course I expect to take, and where is to be my future scene of labor. This I do not know. The present path of duty is plain. The future I can leave with Him who doeth all things well.

57. The Lord is Able
Ipswich, May 16, 1834

To Zilpah Grant

What can any of us do without the blessing of God? I do hope we shall not be forsaken of him. Pray for us all, and especially for the teachers, that we all may be fed with heavenly food, granted day by day, like our daily bread. When there is so much to be done for the blessed and glorious Savior, how important that all our strength, feeble as it is, should be wholly devoted to his service! I am feeling more and more, and with considerable force, that it is much more important that all our powers, greater or less, should be devoted to God, than that our powers should be great; and that it is more important that all our time, whether longer or shorter, should be devoted to him, than that this life should be long. What a privilege to labor, feeling that, while we are spared, God, in his infinite love, can make use of our labors to promote the best of all causes, and whenever he calls us hence, we can lay by our work, as we lay off a garment, and the work can go on just as well without us! How full of wisdom, goodness, and mercy, are all the ways of God! In eternity, we shall forever feast upon his love. Sometimes I have great hope that the Lord will meet with us and bless us this summer; teachers, scholars, and all. To save by few or by many is the same with God. It may be that he will honor his name by remembering us in our weakness, and by taking us all to be his own. It seems to me that this is my heart's desire and prayer to God from day to day.

Last week, I wanted to tell you how weak I felt. In the first place, a pain seemed to play around my head, just ready to seize upon it, and to unfit me for every thing. It became necessary to watch and guard my efforts as carefully as I would a candle in the gentle breeze. In the next place, my mind was locked as in a cage, and my heart was seized with a painful chill. So much for myself. In looking over the boarding-houses and scholars, I could find so little *salt* on which I could depend that it would not lose its savor, that my heart sank within me. The inquiry, "How can these boarding-houses be so regulated, and the school so guided, that every thing may be done, which ought to be done, to prepare the way of the Lord, and make his paths straight?" came home to my soul. I felt like sinking; but the thought that the Lord is able was comforting. Yesterday, I seemed to gather some crumbs from my Father's table, which revived my strength of body, mind, and heart.

58. Best that She Should Leave
Ipswich, June 25, 1834

To Zilpah Grant

I wish very much to give you some more full account of the school than I have done, but have time only to say the same that I have expressed before—that the good hand of our God is upon us in our daily labors and cares. What trials the Lord may see best to bring upon us before the school closes, I know not. The circumstances of Miss –'s unhappiness have terminated, as I expected, in her leaving the school, and were very trying. She did nothing; was at school only now and then half a day; disliked the school excessively; thought she was sick, and wrote to her uncle, without mentioning it to me, that she could not stay; wrote to her guardian, &c. I told her I thought it best that she should leave. I do not know but I have done my whole duty to her. At any rate, she has gone, and I shall meet her no more till I meet her at the judgment seat. How solemn will then be the account which I must render of my stewardship! May I, from this time forward, feel more and more the solemn truth that I must meet every one that I am allowed the privilege of teaching, and render up a strict account. Pray for me, that I may be faithful to every individual.

Three or four young ladies were anxious about their salvation when they entered the school. Others are somewhat interested. Last Sabbath morning, I met twelve at my room, who thought they were decided to make religion their first concern. Two of the number are now indulging some hope.

59. One Honest-Hearted Man
Ipswich, July 4, 1834

To Zilpah Grant

Returning by way of Beverly, I passed the night in the hospitable home of kind Mrs. B., and spent some time in reading to her and another good lady from Mr. Emerson's Life. It was a luxury, indeed, to read to people possessing such hearts. How justly might he say, "O, with what eyes, with what smiles, with what hands, with what hearts, with what words, did they meet the feeble remnant of him they once honored as their minister, so much above his deserving!" I love to read his letters. I delight to dwell on his sincerity. Surely, mine eyes have seen one honest-hearted man in this dark, deceitful world. I am distressed with the apparent want of sincerity among Christians on the first and grand principles of duty; and more than all, with my own real deficiencies in this respect. I am distressed that so many momentous subjects of Christian duty should wear so different an aspect in the pulpit, and in the solemn and attentive audience, from what they do in the social circle, and in the business of life. I have often had seasons of being distressed with this subject. In reading Mr. Emerson's Life, all these feelings have been renewed. Is there real cause for this distress? Is it owing to partial views of things? O that my own heart might be sincere, and my hands clean! But I had almost forgotten that I was going to confine myself to business.

Miss F.'s lucid description of Granville, Ohio, I value very much indeed, and trust I am truly grateful to her for it. Such an aspect of society rouses my soul to almost a flame, when I think what might be done in advancing the interests of the human family, if every good thing might take its proper place.

Last evening, Mrs. – showed me an old tract, Mary and Martha, which her daughter had brought from Vermont. I found it was written more than forty years ago, by my grandmother's sister. She was a good woman, in whom the meek and heavenly spirit of Jesus reigned all her life, almost without a spot. She nursed her aged parents till their death, after which she was married, and had one only son, who was content to be brought up by his mother's side, a stranger to the arts of the world. This child has now three little daughters, and for a son has taken the youngest child of my afflicted sister Putnam.

This little tract brought up a long train of family associations. It seemed an interesting relic of the old, venerated family of my mother's grandfather.

60. Andover
July 5, 1834
To a Gentleman in Andover (No Other Identification)

Rev. Mr. K. called on me yesterday, making some inquiries in your name, relative to my plans for future labors. I have been desirous of an interview with you, that I might learn your views on several particulars.

I have decided to close my connection with this institution, with a hope of using my limited influence towards advancing the belief that female schools of an elevated character may be furnished at a very moderate expense. I have much stronger desires to do something towards establishing some general principles on female education than to accomplish much myself. But I do hope that Providence will open a door, where I may labor directly in a school in behalf of this great and important cause, as I believe I can do more in this way than in any other.

I have no definite spot in view where I may spend the remnant of my strength in behalf of an object which for a long time has seemed to drink up my spirits. I have not been so affected, because this object is more important than many others, but on the same principle that I should be more moved by the cries of a drowning child, where no deliverer was near, than by those of one actually in the arms of relief. I have no doubt there will be many objections raised. To avoid these, as far as possible, as well as to rouse a candid attention to any features which may be somewhat new and peculiar, I have supposed that, in many particulars, it would be of great importance to meet the views of the judicious part of the community. On this account, I have been desirous that a location might be selected by a committee, so appointed that they would be regarded as a kind of representative of the public. Whether it is practicable to create such a committee, I do not know. I have conversed with two or three gentlemen on this point, who think that some plan can be devised by which the thing may be brought about. It was suggested that something towards the object might be done at the General Association, that met at Lee last week. But on such occasions, the multiplicity of objects, each of which has several warm advocates, generally presses out an object of this sort, which has so few warm-hearted friends.

You will, of course, perceive that I cannot now give any definite opinion with regard to Andover as a location. If it should be judged by gentlemen from different parts of New England to be a favorable, or the most favorable, for which there is any probability of raising funds, I should not shrink from undertaking even there, though it would be a location attended with difficulties.

The question of the expediency of my devoting myself to this object in some place farther west has been several times mentioned to me. That influence needs to be put forth in the more western states, as in New England, cannot be doubted. The opinion, which has so universally prevailed here, that female seminaries of the first respectability must necessarily be expensive, has overspread the whole State of New York, and marched on farther still, keeping pace with every effort in behalf of female education. As I believe, with many others, that this opinion is an error, and a highly injurious one, this is the point on which my mind centres more than on any other, and on which I wish to use an influence as far as I can. Considering the vast importance of the more western portion of our country, and the more abundant zeal, and the greater rapidity with which they carry any thing forward, when they are once convinced of its importance, I have been half inclined, at times, to look upon some spot beyond the limits of New England as more desirable for experiments on this subject. But, considering that improvements in education seldom make any progress eastward, my purpose to live and labor in New England has, during the last six months, become fixed and unchanging.

61. Domestic Work
Ipswich, August 1, 1834

To Hannah White

How long, very long, it is since you have written to me, or I to you! I can hardly realize that I have so little intercourse with those whom I so tenderly love, those whom I once met daily face to face, and with whom I held delightful intercourse sometimes from hour to hour. But it is even so. I have not written to dear A. for a great, very great while. How was my soul knit to her soul! Seldom have I loved any one so much, dear Miss Grant excepted. But we have long been separated, perhaps to meet no more on earth. Long separation breaks up the vividness of affection, but the strength still remains. How delightful will it be to have this affection renewed in heaven! I have to bid dear Miss Grant farewell, no more to live with her on earth. This separation has not severed my heart, but it has so shaken it as to render it most tenderly alive to all emotions of affection, which have sometimes seemed to lie dormant in my heart. I love more than ever to dwell on those friends who shared the warmth of my heart in my younger years.

I suppose you have heard that I am endeavoring to establish a *manual labor school* for ladies. I have heard so. But as it is not true, I wish the mistake could be corrected. I will tell you what I should be glad to have done. You know it has become very popular for our highest and best seminaries for young men to be moderate in their expenses. It is not a sufficient recommendation for a college to be expensive. But how different is it with regard to female seminaries! Even at the present time, almost in the middle of the nineteenth century, do not many value them according to their expensiveness? Is it not rather gratifying to young ladies to attend expensive schools, when perhaps their brothers would rather glory in pursuing their studies at a moderate expense? Is there not a general feeling that female education must be costly, and that those who cannot pay the price must do without it? Is not this the reason why ladies are more aristocratic than gentlemen, and why their aristocracy is founded on so much more despicable principles? Would it not be a less evil for the farmers and mechanics through the land, who must spend all their time in laboring to support their families, to have scanty stores of knowledge, than for their wives, who must train up their children, to be thus scantily furnished? I will now tell you what I wish could be done. I wish the same public interest could be excited to extend female education to the common walks of life that exists with regard to the education of young men. If the church would do the same for young ladies that she has done, and is continually doing, for young men, the work would be accomplished. O that the church would take our highest female seminaries under her direct control, protection, and support! And do you not believe that this will be done at some future time? But this cannot be done, unless means are used to secure the confidence of common Christians. And if any institution should ask for public support, would it not be desirable that, in some particulars, it should present certain marked features which would be approved by common Christians? On this account, I have thought that, in the proposed seminary, it would be well to have the domestic work done by the members, not as an essential feature of the institution, but as a mere appendage. But this mere appendage ought, by no means, to give the name of *manual labor* to the scheme. I have not the least faith in any of the proposed kinds of manual labor, by which it is supposed that females can support themselves at school, such as raising silk, attending to grape-vines, spinning, sewing, &c. I should expect that any attempt of the kind would become a bill of expense, rather than an income, to any female seminary. After the acquaintance I have had with many cultivated and interesting families, where the daughters, in a systematic manner, performed all the labor, I have the greatest confidence that a system might be formed, by which all the domestic work of a family of one hundred could be performed by the young ladies themselves, and in the most perfect order, without any sacrifice of improvement in knowledge or of refinement. Might not this simple feature do away much of the prejudice against female education among common people? If this prejudice could by any means be removed, how much would it do for the cause! Some of the specific features of the great object in which I am engaged will seem to some of our friends like new views, different from my former ones. Not so new as might seem; they are of no very recent date. The only difference is, that I did not consider it expedient, while I was connected with Miss Grant and this institution, to say much about these views. I should be very glad to see you a day or two, and talk over this whole subject.

62. A Frail Boat on a Boisterous Sea
Ipswich, August 26, 1834

To Freelove Lyon

Our niece, A. M., has gone to Virginia, to teach. She left us about four weeks ago, and has arrived safely. She has made very good improvement here, and is promising. I think she has some right views about the real object of life, and the real object of education. I do hope she will use her acquirements for the advancement of Christ's kingdom. When you pray for her, I beg you will remember this one thing. What a great mistake has been committed by the followers of Christ, in not believing that every good thing is to be used primarily for the advancement of the Redeemer's kingdom, for the salvation of men! Property, education, time, influence, friends, children, brothers and sisters, all should be devoted to this great object. All can be used, all should be used thus. All who have willing hearts to engage in the great work of cooperating with Christ in saving the world, I do desire should be thoroughly furnished. I would have their power increased, their strength of body and of mind, their knowledge and influence. These things seem to me more and more important and valuable; not, however, for the worldly-minded, but for the followers of Jesus. When will Christians learn the great lesson of doing every thing for the glory of God? This, I believe, means that every thing should be done, and every blessing be made, to promote the salvation of souls. This is the glory of God, as revealed to us. This is that which we are commanded to promote in all that we do, whether we eat or drink. It is by the church that the manifold wisdom of God is manifest. (Eph. iii. 10.) To the angels, too, it seems that the wisdom of God is made manifest by the church, or by the salvation of man.

  I took this sheet to state a few things about myself; but inadvertently I have turned aside, until it is almost full. You already know that I expect to close my labors here, and my connection with Miss Grant on earth, this fall. I am about to embark in a frail boat on a boisterous sea. I know not whither I shall be driven, nor how I shall be tossed, nor to what port I shall aim. I know not what is before me, nor where will be my next field of labor. I know not when I shall find myself engaged in regular labor in the great work of teaching, for which Providence has fitted me more than for any thing else. But I am not anxious. I have decided to close my labors here, because I felt it to be probable that I could do more good in another field. And now, after breaking asunder a thousand cords, to separate myself from this beloved institution, I feel that I must at present keep myself disengaged from any school, because, by so doing, I have more hope that the way will be open for me yet to engage in the specific field in which my heart is so deeply interested. I never had a prospect of engaging in any labor which seemed so directly the work of the Lord as this. It is very sweet, in the midst of darkness and doubt, to commit the whole to his guidance.

  The next winter I want to spend partly in study, and partly in laying out plans for the future, writing, &c. I wish to be in a family where I shall meet friends, and where I shall have access to a good library, and in a town where I shall not be out of the way of society, for I shall often want counsel. Providence has very kindly given me such a home at Amherst, in the family of Professor Hitchcock.

  The religious state of our school has been in some degree interesting. Many are anxious for the salvation of their souls; some deeply so. A few have recently expressed hope. The interest increases from week to week. I want that you and dear mother should pray for us *much* while the school shall continue, which will be about three weeks longer.

63. A Field of Usefulness
1834
To Electa Moore

I have not heard from your daughter A. for a long time. I think she will be prepared to do great good, and I hope she will live to do it. I feel satisfied with her present situation, only as a temporary one. I do not think the sphere of usefulness so extensive as she might have in other places. How much greater is the blessing of enjoying a field of usefulness, than a situation favorable to personal advantage! And do you not, my dear sister, regard it as a higher privilege to have your children prepared to do good, than to have them enjoy great worldly prosperity? This happiness I desire and pray that you may enjoy in all your children.

64. Young Christians
undated fragments (it is unclear if these are a single letter)
To Zilpah Grant

They are talking about erecting a building for a female school in this city; but they have had no idea of doing it, except by shares, with the expectation of an income. They look at schools, generally, just as they would at mercantile business. Some persons, who knew I was coming here, hoped that I would render them some assistance about a plan; but they need *something more than a plan.*

There is more decided religious influence in this place than in any other village of its size in which I am acquainted. There is more equality among the people, and less aristocracy. But, from what I have learned, I should think the people had not knowledge enough, and fixedness of purpose enough, for their security. They have great zeal and ardor in new things, but in their plans and efforts they are among the most changeable. Their zeal is very apt to be of mushroom character.

You see what the views of these ladies are. I could not refrain from saying to myself, if all ladies entertain the same views, what will become of the immense population of our country, whose scale of means and living, in every respect, is so far below these views? How shall the mothers of future generations be so trained, that, with the common blessing of Heaven, they will refuse to give up their children to Catholic influence? What would become of the great multitude of our churches throughout the country, if all our educated ministers were to demand a salary, which should furnish as much better support for their families than the common, enterprising, and industrious farmers and mechanics can procure, as these ladies consider necessary for their personal wants, above what can be obtained by the industry of respectable females in ordinary employments?

How soon your school will close! And where will you then be? How I should love to step in some morning and listen to your instructions, and, as in former days, not only enjoy the truth in my own mind, but enjoy it as reflected from many an impressive countenance! Does the Lord bless the truth? Has there been a growth of grace among professing Christians? Do the teachers and pupils have enlarged views of Christian feeling and Christian action? Are their hearts and minds so enlarged, that they can understand and love the principle, that the commands of the Bible are to be obeyed, at all times, in all places, and under all temptations? I do believe that this is a time when efforts in behalf of young Christians are peculiarly needed. In my intercourse with society of late, I have been more and more convinced of this. I have noticed a tendency to giddiness, volatility, and foolish talking and jesting. In some cases, I have been surprised to learn that those in whom I had noticed these things were professors of religion. I am inclined to think that this is more manifest when young ladies and young gentlemen are engaged in conversation with one another. I recollect meeting a minister and his daughter of fifteen or sixteen. She was introduced to our company. We noticed her apparent thoughtlessness, and spoke of it to each other with a feeling that she was a child, and would need a prudent mother's care. We soon learned, to our surprise, that she professed piety, and would like to go on a mission. This is an extreme case; but I have seen many others, though less marked, which have led me to tremble for the church. Have we not reason to fear that too many of the young persons in our churches lose sight of the distinction between believers and unbelievers? Is not this a time when there is great need of watchfulness and prayer? O, how important that young Christians should take Christ for their example, and become holy as he was holy, harmless and undefiled as he was! How important that all who are united to Christ, should live in such a manner as to avoid the appearance of evil! May the Lord teach the dearly beloved in our seminary as no man can teach them.

Several clergymen travelled some distance with our company. Much of their conversation was interesting; but I have some sighs in my heart for a more holy ministry.

May the Lord guide us in all our plans, and in all our labors. May we feel our dependence, be humble before God, and by his abundant grace be prepared to receive from our heavenly Father great and increasing blessings on the beloved institution which has been our joint care.

65. South Hadley
Worcester, January 1835

To Zilpah Grant

Last evening, about midnight, Mr. Felt came and told me that the question of the location at South Deerfield was decided in the negative. My heart was filled with gratitude to Him who directs all events according to his own infinite wisdom. The other two places are to be considered today. Between them I had no choice, and it did appear to me that I could commit the whole to God more entirely than ever before. The decision, as Mr. Heard will tell you, is in favor of South Hadley.

66.
The Work Goes Forward Very Slowly
Amherst, April 2, 1835

To Her Mother

I would be glad to visit you this spring before I go east, but you know the travelling is bad; and besides, Professor Hitchcock is now giving a course of lectures on geology, which I have long desired to attend, and I have thought I ought to make special efforts to hear them. They are given three times a week, and I have been able, so far, to attend every lecture...I have been to Ipswich twice this winter. The last time I staid two weeks. There, I have enjoyed much that relates to this world, and much, I hope, that relates to a better. There, more than any where else, I have looked out upon this broad and wicked world, till my heart has longed that laborers might go forth to reap the harvest, which is already ripe for gathering. When I have there looked around on those committed to my care, how has my heart gone forth in their behalf, that they might be ready to do with their might what their hands find to do!

I often feel that my life is far advanced, and that I can do but little more myself. But this great work is all to be done through human instrumentality. How small a portion of it has yet been done! O that I might do a little more, before I depart hence! But my greatest hope is, that I may have the privilege of encouraging, stimulating, and strengthening some, who may continue to labor when I am laid in the grave. It is so pleasant for me to go to Ipswich, I am rather glad that I occasionally have business which calls me there. But it awakens many tender and sad emotions. Sometimes I fear that I never shall have another field of labor, where I can do so much good. But if the Lord has more work for me to do in the world, he will provide it for me, and point out the way.

For special reasons, I think it best to keep myself disengaged from any school, till the new school goes into operation in South Hadley. But the work goes forward very slowly. It will be a great while before I can expect the privilege of laboring there. Will you, my dear mother, pray for this new institution, that God will open the hearts of his children in its behalf, and that the Spirit of God may rest on its future teachers and pupils, that it may be a spot where souls may be born of God, and saints quickened in their Lord's service? It is my heart's desire, that holiness to the Lord may be inscribed upon all connected with it, and that a succession of teachers may be raised up who shall there continue to labor for Christ long after we are laid in our graves.

67. The Leadings of Providence
Northampton, July 23, 1835

To Her Mother and Sister

I cannot undertake to tell you where I have been, and what I have been doing, since I last saw you. I seem to be ever busy, and yet I accomplish nothing. I wander about without a home, scarcely knowing one week where I shall be the next. In this way, I expect to live, *at least* until one year from next spring, the earliest possible time that our new institution can open. And then, I may only make a change for a situation of overwhelming cares. But I have no doubt that I am following the leadings of

Providence. His dealings towards this new enterprise have been such as should lead me to trust wholly in the Lord. Every token of success has been rather strongly marked by his hand; and every trial and discouragement have been such, that when good comes, we feel constrained to say, "This is the work of the Lord."

In looking back, I feel that, whatever may be the result, I can never regret that these things were not directed differently. It seems to me more and more that this institution, and other similar ones, are a necessary part of the great system of means now in operation for the conversion of the world. When I look abroad and see how much abounds that is contrary to the spirit of the gospel, I sometimes feel it to be a precious privilege to pray, "Thy kingdom come; thy will be done on earth, as it is done in heaven." Whatever we are permitted to do, in accordance with these desires, is a precious privilege. The feeble efforts which I am allowed to put forth in cooperating with others, in laying the foundation of this new seminary, I feel will probably do more for the cause of Christ after I am laid in my grave, than all I may have done in my life before. Do not cease to pray for this seminary, that in every succeeding age it may be most sacredly the Lord's; and that no wicked hand may ever be allowed to turn it aside from its consecration to the Redeemer.

68. We Shall Not Shrink From This
Northampton, July 24, 1835

To Zilpah Grant

How vain would it be for us to hope by our present efforts to make our situation more comfortable or quiet! We have every reason to believe, that the more we seek to draw the public to aid us in doing good, the more perplexing will be our cares and labors. But then we shall not shrink from this, if we can thus lay a foundation for our successors to labor abundantly for the cause of Christ.

69. This I Have Never Asked
Norton, October 24, 1835

To Her Sister

You will doubtless be glad to know something about the Mount Holyoke Seminary. The work goes on slowly. I hope they will be able to commence building next spring. We have much to try our faith, and much to excite our hopes. I love to look at the hand of Providence as connected with this enterprise. With how much wisdom and goodness are trials and blessings mingled together in our cup! The work of endeavoring to found and build up this seminary is one which I trust the Lord will own and bless. But I do not expect that it will be carried forward as on flowery beds of ease. This I have never asked. I only ask that it may receive the smile of Providence in that way which shall best promote the interests of the great cause to which it is consecrated. I hope that in your prayers you will commend this enterprise to God.

70. The Fountain of Light
October 27, 1835

To Zilpah Grant

I have thought of you very much since we separated. I greatly fear that the trying questions which are now taxing your mental energies, besides the care of the school, just now at the commencement, will be more than you can sustain. May the Lord give you strength equal to your wants, and may he give you wisdom from on high to guide your thoughts, and your views, and your present important decisions. When all human help and human wisdom fail, and all knowledge of future events, as connected with present causes, seems entirely cut off, how sweet it is to go to One who knows all from beginning to end, to One who can direct our very thoughts, and who can take us individually by the hand and lead us in a plain path! Every thing appears to me dark with Egyptian darkness, except as I turn my thoughts to

Him who is the fountain of light. I dare not pray for any thing in particular, but only that the will of the Lord may be done, that all interested in this institution may be humble and submissive, that his will towards this enterprise may be done, as it is done toward those on whom he smiles, and not as it is done toward those whom he chastens and afflicts. My daily language is, "Lord, thou knowest; not my will, but thine, be done."

How often have I endeavored to consecrate all the part, all the interest which God has given me in this contemplated institution, most sacredly and solemnly to his service! And how often have I endeavored to pray that no one who has any thing to do in building it up may ever call aught his own! O that every one who puts a finger to the work, by giving the smallest contribution of time, of money, or of influence, might feel that this is a work of solemn consecration, a work to be reviewed in the light of eternity! For a few weeks past, I have thought a little too much about gaining the approbation of the wise and good, as compared with my desires that every thing connected with it may receive the approbation of God.

71. I Anticipate Trials in the Future
Amherst, December 23, 1835

To Zilpah Grant

It is sweet to review our past years, the time of our first acquaintance, the commencement of our connection, and the many years we spent so delightfully together, and in some degree, as I hope, profitably to the best of causes. When I look back and compare my own views and feelings, fifteen years ago, with what they are now, I am constrained to believe there has been a very great change. Comparatively, it does seem to me now a great privilege to live and labor for the cause of Christ in any place, and under any circumstances, where He may direct; and, if possible, a still greater privilege to lead others to attempt and to do more than I can ever myself accomplish. It seems to me, uniformly, as if my strength was mostly spent, and my years, a great proportion of them, gone. But if I may be permitted to do something more, it will be indeed a great privilege. In this respect, life seems to me a greater and greater blessing.

I anticipate trials in future, such as I have never yet known. I expect them, from indications of Providence already manifested toward the enterprise in which I am engaged. Sometimes my heart and spirits seem to sink under the prospect, and I am almost ready to exclaim, "When will the work of my feeble hands be done, that I may go home?" But through the mercy of God, these seasons do not often occur, and do not continue long. Generally, I feel that the dark, portentous cloud which hangs over the future is under the direction of Him who led his chosen people by a pillar of cloud and of fire. I do hope that in some way the remainder of my life may be instrumental of more good than my past life has been, though it may be in a manner very different from what I anticipate. The years which I have had the privilege of spending with you have done more to fit me to enjoy so great a blessing than almost all other circumstances. Such a view gives a peculiar sweetness to the remembrance.

Have you seen Dr. Channing on Slavery? Really, I did not know that he had such a great soul, so much of the noble spirit of former days, composed of mildness and decision. He deals in great principles, instead of that personality which is the order of the day. In seeking after truth, it is delightful now and then to come to a stream which we can recognize as flowing from the great fountain, and which has not been subdivided into endless ramifications, till we forget that there is *any* fountain-head; or, to speak without a figure, till we forget that there are any great principles, on which we can rest unshaken amid all the clashing of opinions and sentiments. Dr. Channing has a suitable word of reproof, alike in season for the south, in their present excited and threatening attitude, for the abolitionists, in their furious and misguided zeal, and for the anti-ultras, who, in their *prudence* and caution, are in danger of making concessions, tacitly at least, which are suited to endanger our first principles of duty, rather than hazard the odium of being called by some one *ultra*, and of being claimed by some of the ultra parties. This last class need reproof, perhaps, as much as either of the others, though in different degrees. And from this class we have more fear that truth will suffer than from any other. I lament most deeply the havoc which misguided zeal is now making with the dearest interests of our country and the church; but should this fire sweep over the whole country, consuming all that is combustible, the soil will be left, the foundation will be unshaken. But I dread to have the foundations broken up. I dread to have those who are the stability of the times driven, by the scarecrow of ultraism, from their high post in defence of truth, the rights of man, and the duties of the church. Dr. Channing's reproofs must come down with great weight on every conscience that puts on the coat so finely fitted. How much more heavily will reproofs bear upon the conscience, which come from great principles, than those captious fault-findings which fill many of our newspapers! I am delighted with the spirit in which this book is written.

72. Tuition
July 1, 1836
To Catharine Esther Beecher

I thank you for your interest in my plans, expressed in the sincere way of criticism on one point. I think, however, you do not fully understand them.

The terms high, low, and moderate tuition mean very different things in different parts of the country. In the aristocratic south, where all the wealth is concentrated on large plantations, and in some of the speculating portions of the north, where wealth flows in as in a day, and in some of the most prosperous mercantile and manufacturing places, these terms are understood differently from what they are among the general community of New England. The latter, tilling a sterile soil, and uniting economy with prudence, are enabled, by the slow gains of patient industry, to provide comfortably for their children, and send them to school in their own neighborhoods, to sustain the ordinances of the gospel, and to reserve something to be cast into the treasury of the Lord, in order to send the gospel to the heathen, to raise up ministers, to build up colleges and seminaries at the west, and to supply the destitute of our own land, who are less able or less willing than themselves, with the sacred ministry.

Our plan is to place tuition at what will be regarded by the New England community, including the wealthy and the educated, with farmers and mechanics, as moderate tuition.

Here I would have you distinctly understand that we do not adopt this standard because we consider ourselves under any obligation to *man* so to do. Neither do we consider it necessary that other institutions should adopt the same standard, or that this institution should certainly abide by it evermore, though at present it is essential to our success.

I have not been alone in considering it of great importance to establish a permanent seminary in New England for educating female teachers, with accommodations, apparatus, &c., somewhat like those for the other sex. Honorably to do this, from twenty to forty thousand dollars must be raised; and such a sum, raised for such an object, would form almost an era in female education. For years, Miss Grant and myself made continual efforts to accomplish the object; but all our efforts failed.

I am convinced that there are but two ways to accomplish such an object. First, to interest one, two, or a few wealthy men to do the whole; second, to interest the whole New England community, beginning with the country population, and in time receiving the aid and cooperation of the more wealthy in our cities. Each of these modes, if practicable, would have its advantages. The first, if done at all, could be done sooner and with very little comparative labor. The second would require vastly more time and labor; but if it were accomplished, an important and salutary impression would be made on the whole of New England. Having adopted this second course, we have been for some time going forward with as much success as we could expect. We have enlisted for the work. I have regarded it as a work for life. In laying our plans, we examined carefully every step. In the commencement of any great enterprise, the community often are not prepared to act upon the most important considerations, when they can be moved by less important, but more tangible, circumstances. During my long but fruitless efforts in connection with Miss Grant, I became convinced that the community were not disposed to appreciate the most important advantages of an institution thus endowed, such as its superior character and its permanency. I was also convinced that, to give the first impulse to this work, something must be presented which is more tangible, and of real, though of less, value, and be made to stand out in bold relief. For this purpose, we have chosen the reduction of expenses, as compared with other large seminaries, not aided by the public. Every step we take proves it a good selection. We carefully avoid all extravagant statements; indeed, we usually state only general facts, leaving each to make his own estimate and draw his own conclusions. There is an expectation that economy will be practiced in the establishment, and that the funds, gathered by little and little, will be reserved for the good of the institution, and not for private emolument, and that there will be such a reduction of expense as the nature of the case will allow. Here is our pledge, and we must redeem it. In doing this, the first object to be gained is good management in the boarding department. Let that be secured, and all else will be sure to follow. I do not expect to have the direct care of the boarding department, but I hope to secure the cooperation of persons skilled in domestic economy, and disposed to use their skill faithfully for the great cause. The department of instruction, including tuition, I expect to superintend myself; and it is essential to success in the boarding department that I should set an example of economy in my own. Unless I do, I cannot lift up my head in efforts to exert an influence on this point in every other department. I do not mean to ask any other one connected with the institution to make such sacrifices as I can cheerfully make. This may not be necessary for my successor, but it is necessary in my case, at least for a few years.

Again, we have held up to New England people the advantages of a teachers' seminary, with ample facilities for boarding and instruction, free of rent, of so superior a character that a supply of scholars could be secured without receiving those who were immature and ill prepared, and who are always a heavy tax on the time of teachers. We have shown that the same money will, in this way, do more to provide instruction for young women qualifying themselves to teach, than it would do in our country academies. After these professions, shall we ask for higher tuition, at the same time that we are asking for benevolent aid to carry forward our enterprise?

Thus I do feel confident that we must retain our plan for tuition, or abandon the enterprise. But we must not give up the work. To indulge even a fear as to our final success, would be a cruel distrust of the kindest Providence. While I do not consider ourselves under any obligation to *man*, we are under solemn obligations to *God*, to adopt this course. We are compelled by the principles of expediency, so beautifully exhibited in the precepts and practice of the apostle Paul. If any injury should result to the cause of education from our adopting this moderate standard of tuition, it will be as nothing compared with the great good to be accomplished; less far than the injurious results of Paul's example, on the support of the gospel ministry, which results he so carefully guards against in the ninth chapter of I Corinthians.

I express myself with more confidence on this subject, because it has been with me, for two or three years, a matter of careful consideration; but further, because our laborious and indefatigable agent is of the same opinion, and all his intercourse with New England people has tended to confirm it. Having been wholly devoted to the enterprise for a year and a half, he probably knows more of the views of the New England community on this point than any hundred others. Careful in all his movements, he never has occasion to retrace a single step. Whatever may be thought of my sanguine temperament, he cannot be charged with being over-zealous. But his deficiency in zeal is more than made up by his unwearied labors, his never-ending patience and perseverance, his sound common sense, his careful observation of human nature, and his intimate acquaintance with New England people.

You speak of the importance of raising the compensation of teachers. In a list of motives for teaching, I should place first the great motive, which cannot be understood by the natural heart, Love thy neighbor as thyself. On this list, though not second in rank, I have been accustomed to place pecuniary considerations. I am inclined to the opinion that this should fall lower on a list of motives to be presented to ladies than to gentlemen, and that this is more in accordance with the system of the divine government. Let us cheerfully make all due concessions, where God has designed a difference in the situation of the sexes, such as woman's retiring from public stations, being generally dependent on the other sex for pecuniary support, &c. O that we may plead constantly for her religious privileges, for equal facilities for the improvement of her talents, and for the privilege of using all her talents in doing good!

73. An Era in Female Education
October 9, 1836

To Zilpah Grant

I am thinking of going to Boston about a week from this time, and perhaps shall go to Ipswich, if you are there. I should be glad to hear from you, and learn something about your plans. I do not wish you to stay at Ipswich on my account, but I should be glad to know when you will be there. I believe I must have a little mantua making done. I am hesitating whether to make an attempt to have it done in Boston, or at Ipswich or Norton. My black silk dress I had made at Monson. My cloak has had such very hard usage last year, that on examining it, I believe I must have something else for this winter. I am hesitating whether to have a good cloak, or to have something for a pelisse, which I can make into a dress at some future time, perhaps dark silk, perhaps some kind of woollen, merino, or something else.

I could have it lined very warm, and carry it in my trunk on my journeys, and sometimes journey without it. My cloak will do for journeying, and for most occasions, but sometimes, I must have something a little better. What do you think would be most comfortable, and most economical? I should very much like to know what is your opinion. I shall purchase it in Boston probably. Can you ascertain whether there is any thing in Ipswich, you would think suitable? Can you also ascertain whether I could have it made at Ipswich next week. I have not entirely given up going to New York this autumn. I am thinking of going directly to New York from Boston. But it is almost impossible for me to predict my own movements. I spent last Wed. night at Belchertown, Thurs. night at Barre, Friday night at Amherst, and yesterday returned here. I leave tomorrow on an excursion around on the hills for the sake of conversing with some individual about our enterprize. I expect to get round to Belchertown the last of the week, on my way to Boston. If you can mail your reply as early as Friday, direct to Belchertown. If later direct to Boston care of Dea. Safford, No. 3, Beacon Street. I am going to Boston to endeavor to find out whether it is safe for us to attempt anything there this autumn. If it seems expedient, I shall write to Mr. Hawkes, and he will go on and make the attempt. I wish you could render us some aid. There is more than 9 chances out of 10, that the question will be decided in the negative. May the path of duty be made plain. Pray for us. Have you any hints to give on this subject? Perhaps I shall go to Ipswich with very little stop in Boston, and stop more on my return. I went to Barre with Mr. Hawkes. Rev. Mr. Stone has finally decided to accept of an agency for our seminary. He commences immediately. We had a fine day for the laying of the corner stone. I should have enjoyed your being present. The address is generally well spoken of. The general doctrine of benevolence was pretty well discussed. I should have been glad of something a little more specific. Dr. Humphrey made the first prayer, and Mr. Condit the last. It was a day of very deep interest. The associations were very tender. That is an affecting spot to me. The stone and brick and mortar speak a language, which vibrates through my very soul. How much thought, and how much feeling have I had on this general subject in years that are past. And I have indeed lived to see the time, when a body of gentlemen have ventured to lay the corner stone of an edifice which will cost about $15,000—and for an institution for the education of females. Surely the Lord hath remembered our low estate. This will be an era in female education. The work will not stop with this institution. The enterprize may have to struggle through embarrassments for years, but its influence will be felt. It is a concession on the part of gentlemen in our behalf which can be used again and again.

I have not seen you since the first day of July. I do want to see you very much. Can we settle our pecuniary affairs while I am at Ipswich. I do very much want to know how they stand.

74. Give Liberally
May 29, 1837

To Eunice Caldwell

I very much want to see you and others whom I place among the particular friends of Mount Holyoke Female Seminary. We are now in a very great strait about obtaining furniture, &c. If I should visit you, could the whole school devote from one to two hours to the subject? I do not expect that they will contribute any thing to this object while they are members of the school, but only use their influence in its behalf when they go to their various homes.

I would by all means have the teachers choose their object of benevolence, present its claims to the scholars, and lead them to give abundantly and cheerfully; but I do more and more feel it to be important that young ladies engaged in study, and spending freely on themselves for board and tuition, should give liberally to the treasury of the Lord. This is essential to their cultivating right principles, to their forming right habits. Are not young ladies, as well as young men, while engaged in study, in danger of excusing themselves from contributing liberally, because they are spending their money to prepare themselves for usefulness? By fortifying themselves with this excuse, through their whole course of education, may they not almost form the habit of feeling that every thing of large amount, that is to be cast into the treasury of the Lord by their own hands, must first pass through the channel of self, to fit it for the Master's service? Ought not young ladies, in a course of education, carefully to economize in the least expenditures, lest something which ought to be put into the treasury of the Lord should flow into some other channel? I hope the teachers in Ipswich will be faithful on this subject.

75. Sweet Consolation
Norton, July 24, 1837

To Sarah Brigham

I have sympathized with you in your late afflictions. I need not tell you that I feel deeply interested in all that relates to yourself and friends, and that my interest in your behalf is now more deeply enlisted than ever. How sweet, though painful, must it be to think of your dear mother! You do not dwell on her image, which is ever before you, with painful emotions and anxious doubt where she now is, and what is now her condition, and what her present employments. You can rest quietly in the belief that she is now with her God, beyond all dangers and all troubles. When you first awake in the morning, do you not think of her for a moment as still alive? But the next moment the painful reality rushes upon you that she is indeed no more; that she has gone, forever gone, and you are all motherless. But the painful truth scarcely finds its way into your wounded heart, when your soul is filled with the sweet consolation that she is happy, forever happy; that she does not lie distressed on that painful couch, where you watched her by day and by night. She has gone to rest—eternal rest. How important that such afflictions should lead us to do with our might what our hands find to do! What have we to do with this world, except as a place to prepare for eternity ourselves, and to seek the same preparation in behalf of others?

76. The Changeableness of Earth
South Hadley, April 23, 1838

To Zilpah Grant

Do you now and then like to receive a line from me, or have you so many other cares, that it is a tax on your strength more than it is worth? The intimate communion which continued between us for so many years, I do not, I cannot forget. Sometimes former views, and former intercourse, and former mutual duties and obligations, and mutual kindness and faithfulness, in contrast with the present non-intercourse almost between us, come over me, with an overwhelming power. I know it must be so. I know you cannot come to see me, nor can I go to see you; and if I could, I should not feel at liberty to tax your strength with my visits. The same is true with regard to our writing. I am generally entirely reconciled. But occasionally, when I have heard nothing from you for weeks or months, only as I do by the by, as I do from any of my common acquaintances, I find myself involuntarily saying, Is this that same friend with whom I lived and labored so many years, with whom I had so much intercourse from day to day, and with whom I have exchanged so many letters? This is the changeableness of earth. How transitory is every thing here! It seems as if I could say of nothing that it has long been, but only that it once was; or that it now is, and may be a few days longer. Of all the changes that take place, the changing of friends, of companions, of fellow-laborers, of fellow-travellers through this pilgrimage, is the most painful. Rather let these changes come year by year, and month by month, so that there may be no tender and long-strengthened cords to be torn asunder—that there may be no train of recollection and former communion to add to scenes of desolation.

77. Death Has Entered Our Windows
South Hadley, April 12, 1839

To Zilpah Grant

We have just been passing through a trying scene. Death for the first time has entered our windows, and marked one of our number as his victim. It has been a trying, solemn time. It was a disease of the head, and, as is common in such cases, was very deceitful in developing its true nature till a short time before her death. On this account, none of her friends were here to see her breathe her last. Her sister arrived about two hours after, and her father met the remains a few miles from this place, as they were moving towards her last earthly home. She had been with us about a year, and I trust her being here has been the means of preparing her for heaven.

She became serious last summer, indulged a hope in the autumn, has been consistent through the winter as a Christian, and has seemed to share deeply in the late revival. She has not been very well through the whole year, and I now think that the causes of her last disease have been long at work in her system. But it seems as if an unseen hand had kept back its progress, that she might repent and believe, and prepare for eternity.

I will take Rees's Cyclopaedia at the price you mention, but I have not the means to purchase the Annals of Education. If you do not wish to sell all together, perhaps 'the Memorandum Society,' in the seminary, may purchase one set. It is now vacation, and those to whom the question would be referred are not here. The leading objects of the society are to preserve a history of its members, and a general history of the seminary. It is designed also to make it a means of individual improvement.

We are thinking of preparing a written catalogue, with various items attached to each name, as a part of the work of the Memorandum Society.

78. Our Dear Mother is No More
South Hadley, December 3, 1840

To Aaron Lyon

But a few years ago, and we seemed an unbroken circle. Though separated from each other, we seven were all living, and could think and pray for one another from day to day. After the hand of death was laid on our dear father, nearly thirty years passed away before any one of us was called out of time into eternity. Since then, how frequently have we been called to mourning! How great have been the ravages of death! You have heard of sister F.'s departure, and now it becomes my painful duty to tell you that another one is gone. Yes, our dear mother is no more. My dear brother, can you think how lonely it was to me as I followed her dear remains to the grave, with no brother or sister by my side? I felt that indeed our family was but a broken circle. As I passed out of the door where I have often met her gladdened and joyful face, as I went along the way where we have so many times rode together to see sister J., and as I looked on her placid face for the last time, "Can this be," thought I, "my dear mother? And is this my last visit to her solitary home?"

79. The Moral Cause
South Hadley, March 8, 1841

To Zilpah Grant

I thank you for communicating so much about the health of your body, and the health of your soul. I have long wanted to hear from you, and have often attempted to commend you, with all your unknown state, to our covenant-keeping God. The dealings of divine Providence have been such towards me since I last saw you, as to lead me to think with great tenderness of all my friends, and especially of yourself; and more than all, I hope, of that dearest Friend that sticketh closer than a brother. The hand of God has been laid heavily upon me. I have been led through deep waters, but they have not overflowed me. His good hand has been ever my support.

You have heard of the sickness and death of my dear pupils during the fall vacation. Last year we took unusual pains about the health of our young ladies; altogether more than ever before. So true is it that *the race is not to the swift, nor the battle to the strong,* and that *it is not in man that watcheth to direct his steps.* None but my heavenly Father knows how great a trial this was to my heart. While others have been inquiring about the natural cause, I have felt that we who were most nearly connected ought particularly to inquire about the moral cause, and to seek to know what the Lord would have us learn from his dealings with us. I hope the affliction has not been altogether lost on myself, but that in the hand of God it has been used in some degree to prepare me for the events that have since followed. You have heard of *these*. I have now no mother or sister whom I can go and see; and alone I followed my dear mother to the grave. Her prayers, which I have daily had for so many years, I shall have no more. She, to whose comfort I have been expecting the pleasant privilege of administering for years to come, as almost the only child left her, will need nothing more. I feel my family loneliness; but with it eternity seems very near, with all its precious privileges, purchased by the blood of our glorious Savior.

The last stroke touching my health has been to me scarcely a trial. As I have been obliged to give up many labors to other hands, and some weeks nearly all, I have felt that I have nothing to say and scarcely any thing to ask, but that God might be glorified.

After about a month's active labor in organizing the school, I began to find my strength very weakness. I tried to rest, but all seemed only to reduce me still more. I have had but little disease, but a general prostration. For several weeks I could not read much, nor write, nor think, nor feel, nor talk. For about two months I did not go out to church. Now I can go half a day, and do several things of the lighter sort.

I want to tell you many things about our school, and how kind Providence has been to us, and how the way was all prepared beforehand for me to be laid aside. But I must wait till I write to you again. The Spirit of God has been evidently with us all the year. About fifteen have expressed hope, and many others have a long time seemed but a step from the kingdom of God.

80. Cord of Affection
South Hadley, September 1, 1841
To Hannah Chickering Briggs

I have already sympathized with you in your present trial. May the Lord comfort and sustain you, and give our dear Miss Grant all the strength which she needs. How many changes do we meet, and in how many ways are these changes taking place! How does Providence in wisdom set one thing over against another, so that we need not glory in our own strength, rejoice too much in our own happiness, or sorrow above reason! Scarcely a new cord of affection can be spun, but the materials must be drawn from the shattered fibres of some former attachment. On the other side, scarcely are the firmest bonds broken asunder, but they are followed by some new ones of equal, if not greater interest. My feelings were interested on this subject last winter, when Miss Grant informed me that you appeared near your grave. 'How interesting,' thought I, must be your situation, as far as you had power to reflect; at one moment looking with deep sorrow on those many cords which must soon be severed; and the next moment, forward to those new and everlasting bonds in heaven just ready to be bound around your heart! I love sometimes to lose sight of individuals, in thinking of the bundles of eternal life and happiness that are bound up together in heaven. How delightful will be the joys of that happy place! Edwards's views in his "History of Redemption," on God's dealings with his church as a *whole*, are very interesting.

81. Spiritual Interests
South Hadley, March 8, 1843

To Zilpah Banister

I have been absent a short time, and on my return yesterday found your two letters. You ask about the spiritual interests of our school. I was just thinking of writing to you on this very subject, that I might beseech your prayers at this time, for it is one of great darkness, of anxiety, of hope, of fear. In temporal things we have been greatly blessed. We have a much greater supply of teachers than usual. Misses M. and W. have applied their minds closely to reducing every thing under their control to the most beautiful order and symmetry, and with great success. Our young ladies are very youthful, more and more so every year; but there is so much docility, such a sweet atmosphere all around, that I feel, from day to day, that our home is a sweet home. There is more missionary interest than usual, and more desire among some Christians to be prepared for the service of God. But, alas! one thing is lacking—the direct and powerful influences of the Holy Spirit. A few gentle drops have descended, but we have enjoyed no plentiful shower, and this we greatly need. According to all former experience, the harvest time for this year will be past in four or five weeks. Then will come the finishing up of the term and the spring examinations. After that will follow the short summer term, a most favorable time for fixing last impressions, for attempting to lead Christians into green and living pastures, but not a favorable time for the work of the Holy Spirit in breaking up the fallow ground by conviction and conversion. Nearly sixty of our number are without hope. As teachers, as Christians, as an institution, we greatly need the effects of a powerful revival. I fear to make any extra effort; I fear to omit it. I know not what to do. The way seems greatly hedged up. I fear to go forward; I dare not stand still; I cannot go back.

   I went to Boston to help fit off one of our teachers as a missionary to the Nestorians. I made arrangements to be absent a few days longer, that I might have time to look over our sad, very sad state, and that I might inquire of the Lord a right path in which to walk. I wanted exceedingly to go to N., and also to M., on my way home; but I thought it my duty to stay in one place, to make no calls, to do but a little business, and only attend meetings as I could. I have seldom had so profitable a week, when I have had so much physical and mental rest, and so much, as I humbly hope, of spiritual refreshing. I have been greatly interested in examining the subject of prayer. Since I returned, a few more drops have fallen. But how so great a work can be done in so short a time I know not. All is yet darkness, but I hope and trust that light will shine out of darkness. Now, I have one urgent request to make of you. It is, that you would set apart a little time every day to pray in sincerity and in truth for us. Pray that God would, in his own way, do a great work here, and give us a great blessing. Pray that we may be taught what the Lord would have us do. Will you thus pray every day till you hear from us again, which shall be soon? For a few days, I design to study daily two passages of Scripture, praying that I may be led by the Spirit to receive into the understanding and heart just what the Holy Ghost has revealed in these wonderful passages —Luke xi. 5-13, James i. 5-8. Would you like to study these daily with me, as you pray for us?

82. Revival
South Hadley, March 9, 1843

To Eliza Ann Safford

As I have a little business on which I must write this morning, I will take this opportunity to say a few things on the subject so near my heart. On my return, I found things in some respects a little more favorable than when I left. The general seriousness has increased somewhat, and considerably in one small section under the care of one teacher. The teachers have had some increase of interest, and are making some new efforts in their sections. Among those who have most of a heart for such a work there is a growing conviction of the great need of a thorough, powerful revival, to break up the fallow ground, to give a new current to thought and feeling among the younger and least experienced Christians, among the coldest, most lukewarm, and most backward professors, and among some who stand on middle ground. Thursday morning is one of the three mornings in the week when I reserve a half hour for religious instruction and devotional exercises. I have just met the pupils in the hall. I took occasion to spread out before them our present position, with our necessity, our danger, our fear, and our hope, mingling all along my own feelings, my own solemn convictions of the urgency of the case. I stated my own views, that something must be done, though entire darkness was spread over the path of duty. I told them that a little while ago I came to them to ask of them a missionary. I would not go from one to another, lest I should not find the best. And the Lord so stirred up the willing hearts that we all believed that we had sent the one whom he had called and qualified for the work. And now I came to ask for a willing heart to unite with me in prayer for this great thing, as this seemed our last refuge. The scene was very interesting to my feelings. How I should love to have had you with us, to mingle in our sympathies and prayers! There was a very tender spirit this morning, an atmosphere in which it was very easy to breathe and to speak too. Probably little circumstances might have some effect. It is so seldom that I leave this beloved household for a single day, that my meeting them after an absence of only a week and a half is suited to awaken some tender emotions on both sides. Such things are the veriest trifles in themselves; but my sentiment is, that the most trifling circumstances should be used for the same great end. With regard to efforts in behalf of the impenitent, all is dark. But amidst the darkness, and with a burden on my heart which I cannot describe, there is something in my soul which seems like trust in God, that is like a peaceful river, overflowing all its banks. Light can shine out of darkness, and I have great hope that we shall receive a blessing, whether or not the providence of God shall permit Mr. Kirk to come and share with us in our labors, our joys, and our sorrows.

    I have increasing views of the importance of a whole

work of the Spirit, a universal work, one which shall reach our whole church of more than one hundred, all young. You recollect Mr. Kirk's vivid description of the difference between passing through the deep valley and rising up into a revival, and leaping immediately into the sympathies of a revival. We need experience of his first to fit us for the varied and important remaining duties of the year. On this account, I have some query whether it may not be better that Mr. Kirk's visit should be deferred a little longer. If he could stay two or three full weeks, I would as soon that he would come today as ever. But if he cannot stay but one week, and possibly even less, it is very important that he come at the right time, and expend his power in the best way. His fear that he could not stay long enough is my great fear. It seems to me like a very desirable thing that certain minds, certain difficult cases, should come under the influence of a powerful mind and warm heart, like Mr. Kirk's, and we all need some stirring means; but my own will has ever been graciously kept in an even balance concerning this thing. I am prepared to rejoice or to acquiesce as soon as the will of the Lord shall be made known.

Now, whatever may be in relation to these things, let me ask and beseech you three, [Mr. and Mrs. Safford and Mr. Kirk,] my dear sympathizing friends, to grant me one petition. Will you every day offer a short prayer in our behalf, which shall arise from your inmost heart, till you hear from me again, which shall be soon? Only ask God, our heavenly Father, in the name of Jesus, our blessed Redeemer, and you shall have your request.

83. The Spirit of God is Moving
March 17, 1843

To Daniel Safford

The present state of our school is exceedingly critical. May you have a mind and a heart to pray for us. The testimony from every source—from the teachers, from the prayer meetings, from meetings for the impenitent, from individual conversation among Christians and among the impenitent—is all the same, proving beyond doubt that the Spirit of God is moving with a gentle influence on the face of the waters. Still, there is not that point and decision which must be attained, or we shall fail of the blessing. The great and distressing doubt which rested on my mind about using any extra means myself has, in the providence of God, been somewhat removed. That interesting state on many things, such as missions, the general path of duty, &c., seems now changing to an increasing desire for the direct and special influences of the Holy Spirit. Our regular business goes forward just as usual, but many have been looking up their leisure time for religion. The teachers are most of them very much engaged in gathering up the fragments of time, that nothing be lost. I have had a short extra meeting for the impenitent every day. I have been able to meet all my appointments, though sometimes I have concentrated all the strength of three or four hours into half an hour. Every thing I do is such a privilege. It is such a privilege, too, to depend daily and hourly for light, for strength, and for hope on our heavenly Father, through Jesus Christ, our Redeemer!

It is so difficult for me to stop writing! My heart is so full! But I fear you cannot read this. If not, let it go as of no great importance.

84. Unusually Encouraging
March 20, 1843

To Zilpah Banister

When I last wrote to you, I engaged to address you again very soon. I have been very sick for a week, or I should have written some days sooner.

In my last, I requested a special interest in your prayers until you heard from us again. I communicated also something respecting our religious state. Just at that time, I felt that we were in a very trying, critical condition. I had been absent three Sabbaths. After spending another Sabbath here, and becoming more acquainted with the state of things, I began to feel 'surely the

Lord is in this place, and I knew it not.' In all seasons of religious interest in this house the Lord has ever delighted to own and bless the holy Sabbath. For the last week, a work has been going forward with convincing evidence that it is indeed the work of the Lord. I believe I told you in my last that I spent a few days in Boston, that I might have quiet and time to look over our condition, and to seek the right way. The state of our school in general has been unusually encouraging this year. There has been a very sweet spirit, a pleasant docility, and a consistent deportment. Our evening prayer meetings have been like a connecting artery through which the life-blood flowed. Our semi-monthly missionary meeting has been better attended than ever before, and we have all thought that the missionary spirit was advancing in the seminary. This spirit seemed to receive an impulse by Miss Fisk's leaving us, and devoting herself to this work. I have thought we seemed preparing for every thing else desirable except for the reception of the special influences of the Holy Spirit. To this there seemed some great barrier. This was the great thing to be sought. This we needed to convict and convert sinners, to give that living faith in the great atoning sacrifice without which it is impossible to please God. This we needed to overcome the world, to fix our hopes, to establish our joys, to settle forever our confidence. I returned from Boston not knowing whither I should be led, or whether there was any thing special that could be done. But I felt a trust, and a reliance on an invisible arm, greater and sweeter than I can ever describe. What a privilege it is to walk by faith! What a privilege it is to have no wisdom of our own, to have no plan for the future, that the wisdom of God may be more manifest, and that the indications of Providence and the guidance of the Spirit, day by day, may be more precious! I found, on my return, that a spiritual change was passing over the face of things, that the Spirit of God was gently moving on the face of the waters. The teachers I found more active in gathering up the fragments of time for religious duties and privileges connected with those under their care. Some Christians were becoming deeply interested. Many of the impenitent were in an inquiring state, and some very deeply affected. The work appears now to be going directly forward. Some eight or ten expressed a hope at different times along in the winter. This number is now increased probably to about twenty-five. We are passing a very important time. There are some exceedingly difficult, dark cases. Some have passed through revival after revival, have been deeply affected, indulged a hope once or twice, have made one effort after another, and now, as they suppose, are settled down in a state of disconsolate indifference. May the Lord give you a mind and heart to pray for us! May I not hear from you soon? Let me have a page from your own heart.

    I should love to write you a long letter about my own personal feelings. Some views of truth have of late passed before my mind in an exceedingly interesting manner to myself. With what condescension does God come down in the simplicity of truth to our own personal wants! Let God be honored, let Christ be all and in all, and let every created being be less than nothing and vanity.

85. Conversions
South Hadley, March 21, 1843

To Eliza Ann Safford

I must write you a few lines this morning, though I can say but little. I want to ask your prayers especially in two or three respects. Respecting our state generally I have little to say, only that the Lord is doing his own work in his own blessed way. The work is going forward apparently with great rapidity, stillness, universality, gentleness, and power. I believe I mentioned about sixty who entered the school without hope. I should have excepted some eight or ten as the fruits of the drops of mercy which have been falling upon us from month to month during the year. I suppose now not less than one half of the sixty are indulging a hope of pardoning mercy through the blood of Christ. A large number of hopeful conversions have occurred in three days, including the Sabbath. The Sabbath is of indescribable value to us. There can be no community to which it is more important. In times of revival, it seems always to be the day that God delights peculiarly to honor. At other times, it seems to be worth more than all other days in bringing the thoughts into captivity to the will of Christ.

You will ask what means we are using. They are so small that I can hardly tell what they are, and yet they are numerous, simple, and, through the infinite condescension of God, they seem to be adapted to our state. In the use of means, we simply walk, day by day, by the light which is so graciously shed on our path. We cannot, we would not look forward. Our studies go forward, as usual, with all their regularity, our family duties with all their accustomed order. But we feel that we can and ought to turn aside from other sources of social improvement and enjoyment, that all the fragments of time may be gathered up and devoted to the great and grand business of seeking a divine blessing to descend on all this family. The teachers are all of one mind and one heart in this thing. We use our fragments of time just when they happen to come, and just for the object for which they seem at the time to be most needed. The prayer meetings are sometimes fifteen minutes, sometimes half an hour, and sometimes longer, according to circumstances. Some of the teachers have quite a prayer meeting in fifteen minutes at recess in the evening with their sections. They have adopted the practice in these little daily meetings, long ago, of having the prayers unsolicited. This turns to a favorable account just now. Sometimes they find time for three or four prayers in fifteen minutes. They can return to their duties with renewed energy and submission, if not of pleasure in their studies. The teachers really seem to be emphatically the leaders of the flock. In the meetings for the impenitent I have no very definite plan. My waiting eyes are unto God. From day to day, thus far, the path of duty has been plain. The almost Egyptian darkness which rested on my mind about the path of duty was but a contrast to that light which shines from day to day. I have no knowledge of future duty, and I ask for none. It is so sweet to carry every burden and every care to the throne of everlasting love, and of perfect confidence through the Lord Jesus Christ. My lungs have not allowed me the privilege of individual conversation, but the teachers and others are instant in season and out of season.

But my sheet is full, and I fear the mail will be gone, and I have not told my errand. First, I want you should pray daily and unitedly with great fervency for _____. She has some rather peculiar associations, as I suppose. She retains her hope, but something in her character revolts from every thing social in feeling or action. I cannot find that an individual in the house has been able to approach her successfully in the least degree on the religion of her heart or life. I have met minds in a similar state, and, as a matter of judgment in her case, have avoided meeting her on the subject, hoping that some door might be opened in her behalf before the year closes. Many things may be done and said in time of a revival that cannot be done and said at any other time. This may be the favored time for her. I have approached the subject gently, and hope I may have the privilege of doing something more. I think it not best that she should know that the subject passes between us. But I hope you will really pray in her behalf.

We have some individuals that seem among the most hopeless. They are among the righteous towards men. They have passed seasons of conviction, and perhaps indulged hope once or twice. Here they are clothed now in the self-righteousness of not being deceived this time. Do pray for them.

My continued desire and prayer is, that this whole family as a family, and every individual as an individual, may be baptized by the Holy Spirit. We are experiencing some interesting reconversions among those who have long indulged a hope.

86. Day of Fasting and Prayer
South Hadley, March 25, 1843

To Eliza Ann Safford

I cannot tell you how rejoiced I was to receive your letter. I had so long been looking and longing for it. I knew you were praying for us, but I wanted to have you tell me so. We are in greater need than ever of the power of prayer. As you hear from us, from time to time, I trust that you will not cease to give thanks to God, and to pray without ceasing, making all our requests known to God. It is sweet to think of you as praying in our behalf, if you cannot come and see us. We are on the verge of another holy Sabbath. It is a great event for us to pass a holy Sabbath. O that a great, a very great blessing may descend upon us! The past week has been a wonderful time. Of that sixty over whom I mourned so much, and wept so much, and prayed so much, the week I was with you, only a remnant are now without hope. But some very trying cases are left. O for that all-prevailing prayer in their behalf which shall be heard! Several professors of religion have given up their hope, and a few have disclosed the fact that they have had no hope for a long time. Some of them are now walking in light, and others are shrouded in thick darkness. But the Lord has wrought for us such great things that we can but trust him in every time of need.

Monday Morning. —We have decided to devote this day as a day of fasting and prayer. This is the first day this year that we set apart to such a blessing on ourselves as individuals and on our family as a family. It is a great and a solemn thing to set apart such a day. It is a great thing voluntarily to give up all our business for a whole day, that we may meet God in the inner sanctuary of his holy, spiritual temple. I trust this day is brought by many hearts as a willing offering, and that it will be accepted through the blood of the everlasting covenant.

I have many things which I want to write, but I cannot now. I should be glad to tell you how the Lord has led us along by his own right hand. I should love to give you one simple page from my own soul. Do write very soon.

87. Cloud of Mercy
April 13, 1843

To an Unknown Correspondent

I hoped I should have quite a large part of this sheet to tell you what the Lord hath wrought for us since I last wrote you. I believe just at the time that I sent my last letter, a cloud of mercy was gathering over our heads, and a few drops had fallen upon us. The cloud had so long been gathering, and so gently, that we scarcely knew it; but soon the windows of heaven were opened, and the blessing descended, so that there was scarcely room in our minds or hearts to receive it. When I returned from Boston, there were a few more than fifty without hope. In about three weeks, all but six expressed some hope that they had found the Savior; in a single week of this time, more than thirty of the number.

In all my privileged experience connected with the work of the Spirit, this, I think, has been of unparalleled rapidity; and yet I have never witnessed more quietness and stillness than in its progress, or any less of what some call *reaction* to be watched against in the result. It has seemed like a sudden, powerful shower bursting upon us, but descending with so much gentleness that not a leaf or twig among the tender plants is turned out of its place, and then so suddenly giving way to the beautiful sun and refreshing dews. But as teachers, we have a great work to cherish these tender plants. Shall we not have your prayers? O, to follow Christ in the work of cherishing them is what I want. This desire enters almost daily into the very depths of my soul with an untold and unwonted strength.

88. A Very Little Book
South Hadley, June 12, 1843
To Zilpah Banister

I will just communicate to *you* a secret. I have been employing all the time I could take for the last month in writing an article, which I expect to put into a *very little* book. How much I should value a little of your aid in fitting it for the press! But this cannot be with your health and cares, and with my extreme pressure relative to time. As a mere matter of friendship, however, I should love just to read it to you. If the printers can spare it, I shall take it with me, though there may not be time to read it. It would take about one hour and a half. I am extremely anxious that no one should guess at the writer of this little book.

89. The Duties that Devolve on a Missionary
South Hadley, February 6, 1844
To Justin Perkins

Your kind letter, bearing date July 7, I have received, for which please accept my cordial thanks. Perhaps you may occasionally grant me a like favor.

Your testimony to Miss Fiske's happiness and usefulness is very gratifying. Her own letters, too, are all suited to make her friends happy in having given her up for such a work. It is my opinion that the leadings of Providence should be decisive to justify our encouraging an unmarried female to go on a foreign mission. My impressions on this subject were strengthened as I saw Misses Fiske and Myers bidding farewell to friends and home, and kindred and country. How different was their situation from the rest of the company! Every other missionary had *one* intimate friend, and that one the dearest friend on earth. But Miss Fiske has been admirably prepared by the endowments of nature, by the dealings of Providence, and by the influence of grace, for just such a sacrifice. I rejoice that her heavenly Father has called her to this self-denying work, and that she was not disobedient to the heavenly voice. I rejoice, too, that the finger of Providence pointed her out to go, rather than any other one about whom we had conversation. I doubt not that she will find many ways of doing good besides that of teaching. As you wander along together, a lonely band through this vale of tears, and as you are laboring and suffering for Christ's sake, I doubt not that Miss Fiske will often be able, in her own quiet way, to come to one heart and another as an angel of mercy and kindness. Sometimes she may be able to give to some of her companions in toil a cup of consolation, when others, who would fain enjoy the same privilege, have not the time nor the strength granted them.

Miss Fiske has been very faithful and successful in writing letters. I think this not among the least of the ways given her to serve the cause.

You speak with interest of your visit to America, and to our beloved institution. Your remembrance of us is gratifying to our hearts. I rejoice that I was permitted to see so much of you while in this country. I enjoyed your visits here very much, and the memory is still precious. We love to recognize your mission and your name, as well as that of our beloved friend, Miss Fiske. I would rejoice and thank God in your behalf, that your return, your visitation, and your departure, were attended with so many circumstances, comforting to yourselves and favorable to the cause. Among all the duties that devolve on a missionary, it is far from being the least responsible, to be called in providence to visit his native land, and to meet all the people and all things which he must meet, and to make every where an honest, a faithful, and a salutary impression—an impression worthy of Him who came from heaven to earth on a great mission to save a lost and guilty world.

Give my very affectionate regards to Mrs. Perkins. May the Lord sustain and comfort her under all her trials. May you both have strength given you, for many years to come, to enjoy the privilege of laboring and suffering for Christ's sake.

Give my affectionate remembrance to Mar Yohannan. I hope he will live to see many missionaries go from his country to different parts of Asia. My love to Miss Myers.

90. I Wrote as Fast as Possible
South Hadley, March 4, 1844

To Fidelia Fiske

It is one year this week since we were in Boston together. I have often desired to write you some of the passing events, some of deep and thrilling interest, which have transpired since that time. As the mind and heart have been borne along upon the swelling wave, I have thought of you, and thought, too, that I should love to have you know what was passing among us. But I have almost done writing letters, except on business. I can never again sit down to write what will be worth passing so far by mail. But in this little box I cannot refrain from depositing a note. But what shall I write? Every thing must be told you over and over again, except it may be some of the passing things in my own breast. And first I would thank you sincerely for your faithfulness and promptness in writing to me, and to us all. I believe it is one prominent way offered you of doing good to write to this seminary. I hope you will have a mind, and a heart, and strength, and time to continue to do what you have begun. I shall enjoy, in my turn, receiving an occasional letter, though I may never write you again.

You remember the state of the school when you left. After you were fairly gone, I had a little time to look at our real condition. It seemed to me very peculiar and critical, and so it now seems to me in review. I can never forget that week in Boston after you left, which I spent there especially to rest, to meditate, and to try to pray; and I never can forget the scenes of the month which followed, and of the unspeakable grace of God then manifested. But Miss Whitman and others have written you all the particulars. I will just pass that over, and not attempt to describe that remarkable chapter in our history. Suffice it to say, that the grace of God was manifested in a wonderful manner. Those I shall ever regard as among the most striking scenes, exhibiting and illustrating the great scheme of salvation.

I will just take time to describe an incident in the history of my own emotions, which resulted in the little book which I send you with this—the "Missionary Offering." You may inquire how I found time to write a letter long enough to make a book. The truth is, that my spirit was so stirred, and my heart so burdened, that I wrote as fast as possible, without inquiring how I wrote, or whether I had time to write. In the month of April, the scenes of the revival, the prospect of our next missionary subscription, the falling off of the missionary receipts, all combined to give me an unusual current of emotions in view of certain subjects. I was preparing a connected series of topics to present to the school, the substance of which you will find, to some extent, in the first three and last two chapters. I had just commenced before the monthly concert in May, to which reference is made. After reading the affecting circular, which I heard with deepest interest, in behalf of all our school, who were present as well as myself, Mr. Condit invited a young minister, just commencing preaching, to make some remarks. To Mr. Condit's disappointment, and to my distress, instead of following out the subject, he just attempted to make some strictures on our missionary operations, alluding to slavery, and speaking of the want of economy at some of our stations. The defect of the young man was more in the head than the heart. All agreed that his remarks were, at least, ill-timed. But, among other results, they gave existence to the little book. It was scarcely two days before most of the materials were gathered together. They soon assumed a visible and tangible form, merely as a relief to the internal spirit. Thus much for this little circumstance, as little things often interest friends more than greater events.

91. The Cause of Christ
Monson, September 3, 1844

To Zilpah Banister

I am now on my way to Boston, where I shall spend a few days for business, and return to attend the meeting of the Board at Worcester. Mrs. P. sends you her love. Shall we not see you at Worcester? Is it not the duty and privilege of Christians to carry this missionary meeting on their hearts to the throne of grace? Except the Lord build the house, they labor in vain who build it. What a privilege it is to be allowed to cooperate in the least degree in the great work of bringing this world to the love and service of our blessed Redeemer! As we advance in life, may we have a more single eye to the glory of God in all we do, in all we desire, and in all we feel. May we have deeper and more affecting views of the value of the soul, and of the unspeakable and incomprehensible value of the price which has been paid for its ransom. I often feel that my days are rapidly passing, and that I have but a few remaining. But these remaining days are precious days, if they should be spent for the cause of Christ. And what an unspeakable privilege is it to indulge a hope that, when our work is done, through infinite grace, we may be admitted to dwell forever with the Lord!

92. Lightning
South Hadley, July 23, 1845

To Zilpah Banister

I have allowed your letter to lie by one mail, and if you had been with us yesterday morning, you would not think it strange. About three o'clock in the morning, our building was struck with lightning; but it was saved from a speedy and dreadful destruction. Do you recollect a closet over our ovens for drying towels? The frame to hold the towels was moved on a railway made of iron rails. The electric fluid found its way to these iron rails, and, as I suppose, in a moment every towel was lighted to an intense blaze, and in a few minutes the whole closet was like a burning oven. I think I heard the report when the lightning struck, and in less than five minutes I heard the cry of *fire*. In a few minutes more, I think it would have found its way to the wood-work and doors leading to the stairways, in such a manner that it would have been past control. I have not time to tell you how we were delivered. My mind has been affected by this striking illustration of eternal things, and of our dependence on that unseen hand by which we have been saved from everlasting burning.

93. Portrait
South Hadley, December 3, 1846
To Daniel Safford

My health is much better. I can now ride, and I am taking this tonic every pleasant day with great advantage. Let me know how dear Mrs. Safford is when you write. When shall I set my eyes on your faces again? Perhaps you know that cousin Lucy Lyon (now Mrs. Lord) is going to China on a mission under the Baptist board. She and her husband are now here, making us their last visit. They sail from New York some time this month. If my health improves, I may go and be with them at the time they sail. Perhaps you will ask *why* I do not sit for my portrait. I have thought of it, but think I cannot at this time.

How afflicting is the providence which has taken away one of our secretaries of the Board of Missions! But my mind dwells much on his sudden transition to his eternal home. How must that world of glory have burst on his astonished vision! But we are left to mourn. Yet let us remember that it is no accident which has taken him away. It is a stroke of the divine hand, planned, directed, and executed by infinite wisdom and infinite goodness. May we not yet see, and may he not even now see, how it comes in to forward the great work of saving a lost and dying world? What a place does Christ occupy as an atoning sacrifice in all the great things of divine Providence! What a book is there yet to be opened and read in the glorious doctrine of the atonement!

94. The Mercy Seat
South Hadley June 17, 1847

To Mary Rice

When Miss Fiske shall hand you this little note, you will be far, far away. Kind Providence preserving your life, I trust this will find you in your new, your chosen, your adopted home.

Your eyes there will look on the same glorious sun, the same beautiful moon, and the same sparkling stars that ours do in your own native land. Will it not be pleasant, when you are removed from all which once met your eyes, to look up to the heavens, and think that the eyes of your father and your mother may be looking at the same things? But nearer than this can we come together, when we approach the mercy seat. You will be no farther from that precious place of resort, no farther from your God, no farther from your last and best home in heaven. My dear, dear friend, be thou faithful unto death, and thou shalt have a crown of life.

95. Spiritual Food
South Hadley, April 27, 1848

To Zilpah Banister

I am glad to know the communings of your spirit with the wise and good. I have read Upham's "Interior Life" with deep interest and profit. I love to meet with such a heart as is evident in what he writes. It disarms my disposition to criticize. If a sentence does come along, now and then, which might be questioned by the strictest philosophical or theological rules, it is easy to pass it over and gather up the spiritual food.

In our Sabbath privileges we have had such a constant change of preachers, since our dear Mr. Condit's death, that with my deafness I have gained but little profit. Many things relating to our family and the church and parish render the question of Mr. Condit's successor one of great importance and of deep interest to me. I have enjoyed the privilege of praying that God would send us a man after his own heart, and such a one as he knows us to need.

We have again received a spiritual blessing in our family according to the riches of the grace of Jesus Christ. During our first term, about fifty expressed hope. During the last term, there has been a continued, gradual, progressive interest. Some one case of hope has occurred nearly every week; still, there are about thirty without hope.

96. Feeble Strength
South Hadley, June 5, 1848

To Zilpah Banister

Will you not come and make us a visit the week of our anniversary? It happens the first Thursday in August. The examination will occupy two or three days preceding. You have a standing invitation to come, and I enjoy the belief that you always will if you can. I do not know that you can realize what a great pleasure it is to me to have yourself and husband with us on these occasions.

Our dear Mr. Condit! I am reminded of him every way; I shall be especially at the time of our anniversary. I loved him as a friend on earth; if possible, my spirit loves him more as a friend in heaven. His memory is precious, very precious. But we have another man of God in his stead, (Mr. Laurie.) For this I would thank God. I should love to tell you all about the dealings of my heavenly Father in bringing him here, in helping him along, and the various occurrences, all interesting to my own feelings, connected with his becoming our pastor. But this I must leave till I have the privilege of communing with you face to face.

I have recently been reading, or, rather, am now reading, McCheyne's 'Life, Letters, and Lectures.' It is just what I need—the sincere milk dealt out in childlike simplicity and godly sincerity. It is just what I need to feed and refresh me when I am so tired that I can do nothing with strong meat. With my feeble strength, and with the burden laid upon me, I feel that henceforth my reading must be mostly for another world. I do want to commune more with your spirit on earth before we go home to our rest in heaven.

97. Hope and Fear
South Hadley, October 27, 1848

To Daniel Safford

I know you are always interested in our welfare, and especially in our spiritual progress. In many respects we are blessed and prospered. In our religious prospects I scarcely know what to say, my heart is so divided between hope and fear, and has been for many weeks. For a long time, I have hoped that there was a silent influence, which would finally result in the glory of God. There is but little which can be seen by human eyes, or talked about by human tongues. I scarcely dare inquire, lest I may put forth a finger to disturb the gentle onward influence. What, how much, or how little God is now doing we can all say we know not now, but we shall know hereafter. I hope we may then know that it is more than we now can speak about. One thing is sure—it is a time for prayer. I know you will not forget us at the throne of grace. The name of one and another is brought to me by some teacher, from time to time, as one who was venturing to indulge some hope in a Savior's love. But I have made no attempt to designate. Where they will finally be found I know not. Our vacation is very near. Its disturbing influence I very much fear. But we must look to God. In him alone is our hope. How peculiarly true it is that the Holy Spirit is the gift of God! The manner in which inquiries are made sometimes about God's visits of mercy to this institution distresses me, lest we should look for this spiritual blessing in the ordinary course of events. Whenever God comes, it is in his own way, disappointing all human expectations, and taking glory to himself alone. I love to ponder many things of hope and fear in my heart alone, beholding anew our own weakness, our own exceeding unworthiness, and trusting with new confidence in the mighty power and amazing goodness of God.

98.
Weighed Down With Fear and Trembling
South Hadley, October 27, 1848

To Hannah Porter

I do greatly desire to commune in heart with you. I want especially to beg an interest in your prayers. May God give you a spirit of prayer in our behalf. My heart is trembling with hope and fear. The still small voice of the Spirit, which has been whispering in our ears, still hovers over us. I dare not say much, for I know not what to say. I may know hereafter what God is now doing, though I know not now. I fear that I may know hereafter, as I do not now, how the Spirit is grieved. But I hope that I may know that God is even now doing a greater work in the secret recesses of the heart than is visible to our eyes. We transferred our Thursday evening meeting this week to Tuesday evening, (last evening,) and brought all together. Mr. Laurie came in and conducted it. He has not met us before. I trembled, as I fear every change at this time. I had felt it desirable that he should come in once at least this term. If the path of duty was plain, I did endeavor to pray that God would give him some crumbs of bread to scatter to the hungry. My prayer was answered. He spoke extemporaneously from short notes, but with much freedom, and quite to the point. I felt this as a special favor from the hand of God. I think he spoke to our school only once last year, and then he did not seem to enjoy it much. This will explain my solicitude and my gratitude to God for his goodness. I felt before and after the same as I do in my own case. None but God knows how the responsibility of giving religious instruction to those candidates for eternity weighs on my heart. Sometimes, beforehand, my soul is weighed down with fear and trembling and anxious solicitude, which finds no relief but in God. When I have finished, and God has given me some enlargement of heart, I am overwhelmed with gratitude, and with a view of my own unworthiness for such a blessing. Then I can only pour out my heart in prayer that the Spirit may carry truth to the heart, though given in great weakness. Sometimes the spirit within weighs down the body, and sometimes the body treads the spirit in the dust. O this body of death! Thanks to God for the victory through Jesus Christ our Lord! You will see where, and when, and for what to pray in my behalf.

99.
I am Fast Hastening to My Eternal Home
Monson, January 20, 1849

To Abigail Moore Burgess

Here I am again with my dear Mrs. Porter. She proposes that we should again write a joint letter to comfort you in your pilgrimage and voluntary exile for Christ's sake. This I am very happy to do, though I think it will not take a very large part of the sheet to assure you of my continued remembrance of you and of former scenes. I wrote once before in Mrs. Porter's letter, two years ago. I have scarcely had a vacation of any sort since then. But I am now enjoying an old-fashioned vacation of *real rest* in this sweetest of all resting-places. Miss Hazen proposed to stay and take all the care, and let me go away. I decided to accept. I began a week beforehand to arrange all things. I had my plans made out in writing, and left all behind me. Here I can quietly read, write letters, ride, and visit, with nothing to annoy me, and with scarcely a thought of home, except as I attempt to send up my feeble petitions, that the Holy Spirit may come down and dwell with us. This is the more remarkable, as Miss Whitman is away. But one providence meets another. I had many things planned and arranged last year for this, so that this proves one of the *easiest* years. Such years come along now and then.

My health has been unusually good this year, thus far. So unlike has it been to the winter after you left us, that I have great cause for gratitude. But at all times, whether I have more or less strength, I feel that I am fast hastening to my eternal home, my home of rest in the bosom of my God, as I hope. Still, I trust I may have a little more work to do on earth, and that little may I do faithfully. By grace I am the little that I am, and by grace alone would I do the little that I hope to do. The doctrine of grace, in all its aspects and relations, is more and more precious here; and what will it be hereafter, when we shall be permitted to join in that song of Moses and the Lamb to Him who has redeemed us, and washed our robes, and made them white in his own blood! By grace we are redeemed, by grace we are saved, by grace we are received and sanctified, by grace we have our work given us, and by grace strength and a heart to do it.

My work is made up, as you know, of an endless number of duties, of nameless littleness, interwoven if not confused together. But still my work is a good work. By the enduring grace of God am I permitted to enjoy such a goodly heritage of toil and labor. Every hour I feel not only need of divine aid to lead me, but of an internal, divine power, carrying me along in the right path. It is ever a pathway of grace, unmerited grace. When I am about my work, sometimes called unexpectedly and suddenly from one thing to another, I whisper in my heart, 'Lord, help me to be patient, help me to remember, and help me to be faithful. Lord, enable me to do all for Christ's sake, and to go forward, leaning on the bosom of his infinite grace.' How amazing is that goodness that allows us to do all for Christ's sake, and always to pray in his name! May you experience largely of that grace which alone can make your spared life a blessing.

Much love to Mr. Burgess, Mr. and Mrs. Hazen, Mrs. Wilder and Fairbanks, and Mrs. Ballentine. The thought is pleasant to me that an early friend of mine is your fellow-laborer.

100. The Easiest Year
Monson, January 22, 1849

To Mary Whitman

During two or three years past, I have been trying to mature in the literary department the changes which sprung up in the agitation of the waters on Miss Moore's leaving, and I have been trying to mature things, too, in the domestic department. I had every thing about ready for work this year, without much planning, or agitation, or change. Thus it has come out that this has been the easiest year, in itself considered, we have almost ever had. You know the easy years come along now and then, and now and then the hard years. Now that this easy year should come right along when you are called away in Providence, is surely no planning of mine. So it is. If one thing is made comfortable and easy, we may expect some corresponding trial. If trials and perplexities come, then we may look for some comforting, consoling providence. We may always expect enough of trial and difficulties to make us love to sing, —

'Is this, dear Lord, that thorny road
That leads us to the mount of God?'

And enough of consolation, and support, and blessing, and mercy, to make us feel that Christ's yoke is easy and his burden light.

I feel rather anxious about you, and shall till I hear again. I shall not send this sheet till I hear from you. My heart's desire and prayer to God is, that you may be kept in the arms of Him who never slumbereth nor sleepeth, and who numbereth the very hairs of our heads. I pray that you may experience much of the grace of God in your body, in your soul, in your spirit. For myself, I always carry about enough of my own self to be a fit occasion for loathing and abhorring myself, for distrusting myself, for casting off all confidence in the flesh. But from day to day, I think I do find crumbs enough falling from the table to prove the infinite mercy and long-suffering of God, and enough to prove the exceeding grace of the gospel, and enough of strength in the time of extremity to prove that there is an arm on which we may lean with safety. I want to ask you to pray for me in a very special manner about one thing. It is for divine guidance and strength in giving religious instruction. Pray that I may have hid in my own heart all which I attempt to say. Pray that I may speak the words of truth, every jot and tittle—that which God sees and knows to be truth. Pray that hearts may receive the truth in honesty, sincerity, and in faith. Pray that in these seasons God may be magnified, and glorified. We have great reason to fear and tremble about our next term. Vacation came just as the religious interest seemed to be spreading from heart to heart. Miss Hazen will write you all general facts, I suppose. Between twenty and thirty expressed hope. I miss you most of all in the care of souls. But we know not how much you may do by your prayers.

101. The Handiwork of God
February 15, 1849

To Mary Whitman

I need not tell you we were last evening [upon the receipt of a letter from Miss W.] much gratified. First, I thank God for your expressed desires to live for God alone. Next would I thank him for your continued desire to spend your strength for the good of this precious institution, the founding and building up of which I feel more and more to be the handiwork of God. I trust that you will have fifteen years added to your life, if we will all suffer the trial of your taking a thorough rest and recruiting now. I hope fifteen years, too, will be granted to you after I shall cease from my labors.

II
FOUNDING MOUNT HOLYOKE FEMALE SEMINARY

1

NEW ENGLAND FEMALE SEMINARY FOR TEACHERS

1832

Several friends of education and of evangelical religion are considering the expediency of attempting to raise funds to found a permanent female seminary in New England.

General Object

The main object of the proposed institution will be to prepare young ladies of mature minds for active usefulness, especially to become teachers.

Character

1. Its religious character is to be strictly evangelical.
2. Its literary character is to be of a high order.

Location

This has not yet been selected. An attempt will be made to embrace as many of the following requisites as possible in the location:

1. That it be central for New England.
2. That it be surrounded by a community marked for intelligence and public spirit.

3. That a liberal proportion of the funds be raised by the town and its immediate vicinity.

4. That the particular spot be healthy and pleasant, a little removed from public business, and so situated as to be free from all other encumbrances.

Funds

The amount of funds should be sufficient to furnish the following accommodations:

1. Several acres of land.

2. Buildings sufficiently capacious to furnish from one hundred to two hundred pupils with accommodations for school and boarding.

3. Furniture.

4. An ample library and apparatus.

Domestic Arrangements

It is proposed that the domestic department should be under the direct superintendence of such persons as are qualified for the trust. In order to give as much independence and facility to the trustees as possible, in organizing the establishment, and in order to avoid difficulties in filling offices from time to time, it is proposed that all the furniture should be owned by the corporation.

Boarding-House

The plan which has been proposed for the buildings is suited,

1. To give to the young ladies superior privileges, both for retirement and for social intercourse, and in an eminent degree to promote health, comfort, and domestic happiness, and intellectual, moral, and religious improvement.

2. To furnish each member with a small chamber, exclusively her own. The great advantages of such a privilege can scarcely be realized, except by those who have often felt that they would give up almost any of their common comforts, for

the sake of such retirement as can be enjoyed only in a separate apartment. To persons of reflection, the advantages will doubtless appear much greater than the extra expense, especially when it is considered that this institution is not designed for younger misses, but especially for the benefit of ladies of maturer age.

Family Discipline

The family discipline is to be entirely distinct from the domestic concerns. This, together with the general improvement of the pupils out of school, is to be committed directly to the teachers. The family discipline should be very systematic, but of a kind adapted to the age of its members. The whole should resemble a well-regulated voluntary association, where the officers and members are all faithful to their trust.

The plan which has been proposed for buildings is particularly suited to promote family discipline, and to render it at once easy, systematic, and pleasant to all.

1. It is such that the whole family will naturally and necessarily be arranged in a convenient number of sections, each of which can be easily directed by an appropriate head.

2. It is such as to bring all the young ladies under a direct and natural supervision. This will tend at once to secure order and propriety, and at the same time to exclude all necessity of any thing like apparent watchfulness or nice inspection, even if the age and character of the members of the institution should not render every thing of the kind needless.

Specific Objects to be accomplished

1. To increase the number of well-qualified female teachers. The present want of such teachers is well known to all particularly engaged in the cause of education. This deficiency is the occasion of placing many of our schools under the care of these who are not competent to the undertaking.

2. To induce many who have already become teachers, to make further improvement in their education. This institution

will furnish such ladies with a full course of instruction, and with society.

3. To exert an influence in bringing as much of the labor of instruction into the hands of ladies as propriety will admit. This seems important, on account of the many public demands on the time of benevolent, educated gentlemen, and the comparatively few demands on the time of benevolent, educated ladies.

4. To lead the way toward the establishment of permanent female seminaries in our land. That there are no female seminaries of this character is, we believe, a fact. Those which appear to have the strongest claim to such a standing are so dependent on their present teachers, and their funds and accommodations are to such an extent the property of private individuals, that it would not be safe to predict even their existence the next century.

2

Meeting of the Friends of Female Education

SEPTEMBER 1834

To the Friends and Patrons
of Ipswich Female Seminary:

It has long been a subject of deep regret to many, familiarly acquainted with the character and influence of this institution, that numerous promising individuals, for the want of pecuniary means, should be denied its privileges. These friends of universal education and of religion, have fixed their eyes on one and another of their acquaintances, destined to fill some important sphere of usefulness, who would be greatly benefitted by the advantages of this Seminary, and who have ardently desired to enjoy them, for at least one year, but whose desires have hitherto been in vain. In behalf of such individuals, the inquiry has often been made, whether board in some families in Ipswich could not be furnished at a lower rate than usual; whether they could not render some assistance by labor, so as partly to defray the expense, and thus bring these privileges within their reach. Efforts which will meet, in any degree, the wants of this interesting portion of our community, would, without doubt, find a response in many a benevolent heart. Could the common expenses be reduced one third, or one half, a great number, who now almost despair of ever being able to realize the object of their ardent desire, would be made to rejoice in the possession of those opportunities for instruction and improvement, which they would value more than silver or gold. Many others, whose resources will not now permit them to enjoy these privileges more than one term, or one year, would derive scarcely less benefit from such a provision. To effect such an object, could not a separate and independent institution, similar in character to the Ipswich Seminary, be founded and sustained by the Christian public? Could not this be effected by some plan like the following?

1. Buildings for the accommodation of the school and of boarders, and for family arrangements, together with furniture and all other things necessary for the outfit, to be furnished by voluntary contributions, and placed free from encumbrance in the hands of trustees, who should be men of enlarged views, and of Christian benevolence.

2. Teachers to be secured, who possess so much of a missionary spirit, that they would labor faithfully and cheerfully, receiving only a moderate salary, compared with what they could command in some other situation.

3. Style of living neat, but very plain and simple.

4. Domestic work of the family to be performed by the members of the school.

5. Board and tuition to be placed at cost, or as low as may be, and cover the common expenses of the family, the expenses of instruction, &c.

6. The whole plan to be conducted on the principles of our missionary operations; no surplus income to go to the teachers, to the domestic superintendent, or to any other one, but all to be cast into the treasury, for the still farther reduction of the expenses the ensuing year.

From a careful review of the above principles of expenditure, would it not be safe, in the estimate of board and tuition, to calculate on a reduction of one third, and perhaps one half, from the board and tuition at Ipswich? Such a reduction could not, indeed, be expected to meet the wants of the more needy and dependent. The design would be to benefit more directly a very large and interesting portion of the industrious and enterprising, who are able to do something for their daughters, and who would be induced to make far greater efforts in behalf of their education, than they now do, could they secure to them the advantages of one of our best and most respectable female seminaries, at so moderate an expense. If the standard of female education among this class, could, by any means, be raised, and its influence more extensively diffused, every department of society must sooner or later experience the beneficial results.

The difficulty of raising funds would doubtless be the greatest obstacle to such an undertaking. But there are many individuals, in different parts of our country, who confidently believe, that something of the kind could be effected, if the proper course should be taken to interest the public. The object should be brought forward with very broad and liberal views, without any semblance of local interest. It should be presented as a public enterprise, for the public benefit, claiming equally the patronage of every part of New England. To effect this, and to secure public confidence, no special favors should be granted to the town, where the institution is established. For example, none should be received into the school, unless they enter the establishment as boarders, subject to all its regulations, in the same manner as those from abroad.

The location would be a matter of special importance. It should be one, which would be viewed with a favorable eye, not only by the immediate vicinity, but by the community in general; and one for which funds could as easily be raised, as for any other location. The spot selected, should be adapted to the growth and prosperity of such an institution. It should be alike suited to nourish the tender plant, and to support the lofty oak.

The preceding communication has been extensively circulated during the last six months, and the object of it has been generally approved, and it has excited in many persons no small degree of interest.

Relative to the object, a meeting of friends of Female Education was held at Ipswich, September 6, 1834, and the subsequent business was then transacted.

Rev. Theophilus Packard, D. D., of Shelburne, having been chosen Moderator, and Rev. Joseph B. Felt, of Hamilton, Scribe, the former opened the meeting with prayer.

After free and full remarks on the subject under consideration, the following resolutions were unanimously adopted.

Resolved, That it is desirable, that a Female Seminary, in accordance with the general plan of this circular, be established, and that we proceed to take measures for the advancement of this object.

Resolved, That a Committee be chosen to commence immediate operations towards the founding of such an Institution; and that, if the Committee be successful in their preparatory efforts, they be authorized to transact all other business, necessary to carry forward the enterprise, till they shall have appointed a Board of permanent Trustees; and that this Committee consist of the following gentlemen—Rev. Daniel Dana, D.D., of Newburyport, Rev. Theophilus Packard, D.D., of Shelburne, Rev. Edward Hitchcock, Prof. in Amherst College, Rev. Joseph B. Felt, of Hamilton, George W. Heard, Esq., of Ipswich, Gen. Asa Howland, of Conway, and David Choate, Esq., of Essex—and that they be allowed to increase their number at discretion, provided the whole of this number do not exceed fifteen at any one time.

Resolved, That the Committee be particularly instructed to assure the public, that the course of instruction in the proposed Institution, if it be carried into operation, shall be, at least, of as elevated a character as that pursued at the Ipswich Seminary; and that the reduction of the expenses of the pupils shall not, in any degree, diminish their improvement, or retard their progress in study.

Resolved, That to meet the expense of agencies, and other necessary preparatory measures, the sum of about one thousand dollars be raised exclusively by ladies, (with the understanding, however, that any surplus remaining shall be applied towards procuring furniture) that contributions from the principal donors may be wholly reserved for the main subscription, without liability to reduction for incidentals.

Joseph B. Felt, Scribe.
Ipswich, (Mass.) September 8, 1834.

NOTE.—At a subsequent meeting of the Committee, Rev. Joseph B. Felt, of Hamilton, was chosen Secretary, and George W. Heard, of Ipswich, Treasurer of the Board.

We approve of the enterprise of extending the benefits of female education, as disclosed above; and think the arrangements adopted to carry it into operation are judicious; and we cheerfully commend it to the liberality and patronage of the Christian public.

Andover, September 10, 1834.

Leonard Woods, *(Professor in Theological Seminary, Andover.)*

Heman Humphrey, *(President of Amherst College.)*

Lyman Beecher, *(President of Lane Seminary, Cincinnati, Ohio.)*

John H. Church, *Pelham, N. H.*

Warren Fay, *Charlestown.*

B. B. Wisner, *(Secretary of A. B. C. F. M. Boston.)*

J. Edwards, *(Secretary of the American Temperance Society.)*

Wm. B. Banister, *Newburyport.*

Isaac Braman, *Rowley.*

Phineas Cooke, *Lebanon, N. H.*

Samuel Green, *Boston.*

John Nelson, *Leicester.*

Reuben Emerson, *South Reading.*

Ansel Nash, *Windsor, Conn.*

G. A. Calhoun, *Coventry, Conn.*

3

Mount Holyoke Female Seminary

SEPTEMBER 1835

The character of the young ladies, who shall become members of this Seminary the first year, will be of great importance to the prosperity of the Institution itself, and to the cause of female education. Those, who use their influence in making out the number, will sustain no unimportant responsibility. It is very desirable, that the friends of this cause should carefully consider the real design of founding this Institution, before they use their influence to induce any of their friends and acquaintances to avail themselves of its privileges.

This institution is to be founded by the combined liberality of an enlarged benevolence, which seeks the greatest good on an extensive scale. Some minds seem to be cast in that peculiar mould, that the heart can be drawn forth only by individual want. Others seem best fitted for promoting public good. None can value too much the angel of mercy, that can fly as on the wings of the wind to the individual cry for help as it comes over in tender and melting strains. But who does not venerate those great souls—great by nature—great by education—or great by grace—or by all combined, whose plans and works of mercy are like a broad river swallowing up a thousand little rivulets. How do we stand in awe, when we look down, as on a map, upon their broad and noble plans, destined to give untold blessings to the great community in which they dwell—to their nation—to the world. As we see them urging their way forward, intent on advancing as fast as possible, the renovation of the whole human family—and on hastening the accomplishment of the glorious promises found on the page of inspiration, we are sometimes tempted to draw back their hand, and extend it forth in behalf of some traveller by the wayside, who seems to be overlooked. But we look again, and we behold the dearest personal interests of the traveller by the wayside, and those of a thousand other individuals, included in their large and warm embrace.

This is the class of benevolent men who will aid in founding this Seminary; these the men who are now contributing of their time and money to carry forward this enterprize.

It is ever considered a principle of sacred justice in the management of funds, to regard the wishes of the donors. The great object of those, who are enlisting in this cause, and contributing to it, as to the sacred treasury of the Lord, cannot be misunderstood. It is to meet public and not private wants. They value not individual good less, but the public good more. They have not been prompted to engage in this momentous work by a desire to provide for the wants of a few of the daughters of our land for their own sakes as individuals, but by a desire to provide for the urgent necessities of our country, and of the world, by enlisting in the great work of benevolence, the talents of many of our daughters of fairest promise. This Institution is expected to draw forth the talents of such, to give them a new direction, and to enlist them permanently in the cause of benevolence. We consider it as no more than a due regard to justice, to desire and pray, that a kind Providence may send as scholars to this Seminary, those who shall go forth, and by their deeds, do honor to the Institution, and to the wisdom and benevolence of its founders. The love of justice will also lead us to desire and pray, that the same kind Providence may turn away the feet of those, who may in after life dishonor the Instituion, or be simply harmless cumberers of the ground, though they should be our dearest friends, and those who for their own personal benefit, need its privileges more than almost any others.

The grand features of this Institution are to be an elevated standard of science, literature, and refinement, and a moderate standard of expense; all to be guided and modified by the spirit of the gospel. Here we trust will be found a delightful spot for those, 'whose heart has stirred them up' to use all their talents in the great work of serving their generation, and of advancing the Redeemer's kingdom.

In the same manner, we doubt not, that the atmosphere will be rendered uncongenial to those who are wrapped up in self, preparing simply to please, and to be pleased, whose highest ambition is, to be qualified to amuse a friend in a vacant hour.

The age of the scholars will aid in giving to the Institution a choice selection of pupils. This Seminary is to be for adult young ladies; at an age when they are called upon by their parents to judge for themselves to a very great degree, and when they can select a spot congenial to their taste. The great and ruling principle—an ardent desire to do the greatest possible good, will we hope, be the presiding spirit in many hearts, bringing together congenial souls. Like many institutions of charity, this does not hold out the prospect of providing for the personal relief of individual sufferers, nor for the direct instruction of the ignorant and degraded. But it does expect to collect, as in a focus, the sparks of benevolence, which are scattered in the hearts of many of our daughters, and after having multiplied them many fold, and having kindled them to a flame, and given them a right direction, to send them out to warm and to cheer the world. Some of them may be the daughters of wealth, and the offering will be no less acceptable, because they have something besides themselves to offer to the great work. Others, may be the daughters of mere competency, having been fitted for the service by an answer to Agur's petition. Others, again may struggle under the pressure of more moderate means, being called to surmount the greatest obstacles by persevering effort, and the aid of friends. But provided they have kindred spirits on the great essential principles, all can go forward together without a discordant note.

It has been stated, that the literary standard of this Institution will be high. This is a very indefinite term. There is no acknowledged standard of female education, by which an institution can be measured. A long list of branches to be taught, can be no standard at all. For if so, a contemplated manual labor school to be established in one of the less improved of the western states, whose prospectus we chanced to notice some two or three years since, would stand higher than most of our New-England colleges. Whether the institution was ever established we know not, nor do we remember its name or exact location. But the list of branches to be taught as they appeared on paper, we do remember, as for the time, it served as a happy illustration of a general principle, relating to some of our attempts to advance the cause of education among us. In a seminary for females, we cannot as in the standard of education for the other sex, refer to established institutions, whose course of study and standard of mental discipline are known to every literary man in the land. But it is believed, that our statement cannot be made more intelligible to the enlightened community, than by simply saying, that the course of study, and standard of mental culture will be the same as that of the Hartford Female Seminary—of the Ipswich Female Seminary—or of the Troy Female Seminary—or of some other institution that has stood as long, and ranked as high as these seminaries. Suffice it to say, that it is expected, that the Mount Holyoke Female Seminary will take the Ipswich Female Seminary for its literary standard. Of course there will be room for a continued advancement; as that institution has been raising its own standard from year to year. But at the commencement, the standard is to be as high as the present standard of that seminary. It is to adopt the same high standard of mental discipline—the same slow, thorough, and patient manner of study; the same systematic and extensive course of solid branches. Though this explanation will not be universally understood, yet it is believed that it will be understood by a great many in New England, and by many out of New England—by those, who have long been intimately acquainted with the character of that seminary, or who have witnessed its fruits in the lives of those whom it has sent forth to exert a power over society, which cannot be exerted by mere goodness, without intellectual strength. 'By their fruits ye shall know them.'

The following is an extract from the last catalogue of the Ipswich Female Seminary.

COURSE OF STUDY, &c.

The regular course will consist of primary studies, and a two years' course in the regular classes, denominated Junior and Senior.

It is not expected that all who enter the school, will pursue the regular course. Those among the more advanced pupils, who design to continue members of the school no more than one year, may either pursue an outline of the branches here taught, or make it an object to gain a thorough knowledge of such studies as seem best suited to promote their individual improvement. In recitations, the regular classes are not kept distinct; but all the pupils are arranged in temporary classes as may best promote the good of individuals.

PRIMARY STUDIES

- Mental Arithmetic,
- Written Arithmetic,
- English Grammar,
- First Book of Euclid's Geometry,
- Modern and Ancient Geography,
- Government of the United States,
- Modern and Ancient History,
- Botany,
- Watts on the Mind.

STUDIES OF THE JUNIOR CLASS

- Written Arithmetic completed,
- English Grammar continued,
- The Second, Third, and Fourth Books of Euclid's Geometry,
- Natural Philosophy,
- Chemistry,
- Astronomy,
- Intellectual Philosophy,
- Rhetoric.

STUDIES OF THE SENIOR CLASS

- Some of the preceding studies reviewed and continued,
- Algebra,
- Ecclesiastical History,
- Natural Theology,
- Philosophy of Natural History,
- Analogy of Natural and Revealed Religion to the Constitution and Laws of Nature,
- Evidences of Christianity.

Reading, Composition, Calisthenics, Vocal Music, the Bible and several of the above branches of study, will receive attention through the course. Those who are deficient in spelling and writing, will have exercises in these branches whatever may be their other attainments. Linear drawing will also receive attention. It is desired, that so far as practicable, young ladies before entering the Seminary, should be skilful in both mental and written Arithmetic, and thoroughly acquainted with Geography and the History of the United States.

TEXT BOOKS

The Bible, Worcester's Abridgement of Webster, or some other English Dictionary, the Eclectic Reader, by B. B. Edwards, Porter's Rhetorical Reader, Colburn's First Lessons, Adams's Arithmetic, Smith's and Murray's Grammar, Simson's or Playfair's Euclid, Woodbridge's Larger Geography, Sullivan's Political Class Book, Goodrich's United States, Worcester's Elements of History, with Goldsmith's England, Greece and Rome, Mrs. Phelps's Botany, Olmstead's Natural Philosophy, Wilkins's Astronomy, Abercrombie on the Intellectual Powers, Newman's and Whatley's Rhetoric, Baily's Algebra, Marsh's Ecclesiastical History, Paley's Natural Theology, Smellie's Philosophy of Natural History, Butler's Analogy, Alexander's Evidences of Christianity.

The time for admitting into the regular classes is near the close of the winter term. The pupils, who at that time have been members of the seminary a year, and in some cases only six months, on passing a thorough examination on the primary studies, or on such studies of the course as shall be equivalent to the primary studies, can be admitted into the Junior Class: and those who can pass a similar examination in such of the studies as shall equal all the primary studies, and those of the Junior Class, can be admitted into the Senior. Those who in addition are well acquainted with the studies of the Senior Class, receive at the close a testimonial of having completed with honor the course of study in this institution.

In order that this new institution may accomplish the greatest good to the cause of female education, it is desirable that the pupils should advance as far as possible in study before entering the Seminary. To many who are expecting to become members, it is a subject of deep regret that the commencement of operations should be delayed so long. To all, who are expecting to enter this seminary when it opens, it is earnestly recommended to spend as much of the intermediate time as possible in study. It is very desirable that the *least* improved of the pupils should have a thorough knowledge of arithmetic, geography, history of the United States and English grammar, though this may not be rigidly required of every individual the first year. These branches may be pursued privately without a regular teacher, or in the common district school, or in the young ladies' village school, or in any other situation, which may be convenient.

Those who wish to pursue these branches without a regular teacher to direct them, may derive advantage by pursuing something like the following order of study,

1. Colburn's First Lessons to the 11th Section;
2. A general course of Geography;
3. Adams' New Arithmetic to Fractions;
4. Rudiments and general principles of English Grammar;
5. Colburn's First Lessons completed;
6. Adams' Arithmetic to Proportion;
7. History of the United States;
8. Thorough course of Geography;
9. Thorough course of English Grammar.
10. Adams' Arithmetic completed.

MANNER OF STUDYING

Colburn's First Lessons

This book should be studied through so many times, and with such close attention, that all the difficult questions in every part of the book can be solved with great readiness, and the manner of solution described. In studying this, recitations are very important. In recitations the book should not be opened by the learner. If the questions cannot be remembered, and all parts comprehended, as they are received from the lips of a teacher, it may be safely inferred, not that there is any deficiency in the ability of the learner, but that more hard study is still requisite. If a young lady attempts to gain a thorough knowledge of this book by private study at home, it is important for her to recite daily to a brother, or sister, or some other friend. In recitations, whether of a class, or of an individual, every answer, and every description should be given with great clearness, accuracy, and promptness. The effects of a continued practice of reciting in this way, both on the mind, and degree of intelligence in the manner of an individual, can rarely be realized by those unaccustonmed to observe them.

Adams's New Arithmetic

(Some other book may be used as a substitute.)

In pursuing this branch of study, two things should be gained.

1. *Perfect Accuracy.* It should not be considered sufficient, that a question is finally solved correctly. No standard of accuracy is high enough, except that which will enable the learner to avoid all wrong steps in the statement, and all errors in every part of the process to be corrected by a second trial. Where a deficiency is observed in these respects, more close and careful study should be applied—the preceding parts of the book should be slowly and carefully reviewed—and every question should be solved the first time very slowly, and with an undivided attention, till accurate habits are acquired.

2. *Readiness and Rapidity.* These habits can be gained only by abundant practice. Reciting, that is, solving questions given out by another, will be very useful. This study may be pursued without a regular teacher, but the learner should recite daily to some friend as recommended in Colburn's First Lessons. If any one is under the necessity of being her own teacher, of solving her own questions, and of overcoming her own difficulties, she will receive aid from observing the following rule. Whenever you are involved in difficulties, from which you know not how to extricate yourself, go back to the beginning, or nearly to the beginning of the book, and solve every question in course till you come to the point of difficulty.

Most individuals will probably find it necessary to go through the whole book two or three times, in order to gain the needful accuracy and readiness.

ENGLISH GRAMMAR

But few succeed in studying this except with a regular teacher. Though the manner of pursuing this branch is very important, it is not easy to give short and specific directions. We will only say, be very thorough. Study every lesson closely and carefully.

GEOGRAPHY

The manner of studying this branch must depend much on the teacher. One direction may be given for the use of those who study it without a teacher. After studying regularly through some book, and reviewing it carefully once or twice, let the learner select a complete outline, embracing prominent facts relating to every part of the world. This outline should be reviewed weekly or monthly for months, or for a year or two, till the facts are so indelibly fixed on the memory, that the lady at any future time of life, could recall anything in this outline almost as readily as she could recollect the order of the letters of the alphabet. The learner is referred to a lecture delivered before the American Institute in 1833.

HISTORY OF THE UNITED STATES

In studying history, some systematic method is very important. But very little dependence can be placed on mere reading. Here and there a mind can be found, which will by a regular reading of history, select and arrange its materials so systematically, that they can be laid up for future use. But such minds among young ladies in the present state of female education are rarely found. History furnishes to the teacher an almost boundless field for the exercise of the inventive powers. But the most successful parts of almost every system of teaching history, cannot be so described as to be used by a young lady without a teacher. An intelligent young lady might use the 'Topic System' as it has been called to considerable advantage in the following manner. After gaining a general view of the book to be studied, let the young lady select a list of topics or subjects through the whole, to be learned and recited to some friend, like a connected narration. In learning these topics, it would not be well to charge the memory with every item which can be found, but with those which are the most important. In reciting, she should not attempt to state any thing, of which she is not confident, but in what she does attempt to communicate, she should not allow herself the least indulgence for inaccuracy. She should charge herself with deficiency for the least inaccurate statement, even though she should correct it the next moment. The list of topics might with profit be recited through two or three times. If Goodrich's History of the United States is studied, Emerson's Questions may be used with advantage in connexion with the topics. Any one not accustomed to recite by the topic system, might use the Questions as a general guide in selecting items under each topic. Beginners have often found it useful in a few of the first lessons, to write out the items under each topic. But very soon, the mind will be able to collect and arrange its materials without consuming so much time. When topics are written, no use should be made of the notes during recitations.

If the whole of this course cannot be completed before entering the Seminary, let the first part be taken in order, and let what is done, be done thoroughly. After completing the preceding course in the manner described, young ladies can select for themselves from the regular course of study pursued at Ipswich. It is desirable to advance in study as far as possible before entering the seminary, provided that every branch taken up receives thorough attention. A superficial passing over any branch before commencing it regularly in school, is always an injury instead of a benefit. But the greater the real capital, which any one possesses of improvement on entering the institution, the greater will be her proportionate income. Any who hope to be so far advanced as to enter the Senior Class at first, and complete the regular course of study in one year, may need some more specific directions and information relative to preparatory studies, to prevent disappointment. Such can obtain further information by directing a letter to Miss Mary Lyon, South Hadley, Mass. A thorough knowledge of a definite number of branches, is a term, which to different individuals has very different meanings. Some of the members of the Ipswich Female Seminary, who had gone through the regular course, except the studies of the Senior Class, have been successful teachers in some of the most important female seminaries in our country. The same high standard will be taken in this institution. But notwithstanding this, a few individuals, who are now making their arrangements with reference to a hope, that they shall be its members the first year, can be prepared to complete the course, and others there doubtless will be, who could do it by devoting all the time that they can command, before the institution commences, to pursuing the most important studies, and to reviewing those which they have gone over.

This institution will do much, we hope, to raise among the female part of the community a higher standard of science and literature—of economy and of refinement—of benevolence and religion. To accomplish this great end, we hope by the influence of the institution on the community, to lead many to discover and use the means within their reach, instead of mourning in indolence after those they can never enjoy. We hope to redeem from waste a great amount of precious time—of noble intellect, and of moral power.

** This was written for the benefit of those, who are making inquiries about the qualifications for admission into this Seminary. It has been printed to save the labor of transcribing. Those into whose hands it may fall, are requested to make no other use of it than they would of a written communication.

4

Fundraising Letter

NOVEMBER 1836

Dear Madam,

Wishing to write to yourself and several other ladies, relative to the MT. HOLYOKE FEMALE SEMINARY, I shall take the liberty to send you a printed sheet. I doubt not that I shall be able to accomplish the principal object I have in view, by writing to those whom I have the privilege of numbering among my personal friends, and to those with whom I feel acquainted through some mutual friend.

The enterprise of founding this institution was commenced about two years ago. The work has since been going forward slowly and with care. The first edifice is now erecting. It is to be 94 feet by 50, and four stories besides the basement. It will furnish good public accommodations for the school and the family, and private chambers for the teachers, and for 80 young ladies. Additions are to be made hereafter as the liberality of the Christian public shall furnish the means. If there is no delay on account of funds, this first building can be finished and a school of 80 scholars commenced the latter part of next summer.

The time has now come, when we must make our arrangements for furniture. For this we must depend principally on ladies. And we have no doubt but the call will be promptly met.

In all our progress, ladies have been prompt to do all that we have asked. It is true, that we have been careful to avoid extending our requests beyond their possible ability. The first contribution in behalf of this object was made by ladies. The institution had then assumed no name, nor place, nor legal standing. The whole enterprise was less in appearance than a man's hand, when a few ladies came forward, and generously raised one thousand dollars to meet incidentals. Of this, $269 was given by the teachers and pupils of Ipswich Female Seminary, and $475 by the ladies of the town of Ipswich. The remainder was soon made out by a few ladies in other places. This was a noble beginning. It was guided by a view of the anticipated greatness of the work.

Though I have no doubt, that all the furniture can be easily made out by ladies, and merely by a written invitation, without the interference of an agent, yet to effect it promptly some regular plan will be necessary. We shall propose to distinct towns or parishes the plan of furnishing one chamber each by a united contribution from the ladies. The recognition in future years of each chamber as having been furnished by some particular town, will be a pleasant little circumstance. The other parts of the furniture will, we hope, be promptly furnished by other means, perhaps principally by donations from individuals. This plan has been examined and approved by several judicious ladies. Some towns are now ready to commence the work of furnishing a chamber, and the teachers and pupils of one school under the care of a lady from Ipswich Female Seminary, have already given a donation of $100, to be expended in other articles of furniture. Will not other schools, with their teachers, follow this example?—and especially those instructed by ladies from the Ipswich Seminary, on whose influence over the community, this enterprize has been able to rely with so much confidence? Will not many ladies feel it to be a privilege to make a large donation, to furnish some specific articles of furniture?

But the business of furnishing chambers needs immediate attention. The sum necessary for one chamber will be from $50 to $60—$50 will furnish the essential articles, though some other conveniences would be very desirable, and might be procured for a few dollars more. This will be left optional with the donors. Let one efficient lady, in almost any place, either alone, or with one or two to aid her, commence the work, with decision, and perseverance to carry it through, and the work will be done; while in the most flourishing town it would not be accomplished, unless some one lady should undertake the work as her own business. I should advise, that the contribution should be very general, embracing a great number of ladies. It may be best to request, that the largest contribution should not exceed $5. Individuals who are able to do more, might give an individual donation in addition, to be appropriated to some other articles of furniture. Perhaps in some cases the bedding, and some money, might be advanced by some young ladies' sewing society, and the remainder raised by a general contribution from ladies of all ages. The plan of operation must however vary according to the circumstances of different towns.

And now, dear Madam, would not the ladies in your place consider it a privilege to furnish one of these chambers? Would you not consider it a privilege to bring the subject before them so fairly, that they will do it with promptness. In your efforts to interest others, you may feel the need of something more on the principles and designs of the institution; I will, therefore, employ the remainder of this sheet in giving you a little sketch.

This institution is to be a seminary for the raising up of female teachers. It is to possess all the advantages which can be derived from its being founded and built up by the united liberality of the Christian public, and placed on a permanent basis. The vast importance of supplying our country with well qualified female teachers is felt and acknowledged by many, and the conviction is increasing from year to year. How can we so effectually strengthen the hands of the most judicious mothers, or supply the deficiencies of those less judicious, or counteract the evils of those more defective still, without weakening filial respect, as to plant every where side by side, female teachers of enlarged views, of active benevolence, and self-denying zeal in laboring for the good of our country, and for the salvation of a world! O that our New England could be filled with such teachers for fifty years to come. What a change should we witness in all our domestic and social relations—what a change in our political men, who are wielding the destinies of the nation—what an improvement in the health, habits, and disinterested zeal of many of the ministers of the gospel—what a change in the active benevolence of our churches. Would the cause of foreign missions again be weighed down under a debt of $40,000, while every thing in the land bears the aspect of increasing wealth and luxury? Would fathers and mothers be so slow to give up their sons for the ministry, or their daughters to labor on heathen shores, or perhaps in more self denying stations in our own country?

But suppose our beloved New England be thus supplied, the work would be but just commenced. A boundless field would lie before us. How shall this vast field be supplied not only the cities and large villages, and the more inviting stations, but the whole land in all its length and breadth, including every nook and corner, and every hamlet which is made the habitation of men! This is a question of great interest to many, who are laboring in the great Western Valley, and who are deeply affected in view of the dangers to which our country is exposed. They have witnessed the great and increasing efforts of the Catholic Church to add these United States to her dominions, and the feeble and tardy movements of the friends of the Redeemer to resist her encroachments. Thousands and thousands of dollars are annually poured in upon us from Catholic Europe, and are appropriated with a discrimination worthy the attention of the friends of the Redeemer. More than half of the thousands thus landed on our shores have been devoted to the educating of females. Schools have been founded and built upon and teachers have been carefully trained for their work. Every effort is thus making to prepare the females of our land, and through them the children and youth of the coming generations to lend their aid in converting this nation to the Church of Rome. In the comparative appropriation of the funds of the Catholic

Church to prepare the two sexes for his service, has she not been wiser in her generation than the children of light? A few weeks since, a gentleman standing on the site of our new institution at South Hadley, and rejoicing in this noble effort now making by the friends of Christ, which if carried through according to the original design need not blush to stand beside the Catholic efforts, remarked that he had the means of knowing, that during the last summer, $100,000 was landed in the city of New York from Catholic Europe, three fourths of which was to be devoted to the education of females. Many who are laboring at the most important posts of observation, are trembling for the safety of the nation. They tremble for the results of the next ten years.

Among the means essential to the safety of the nation, many are convinced of the necessity of urging into the field a multitude of benevolent, self-denying female teachers. Many of the most candid and discriminating, who have the advantage of observation on this subject, are convinced that all other means without this will be insufficient. Fill the country with ministers, and they could no more conquer the whole land and secure their victories, without the aid of many times their number of self-denying female teachers, than the latter could complete the work without the former. But what can be done? Most of the calls which come over to New England and are multiplying every year, must be returned unanswered. The seminary at Ipswich, whose teachers are found in every part of our country, and whose influence has done so much to prepare the way for this enterprize, is compelled even now to return a negative reply to a multitude of calls every year. And the necessities of the country are yet scarcely beginning to be known—and but very few of those who feel their wants have faith enough in the benevolence of our New England ladies, to seek a supply. Ministers have long been regarded by many as a class of men who listen to the loudest calls, as they are measured by the amount of salary, by the refinement of the people, and by the prospect of receiving a temporal reward. But this error is fast melting away before the self-denying labors of a great multitude of men of rare spirits, who have been drawn together and prepared and sent out to their work by the disinterested efforts of the Church during the last thirty years, and who are now toiling and suffering amidst the wilds of our own country, or amidst the distressing pollution of heathen lands. In the same light do many still regard the motives of female teachers. O that the willing hearts of a great multitude of our New England daughters might be encouraged—that they might be invited to come forward and prepare themselves for the work and enlist in the service, till it shall no longer be doubted whether we will do good, except to those who do good to us.

This work of supplying teachers is a great work, and it must be done or our country is lost, and the world will remain unconverted. If we begin we must go on—the more we do, the more we must do. The more we attempt to supply in this particular the wants of our country, the more the wants will be made manifest. What instrumentality shall ever meet this demand? Why is it, that so much could have been seen, and acknowledged, and felt on this subject, without an attempt to apply the sovereign remedy, which has been so successfully applied to every other want? It has seemed that the Church had been fully convinced, that there was but one grand means of meeting any great public demand of the Redeemer's kingdom. A union of disinterested labors and contributions is this grand means. When the Church early felt her need of the services of young men, she began to found colleges, and as the demand for their services increased, and became more manifest, she went on founding colleges, till more than eighty have been reared in our country, and more than thirty theological seminaries. But this was found to be not sufficient, and the American Education Society comes into existence, and has been going forward with an increasing magnificence and glory, scarcely equalled except by the importance of its object. All these are so many public voices from the Church, calling upon young men, and entreating them to enlist in her service. But what has been the voice of the Church to female teachers? Has it not been, *"We need not your services—Go on to serve yourselves—to serve the children of this world—to serve the mammon of unrighteousness. We can save our country, and convert the world without your aid."*

After these general remarks, you would expect that I should feel deeply interested in the success of Mt. Holyoke Female Seminary. Had I a thousand lives, I could sacrifice them all in suffering and hardship for its sake. Did I possess the greatest fortune, I could readily relinquish it all, and become poor, and more than poor, if its prosperity should demand it. This institution proposes to be founded on the principle of enlarged Christian benevolence, and every step of the progress has been in accordance with this profession. Its grand object is to furnish the greatest possible number of female teachers, of high literary qualifications, and of benevolent self-denying zeal; and every other good must, if need be, be sacrificed to this great object.

1. The institution is to be only for an older class of young ladies.

2. Every scholar is to board in the establishment. This will give great unity to the plans of the institution, and great regularity to system, and will greatly facilitate the improvement of those for whom it is designed.

3. In laying out the minutiae of the plans, great care is taken to furnish points of attraction to those, who would gladly become benevolent, self-denying teachers, should the cause of Christ demand it, and points of repulsion to the more inefficient and self-indulgent, and to those whose views and desires are bounded by themselves, and their own family circle.

4. This is to be an institution of the highest privileges for improvement, and of very moderate expense. This is a union not yet found in so high a degree, in any large female seminary in the land, and not to be formed, except it be the production of disinterested benevolence.

5. The general course of study, and the general character of the instruction, is to be like that at Ipswich.

6. The institution is placed on a firm legal basis. An Act of incorporation has been obtained and the Board of Trustees consists of the following gentlemen: Dr. Humphrey, and Prof. Hitchcock, of Amherst College, Rev. Mr. Condit, of South Hadley, Rev. Mr. Tyler and William Bowdoin, Esq. of South Hadley Canal, Rev. Mr. Hawks, (permanent Agent,) David Choate, Esq.

of Essex, Dea. Andrew W. Porter, of Monson, and Mr. Joseph Avery, of Conway.

7. The institution is to be permanent, continuing onward in its operations, from generation to generation. The trustees and teachers will be bound by the strongest and most sacred cords of obligation, to be faithful to their trust. The institution is to be founded and built up by the cheerful contributions of the most benevolent and disinterested Christians all over the country, who ask no reward, except a faithful and judicious appropriation of the funds. A considerable sum has already been subscribed to this object, and by some hundreds of individuals in more than 60 different towns. How unlike the principle so long acted upon, that Christians are not required to contribute for the building up of any female seminary, unless it be established in their own town. How solemn will be the responsibility to use every possible effort to perpetuate the existence, the character, and the increasing usefulness, of this institution. As the number of self-denying friends is continually increasing, the sacred cords of obligation are becoming stronger and stronger.

These are some of the general principles, and this the grand object of the institution. And is it too much for Christians to indulge high hopes of usefulness to the cause of Christ from this institution, founded on such principles, and contemplating such an object, and going forward in improvement and in increasing usefulness, from generation to generation? May the Lord grant, that the high, but reasonable hopes of the friends of the Redeemer, may be more than realized in coming years. In the many hundreds, if not thousands, of teachers which it will send forth, it will doubtless be an instrument of good, far beyond the present grasp of my feeble comprehension.

But this is not all. This, in my view, is not the most important result of this grand experiment on the benevolence of the Christian community. It has an important bearing on the grand subject of adopting suitable means for supplying our country with well qualified female teachers, and it is testing the great question of duty on this subject. This constitutes its chief importance. It is like the signing of the Declaration of Independence; the battles were still to be fought, but the question of independence was then settled. It is like fitting our first little band of missionaries. The great work of evangelizing a world was still before the American churches; but the grand question of duty, and the mode of meeting duty, was then settled, never again to be seriously doubted. Let this enterprise be carried through, and sustained by the prompt liberality of the Christian community, and it will no longer be doubted, whether the great work of supplying our country with well qualified female teachers, shall be allowed a standing among the great benevolent operations of the day. The great principle will be settled forever. The work will still be before us, but the grand principle on which it is to be accomplished will be settled. Another stone in the foundation of our great system of benevolent operations, which are destined, in the hand of God, to convert a world, will then be laid. When the last stone in this foundation shall have been laid, we shall only need to go forward and build—to modify and mature—to carry out our principles and the results, till the work is finished. But the foundation stones must all be laid. Every fundamental principle must be settled. They are mutually to sustain and support each other. Take away any one, and all the others will suffer by the loss. And who can tell how much every great effort of the Church during the last thirty years has been kept back, because it has never been acknowledged in practice, that the work of supplying our country with a sufficient number of well qualified female teachers, must be accomplished by a voluntary sacrifice of time and money, proportioned to the greatness and importance of the object. The work of bringing this institution into operation has been longer than was anticipated. But the progress of the enterprise in taking an acknowledged standing among the benevolent operations of the day, has exceeded the expectations of its warmest friends. I doubt whether any benevolent object, not excepting even the Missionary cause, has ever, within two years from its commencement, made a greater advance in gaining access to the understanding and hearts of the people. How true it is, that Christians will have but little faith in any object, till they have made sacrifices for its sake. The eyes of many are now turning towards this new enterprise. Many have rejoiced that so noble a design has been formed in the heart of New England. They have hoped that it may be only the beginning of a great and glorious work of benevolence, which shall in this department meet the demands of the Church. Many hearts have been filled with hope, as they have beheld this enterprise commenced and carried forward in obedience to the great command, "Love thy neighbor as thyself."

And now, dear madam, will you allow me to appeal to your benevolence in behalf of this cause? There may be some gentlemen in the circle of your friends whose heart the Lord will incline to favor this object, and whose hand the Lord will open in its behalf. If so, you will bear it in remembrance that several circumstances combined place the institution just now in circumstances of great necessity. I do most earnestly desire that all, who have it in their hearts to do something for this object, may speedily do that which has been put into their hearts. There may be some ladies in your circle of acquaintance, who will feel it to be a privilege to make an uncommon sacrifice for the benefit of this cause, and make out in its behalf a generous donation, either to the principal fund, or to furnish some of the more expensive articles of furniture. But the question of furnishing a chamber is one to which a direct reply is particularly requested. It is important that the reply should be DECISIVE, and as early as convenient, at least before the first of next [blank space] so that in case the answer should be negative, (which however I do not expect) a substitute may be found. Letters to myself may be addressed to Northampton.

May the Lord guide you in all your labors of love. In all our efforts in behalf of this cause, the good hand of our God has been upon us. His kind Providence has been most strikingly manifest in every stage of this enterprise. May his blessing ever rest on this institution, and on all connected with its interests, and with its present and future prosperity.

Yours with high sentiments of esteem,
MARY LYON.

5

General View of the Principles and Designs of the Mount Holyoke Female Seminary

1837

This institution is established at South Hadley, Mass. It is to be principally devoted to the preparing of female teachers. At the same time, it will qualify ladies for other spheres of usefulness. The design is to give a solid, extensive, and well-balanced English education, connected with that general improvement, that moral culture, and those enlarged views of duty, which will prepare ladies to be *educators* of children and youth, rather than to fit them to be mere teachers, as the term has been technically applied. Such an education is needed by every female who takes the charge of a school, and sustains the responsibility of guiding the whole course and of forming the entire character of those committed to her care. And when she has done with the business of teaching in a regular school, she will not give up her profession; she will still need the same well-balanced education at the head of her own family, and in guiding her own household.

    1. This institution professes to be founded on the high principle of enlarged Christian benevolence. In its plans, and in its appeals, it seeks no support from local or private interest. It is designed entirely for the public good, and the trustees would

adopt no measures, not in accordance with this design. It is sacredly consecrated to the great Head of the church, and they would not seek for human approbation by any means which will not be well-pleasing in his sight.

2. The institution is placed on a firm legal basis. An Act of Incorporation has been obtained, and the Board of Trustees consists of the following gentlemen: —Rev. Heman Humphrey, D.D. President of Amherst college; Rev. Edward Hitchcock, Professor in Amherst college; Rev. Roswell Hawks; Rev. Joseph D. Condit, of South Hadley; Rev. William Tyler, and William Bowdoin, Esq. of South Hadley Canal; David Choate, Esq. of Essex; Deacon Andrew W. Porter, of Monson Mr. Joseph Avery, of Conway; and Deacon Daniel Safford, of Boston.

3. The institution is designed to be permanent. The permanency of an institution may be considered as consisting of two particulars—first, its perpetual vitality, and second, its continual prosperity and usefulness. The first is to be secured in the same manner, that the principle of perpetual life in our higher institutions for young men, has been so effectually preserved. A fund is to be committed to an independent, self-perpetuating board of trustees, known to the churches as faithful, responsible men—not as a proprietary investment, but as a free offering, leaving them no way for an honorable retreat from their trust, and binding them with solemn responsibilities to hundreds and thousands of donors, who have committed their sacred charities to their conscientious fidelity. Give to a literary institution, on this principle, an amount of property sufficient to be viewed as an object of great importance, and it is almost impossible to extinguish its vital life by means of adversity. How firmly have our colleges stood amidst the clashing elements around us, and the continual overturnings which are taking place in the midst of us. How safely have they outlived every trying struggle, and survived every protracted season of inefficiency, and all indications of final decay.

The usefulness of this institution, like all others, must depend on its character. This may be very great for a time, where there is no principle of perpetual life, as is the case with some of our most distinguished female seminaries. Amidst all their prosperity they have no solid foundation, and in themselves no sure principle of continued existence. Could we secure to our public institutions the continued labors of the same teachers through an antediluvial life, the preservation of the vital principle would be a subject of much less consequence. But in view of the present shortened life of man, rendered shorter still by disease and premature decay, and in view of the many changes which are ever breaking in upon the continued services of those to whose care these institutions are committed, every reflecting mind must regard it as of the very first importance, to secure to them this principle—especially to a public seminary for the raising up of female teachers.

4. The general course of study, and the general character of the instruction, will be like those of the Ipswich Female Seminary. The successful labors of many who have been educated there, and the powerful influence which they have been able to exert over the school, the family, and the neighborhood, prove, that the intellectual discipline and moral culture of that Seminary are of no inferior order—and the continual applications for teachers, not only from our most important schools in New England, but from almost all the States and territories in the Union, show the estimation in which it is held by the community.

5. The institution is to be entirely for an older class of young ladies. The general system for family arrangements, for social improvement, for the division of time, for organizing and regulating the school, and the requirements for entrance, will be adapted throughout to young ladies of adult age, and of mature character. Any provision in an institution like this for younger misses, must be a public loss far greater than the individual good. Their exclusion from the institution will produce a state of society among the members, exceedingly pleasant and profitable to those whose great desire is to be prepared to use all their talents in behalf of the cause of education, and of the Redeemer's kingdom; and it will secure for their improvement the entire labors of the

teachers, without an interruption from the care and government of pupils too immature to take care of themselves.

6. Every member of the school will board in the establishment. All the teachers and pupils, without exception, will constitute one family. This will give great unity and regularity to the system. It will furnish aids to improvement, which are peculiarly adapted to adult young ladies, and are greatly needed by them in developing and maturing all their talents for usefulness, and which it is difficult to secure to them in any other manner.

7. This institution is designed to furnish the best facilities for education, at a very moderate expense. The way by which these two advantages are to be secured in the same seminary, has been extensively adopted in our higher institutions for young men. How moderate are the charges in our colleges, compared with the real expense of the privileges. But these two advantages are not found thus united in any large female seminary in the land, and probably never will be united, unless it be by the power of disinterested benevolence on an extensive scale.

The present effort in behalf of this institution is to raise a fund for the erection of buildings for the school, including a large seminary-hall, recitation-rooms, a library and reading-room, chemical-room, etc., and accommodations for all the domestic work, and all the family arrangements, and private chambers for the teachers and pupils, together with the furniture for the whole, and also library and apparatus for the school. The charges to the pupils for board and instruction will be placed at cost, without rent for buildings or furniture. Additional funds for other purposes would be highly valuable to the institution. But nothing farther is proposed in the present effort.

8. The principle of entire equality among the pupils is to be adopted. The charges will be the same to all without reference to their means. Whatever of favor in this respect they receive, will come to them not as an individual charity, demanding individual gratitude, but through the medium of a public institution, founded by the liberality of the Christian community, not for their sakes as individuals, but for the sake of the children and

youth of our country, who must come successively under their care. It comes to them as a high and valuable testimonial of the estimate in which are held the services of female teachers, and though it imposes on them a debt of gratitude, it will be a debt which shall ennoble and elevate the soul—one, which can never be cancelled by gold and silver, but which demands a far richer return, even the consecration of time, talents, and acquisitions to the cause of Christ.

9. The young ladies are to take a part in the domestic work of the family. This also is to be on the principle of equality. All are to take a part—not as a servile labor, for which they are to receive a small weekly remuneration, but as a gratuitous service to the institution of which they are members, designed for its improvement and elevation. The first object of this arrangement is, to give to the institution a greater degree of independence. The arrangements for boarding all the pupils in the establishment, will give to it an independence with regard to private families in the neighborhood, without which it would be difficult, if not impossible, to secure its perpetual prosperity. The arrangements for the domestic work will, in a great measure, relieve it from another source of depressing dependence—a dependence on the will of hired domestics, to which many a family in New England is subject.

The other object of this arrangement is to promote the health, the improvement, and the happiness of the pupils—their health, by its furnishing them with a little daily exercise of the best kind—their improvement, by its tending to preserve their interest in domestic pursuits—and their happiness, by its relieving them from that servile dependence on common domestics, to which young ladies, as mere boarders in a large establishment, are often subject, to their great inconvenience. The adoption of a feature like this, in an institution which aims to be better endowed than any other existing female seminary in the country, must give it an attitude of noble independence, which can scarcely fail to exert an elevating influence on its members.

The vast importance of supplying our country with well-qualified female teachers, is felt and acknowledged by many. The number of teachers must be greatly increased, and the standard of their education raised. They must have more benevolence and self-denying zeal, and more enlarged views of the great end of education. Many of the most candid and discriminating fully believe, that all other means without this, will be insufficient to save our nation from threatening destruction. And is it not evident, that we cannot depend principally on the other sex for teachers? Let us, for example, undertake to fill the great Valley of the West with male teachers—not only the cities and larger villages, and the more inviting stations, but the whole territory, in all its length and breadth. Will those men who can resist the urgent claims of the ministry, and the pressing calls from the missionary field, cheerfully settle down as teachers in the more self-denying and less lucrative stations, while they are met on every hand by many a fair promise of competence and wealth, rendered more flattering by the increasing wants of a rising family? The prospect of supplying the children generally in New England with competent male teachers, is scarcely more promising. If we chance to find one for a few short months in the winter, how can he give to his charge the first energies of his soul amidst all his dreams of future usefulness, or of future greatness and wealth? Not so with the female. On the side of benevolence, she is left happy and contented with her work. The office of a teacher is all she seeks. Here she finds a sphere of usefulness, the most appropriate and extensive. And, on the side of self-interest, she is almost as safely guarded. A wise Providence has relieved her from the duty of providing for the support of a family, and a corresponding Providence has closed against her the principal avenues of business, which are lucrative, and at the same time honorable. Is not this a wise and kind provision, designed to furnish the church with materials, to be faithfully used in the great work of training the children and youth of our land for the service of the Lord? O that these materials might be faithfully employed.

It is not to be understood, that we would supply the

country with female teachers, who shall devote their lives to the business as a profession. In the first place, this is not necessary to furnish good teachers. Females, thoroughly prepared for their work, and devoting to it the whole uninterrupted energies of their minds and souls, are often very successful, though they continue to teach but for a short time. In the second place, it would not have the best effect on the usefulness of other females. What class of men or women among us, are suffering so much from idle and vacant hours, and from time half improved, and from days busily occupied without any important end, as our adult unmarried females? The few short years of this period, committed to almost every female, forms an important link between the two great portions of her earthly existence—one the preparatory, and the other the active. What period more needs some great and noble object of pursuit, calling forth all the talents, and the best energies of the soul? The anticipation of such an object is greatly needed in the whole preparatory course, to furnish a high and definite motive, without which it is difficult to make the greatest and most valuable attainments; and its salutary and energetic influence on the character is no less needed in future years of increasing labors and responsibilities. The business of teaching, in its highest sense, and in its most benevolent aspect, furnishes the most appropriate object. Without this wide and increasing field of usefulness for females, that would be a dark providence, which, by means of manufacturing establishments, has taken from families so much domestic labor, which had its influence in forming the character of our maternal ancestors. But "providence meets providence." And when we behold the opening and increasing field of usefulness and beneficence in this department, and listen to its urgent claims on the time and talents of females, can we not discover the hand of One, wiser than Solomon, in all the labor-saving machinery of the present day?

  The demand for female teachers is very great and urgent, while the materials are abundant. But the materials will never be drawn forth, and the demand will never be met, unless by the same grand means, by which the church has attempted to meet almost every other great demand of the Redeemer's kingdom. A union of disinterested labors and contributions is this grand means. When the church early felt her need of the services of young men, she began to found colleges, and as the demand for their services increased, and became more manifest, she went on founding colleges, till more than eighty have been reared in our country, and more than thirty theological seminaries. But this was found to be inadequate, and the American Education Society came into existence, and has been going forward with an increasing strength, corresponding with the importance of its object. All these are so many public voices from the church, calling upon young men, and entreating them to enlist in her service. But what has been the public voice of the church to female teachers? Has it not been, "We need not your services, Go on to serve yourselves—to serve the children of this world. We can save our country, and convert the world without your aid?"

This delusive voice has been heard, and its power has long been operating on the community. It has gone out from New England, and extended over the land. Teachers have felt its influence. The sound in their ears, "Wo be unto us, and wo be unto this whole nation, if we teach not the children," has been stifled. The question of engaging in this business at all, and of seeking for suitable qualifications to discharge its responsible duties, is often a mere matter of choice—of personal convenience. Mothers too have felt its influence. They have learned to believe, that the selection of teachers for their children is a subject of inferior importance. At first, they become willing to commit them to the guidance of those, whom we would not send to a foreign land to teach the ignorant heathen. At length, we find them cheerfully giving them up to Roman Catholic schools, fearing not their secret and sure influence, though they would tremble at the thought, that the Pope of Rome may yet set his foot on the neck of this great nation, and on the necks of their children and children's children.

Once the public voice of the community was equally erroneous on many other subjects, which are now regarded as of vital importance. American Christians have done much, by voluntary union, to guard our country, and to promote the salvation of the world. But the great work of furnishing a supply of well-qualified female teachers has been left entirely to chance, or to the private efforts of individuals, without co-operation, and without the public encouragement of the Christian community. Why is it, that in this thing, the church should be fifty years behind herself in other respects? She has been fortifying our Zion, and building around it a strong and high wall, and why has she left the foundation unprotected—that very part most accessible to our two great enemies, infidelity and Romanism? These, our foes, may laugh at our folly, while they are secretly finding their way every where, under the walls of the city. They are beginning to enter our houses and our palaces, and to take possession of our wealth and our merchandise, and step by step, to secure to themselves offices of influence and trust. And may they not, by becoming apparent friends, and uniting their forces, ere long take possession of the highest chair of state, and the highest offices of power, till they shall be able to wield the destinies of this great nation? And may it not be, that we shall yet be roused from our dreams of prosperity, wealth, and luxury, and like the voluptuous monarch of the East, find that we have been weighed in the balances and found wanting, and that our enemies, having marched under the walls, and having taken possession of the city, are bringing upon us speedy and inevitable ruin?

In all the movements of the Catholic church in the old world, what can be found more artful than her operations in the new? She cannot conquer this nation by the sword. She cannot at once convert our enlightened and educated men. Her hope is through female schools, and to them she is devoting her principal efforts. For this object, thousands and thousands of dollars are annually poured in upon us from Catholic Europe. For the same object, it is said, that $100,000 were brought into the city of New York during the last summer. More than a hundred female schools have been founded, and the work is rapidly going forward. Every effort is thus making to prepare the females of our land, and through them, the children and youth of the coming generations, to lend their aid in converting this nation to the church of Rome. How unlike are the efforts of the Protestant church. "The children of this world are wiser in their generation than the children of light."

But this work of supplying teachers is a very great work, and it will never be accomplished, till it is allowed a fair and honorable standing among the important benevolent objects of the day. If it has any claims to such a standing, they are very high and extensive. The more we attempt to meet the wants of the community in this respect, the more these wants will be made manifest.

This work requires haste. The state of our country, and the nature of the subject demand, that what we do, we do quickly. This is a remedy, which strikes at the root of the disease; but it is slow in its results. It promises much in recovering this nation from impending destruction, but only on condition, that it be applied speedily, and to an extent corresponding with that of the disease. It holds out but little prospect of relief to the present generation, but it fixes the eye of hope on those who are coming after, and seeks through them, to secure the nation from increasing danger.

It is immensely important, that the great principle should be speedily settled, that the work of supplying teachers is to be accomplished by a voluntary sacrifice of time and money, proportioned to the greatness and importance of the object. How much does the public sentiment on this subject need the influence of some bold enterprise in its behalf, which shall form a high standard, around which liberal and disinterested benevolence may gather. Such we hope will prove the humble work of founding Mount Holyoke Female Seminary.

This enterprise was commenced nearly three years ago. The work has ever since been going regularly, though slowly, forward. The first edifice is now erecting. It is 94 feet by 50, and four stories besides the basement. It will furnish good accommodations for the school and the family, and private chambers for the teachers and for eighty young ladies. It is to be ready for the reception of scholars early next autumn. Additions are to be made afterwards to the buildings, as the liberality of the Christian public shall furnish the means.

The work of bringing this institution into operation has been longer than was anticipated. But the progress of the enterprise in taking an acknowledged standing among the benevolent operations of the day, has exceeded the anticipations of its warmest friends. It may be doubted, whether any benevolent object, not excepting even the missionary cause, has ever, within three years from its commencement, made a greater advance in gaining access to the minds and hearts of the people to whom it has been presented. It is evidently testing, in the view of the community, the question of duty on the whole subject. Let this enterprise be carried through by the liberality of the Christian community, and will it any longer be doubted, whether the great work of supplying female teachers shall be allowed a fair and honorable place among the benevolent objects of the day? May it not settle the great principle forever? And may not every liberal donation to this institution, bear an important part in settling this principle? Will not every such donation be an invaluable testimony in behalf of the claims of the many institutions for females, which are yet to be founded in different parts of our country, by the hand of benevolence? Will it not prove to them like seed sown in good ground?

This institution now presents its claims to the Christian community. It asks for aid, not for its own sake alone—nor merely for the sake of the many hundreds and thousands of teachers, which it may send forth to bless the world—but it asks, as the representative of the great cause of raising up female teachers by benevolent effort.

1. *We appeal to men in moderate pecuniary circumstances.* This class of individuals have ever taken a prominent part in establishing all the branches of the great benevolent operations, which are promising so much good to this dark and wicked world. They have bestowed liberally of their substance, and they have given

nobly of their time. What could the missionary cause have done without them?—and what the temperance cause? This object now asks for their special aid, and proof has been given, that it will not ask in vain. The donations have hitherto been principally from this class of men, and many of them are of a high and honorable standard, compared with the means of the donors. We might mention one case of $1,200 from about twenty individuals in a little town on the hills of Massachusetts, and several others of scarcely less interest. These men think for themselves, and they are not afraid to take the first step in any important object, and if need be, to stand alone. They will not retreat in an hour of trial. When they are convinced of the importance of an undertaking, they will not wait to see what others will do, and withhold their hand from the work, till their aid is scarcely needed.

2. *We appeal to men of wealth.* This class of men sustain responsibilities peculiar to themselves. When any enterprise is struggling for a standing among the benevolent operations of the day, to them is often given the high privilege of settling the claim, and of affixing the final seal. The elements must be prepared by others. Every thing must be brought into a state of readiness, and then the discriminating man of wealth can cast in his thousands and accomplish the object in view. This enterprise has now come to this favorable and important time. The elements have long been preparing. Under the guidance of Providence, every thing seems brought to a state of readiness. Public sentiment is inclining, not only towards this institution, but towards the whole cause which it represents. One difficulty after another seems vanishing away. One obstacle only to gaining entire public confidence, seems to remain. It is this—the doubt, whether Christians are now prepared to admit another branch of benevolence, so extensive in its claims—the doubt, whether it must not be delayed another generation, till the speculating age shall be past, and till the desire to become rich shall have effected its own cure, and men shall be willing to stand in property, as they did in other days. One and another is waiting to see how this point shall be determined. But the man of wealth and acknowledged benevolence, may settle

this point at once, and prove to the world, that Christians are prepared for the work.

We are aware, that we come to men of wealth in an unpropitious time. But shall we venture to delay this work till a more convenient season—perhaps till the present generation shall have passed away, and another shall have come on the stage, bringing along with it, all the darker clouds of impending ruin? There are men of wealth, who do love the cause of Christ, more than others love their houses and their lands, and who will do, and venture more for its sake, than they would to promote their own personal interests. To such we would commend this object, as one of the first importance—we commend it to them, as the neglected child of benevolence, sought out by divine Providence, and brought to their door.

3. *We appeal to aged men.* A few of the fathers in Israel, whose heads are whitening for the grave, still remain. They have been permitted to witness the wonderful events of the last fifty years, and they have put their own hands to the work. They have broken up the fallow ground, and cast in the first seed, and have borne the heat and burden of the day and they have rejoiced as they have been gathering in the harvest. But some have trembled on observing indications, that all was not right. They have feared, lest we may have overlooked some branch of the benevolent system, and lest somewhere, we may have been asleep, while the enemy has been sowing tares. And is it not even so? The females have been passed by. In all the public munificence of the church, they have been overlooked. Their work is humble and unassuming, but it lies at the foundation of things. It operates secretly and slowly, but like leaven, leavening the whole lump. Is there not here and there one of our aged fathers remaining, who will rejoice in living to see one noble effort to qualify female laborers, for their appropriate duties, and who will delight to give his last testimony in its behalf, and to do his last and greatest deed of benevolence for its sake? One of the largest donations to the institution is from one of our fathers amidst the hills of Massachusetts, who has seen eighty-six years pass away; and are there not others of

similar minds to see, and of similar hearts to feel for this cause?

4. *We appeal to young men.* If it is a privilege to increase the velocity of the various wheels of benevolence put in motion by our fathers, how much greater the privilege to give the first impulse to one of the most important. Such a privilege can now be enjoyed. In our great system of benevolent labors, one essential wheel has been omitted, and the whole has been retarded and embarrassed in its operations. One and another has discovered this omission, but "he has passed by on the other side." After so long a time, who will now lend his aid in putting this wheel into its proper place, and in giving to it, its first happy motion? We look for aid to young men, who are strong, and on whose strength, the church, under God, is beginning to rely. They can withstand the greatest difficulties, and overcome the greatest obstacles. They can venture much—either for God or for mammon, as they severally shall have consecrated their hearts and their lives. We have much hope in commending this cause to the younger class of benevolent men, and from them, we have received abundant testimony, that our hope will not be disappointed. Many of this class have already opened their hands liberally, and some, in view of the magnitude of the object, and its reasonable claims, and in view of the present important crisis, have ventured to pledge in its behalf, far beyond what they have done for any other Christian enterprise. These deeds of benevolence, performed at the most important time, shall, in their favorable results to the great cause, be multiplied a hundred fold. Will not many others go and do likewise?

5. *We appeal to ministers of the gospel.* The church has long been engaged in a great benevolent work in behalf of education. And for whose sake has she been thus engaged? For whom have all the colleges, and theological seminaries, and other institutions been founded? For whom have the streams of benevolence from all parts of the country been flowing into the fountains, opened by our education societies? For whom have hundreds and thousands of dependent females been economizing their scanty means, and toiling with their own hands? For whom have the rich

every where cast in of their abundance, and the widow her two mites? Have not ministers and educated men been the immediate recipients of all this bounty? It is true, that it has not been for their own personal benefit, that all this has been done. But it has bestowed on them a far richer treasure—the precious privilege of being better prepared to serve the cause of our blessed Saviour. And who better than they should know the value of such a provision? And who have given better proof of it than they? To whom are we indebted for the forming of the various plans of adding college to college and institution to institution, and one branch of education to another? Who have gone through the land, arousing the whole church to this subject—enlightening dark minds, softening hard hearts, and opening the hand of charity in unwonted liberality? And who have given more liberally than other men, according to their means, to our colleges and education societies? The ministers of the gospel.

After all the abundant experience in both receiving and giving, who better than ministers, can understand the merits of this cause, and its imperative claims? Others may feel, that the work of the female is humble, and therefore unimportant—they may feel safe in leaving her preparation to take care of itself. But not so with the minister. His experience among his own people bears testimony on this subject, and the same testimony is repeated and reechoed from one part of the land to the other. And who is it, that here and there has been looking with painful solicitude on this subject for years, till he has been half compelled to break away from his labors, and devote himself *alone*, the great work of directing the attention of the community to the vast importance of making efforts in behalf of females? It is the faithful and observing minister, whose desires and efforts, having been matured and put forth among his own people, have extended over our nation, and over the whole world. As might be expected, this subject meets a most cordial and hearty response from the ministers of the gospel. They have given of their time, and of their influence, and they have contributed of their substance, notwithstanding the pecuniary trials of the last year. They have given a precious and interesting pledge, that as they have done for the education of young men, so they are ready to do for females, according to their ability, and even beyond their ability.

6. *We appeal to females themselves.* Females have manifested their interest in this cause in a most decisive manner. "If there be first a willing mind, it is accepted according to that a man hath, and not according to that he hath not." The first contribution in behalf of this enterprise, was made by ladies. The institution had then no name, nor place, nor legal existence. The whole enterprise was less in appearance than a man's hand, when a few ladies came forward, and generously raised one thousand dollars. Of this sum, $259 were given by the teachers and pupils of the Ipswich Female Seminary, and $475 by the ladies of the town of Ipswich. The remainder was soon after made out by a few ladies in other places. This was a noble beginning.

Other ladies have followed this example. Among the contributions, will be found many a valuable token of interest from females. From them have been received several of the larger donations to this cause. We might mention one of $230 from the teachers and pupils of a female seminary. We could mention too the name of one female, lately deceased—the widow of a departed minister, who has bequeathed to this seminary one-fourth of all she possessed, which will amount to several hundred dollars; and also, that of an aged female, who recently died, leaving a bequest to about the same amount. This property was acquired by the labor of her own hands, and it was all she possessed. The intelligence which she had gained by a careful study of the sacred Scriptures, and her devoted piety, gave her a lively interest in appropriating her earthly all to the purpose of preparing females for usefulness.

The hearts of those deeply enlisted in this cause, have been greatly cheered by the intelligent interest and active labors of many ladies. And may we not depend with the greatest confidence on their continued co-operation, and increasing efforts? Will they not labor for this cause more and more abundantly? And will they not invite the attention, and secure the efforts of many others in its behalf? Let discriminating and benevolent females, look at the claims of this cause, and examine its merits, and they will be more and more affected in view of its importance. They will feel, that "one half cannot be told." The influence on their own minds will not be lost. "Out of the abundance of the heart, the mouth speaketh." Guided by their own convictions, and by their own just and comprehensive views of the subject, they will be able to carry it to the minds and the hearts of their husbands and their fathers—of their brothers and their friends. And we trust that their appeal will not be in vain—that it will meet with a liberal and cheerful response.

7. *Finally, we appeal to the intelligent of all classes.* We come to those, who can appreciate this object—to those, in whose view the education of the female for her appropriate sphere of usefulness is no dream of the fancy, and the supplying of our country with well-qualified female teachers, is no game of chance. We come to those, who believe, that in this thing, "whatsoever we sow, that shall we also reap." This cause is the humble, but firm and efficient patron of all other branches of benevolence. What the present generation is beginning to accomplish for the salvation of a world, it seeks to preserve and carry forward with increasing rapidity. Whatever of conquest is now gained, it seeks to secure forever from the encroachments of the enemy. It seeks to lay the foundation strong, on which, under God, the temple, with all its increasing weight, is to rise, and be sustained, and to secure it from injury and decay. It looks abroad on a world lying in wickedness. It beholds with painful interest the slow progress of these United States in carrying the blessings of salvation to the 200,000,000, the estimated proportion of the inhabitants of this benighted world to be converted to God through our instrumentality. And as it attempts in vain to calculate the time, when the work shall be accomplished, it would fain increase its progress a hundred fold, by training up the children in the way they should go. It has endeavored to fix an eye on the distant point of futurity, when, according to a fair and reasonable computation, this nation with all its increasing millions, and the inhabitants of the

whole earth, shall be supplied with faithful, educated ministers of the gospel. And as it inquires, in vain, "When shall these things be?"—and as it attempts, in vain, to count up the millions on millions, who shall go down to everlasting death, before that time *can* arrive, it would fain strive with unparalleled efforts, through the children of our country, greatly to multiply the number of ministers during the next generation, and to carry forward the work in an unexampled and increasing ratio through the generations which shall follow.

The object of this institution penetrates too far into futurity, and takes in too broad a view, to discover its claims to the passing multitude. We appeal in its behalf to wise men, who can judge what we say. We appeal to those, who can venture as pioneers in the great work of renovating a world. Others may stand waiting for the great multitude to go forward, but then is the time, when these men feel themselves called upon to make their greatest efforts, and to do their noblest deeds of benevolence. Thus we hope it will be in behalf of this institution.

We commend this enterprise to the continued prayers and efforts of its particular friends—of all those, who have enlisted in its behalf, and have given of their time, their influence, and their substance. We would invite them to come with us around the same sacred altar, and there consecrate this beloved institution, as first fruits, to the Lord, to be devoted forever to his service.

This enterprise, thus far, has been under the care of a kind Providence. It has not been carried forward by might, nor by power; but in every step of its progress, the good hand of God has been upon it. Let all its friends bring in the tithes and the offerings, and let them commit the disposing of the whole to Him, who can accomplish the work, which his own hands have commenced, and he will pour out upon this institution, and the cause with which it is connected, and upon the children and youth of our country, and of the world, a blessing, that there shall not be room enough to receive it.

South Hadley, Mass., May, 1837.

NOTE.— Rev. Joseph D. Condit, of South Hadley, is Secretary, and William Bowdoin, Esq., of South Hadley Canal, Treasurer of the Board of Trustees. Donations to this Seminary may be forwarded to the Treasurer, or to Deacon Daniel Safford, Boston. A Prospectus of the institution will be forwarded to any who may apply for it, by letter, postpaid, directed to the Secretary, or to Deacon Daniel Safford, Boston, or to Prof. Hitchcock, Amherst.

6

Procuring Furniture

1837

It has been expected, that this institution would be ready for the reception of scholars the ensuing autumn, and nearly 30 pupils are already engaged most of whom are to be teachers, and some of them are to be missionaries, who must be deprived of the anticipated privileges of this Seminary, if the commencement should be delayed. But late failures on subscriptions not yet collected, and other disappointments, arising from the peculiar state of the commercial affairs, will render it exceedingly difficult to accomplish the object at the specified time. There are those, however, who regard this enterprize as one of the most important, and one destined to aid every other branch of benevolence, to assist in giving to the community that moral principle, and that moral feeling, which are so much needed in the great work of renovating the world. There are those, who would deeply regret the extensive disappointment, which would be occasioned by delaying the commencement of the school till another year, when the walls of the building are already erected. They would regard it as a loss to the whole cause of benevolence, too great to be sustained without vigorous exertions to prevent it. Such friends are ready to make an outstanding effort to complete the building, provided the furniture can be procured by other means. For this, their dependence is principally on females. They have done many voluntary deeds of benevolence, perhaps a greater number without any public agent to lead them forward than have been done by the other sex. Let ladies now come forward with their voluntary and cheerful contributions, and let the encouragement be given, that the building can be furnished as soon as completed, and the work will soon be accomplished, and the Seminary will be ready for the reception of scholars the ensuing autumn.

In view of the present trying emergency of the Mount Holyoke Female Seminary, we the subscribers, engage to pay the sums set against our names to aid in procuring furniture for the institution.

Furniture for chambers.

It will require from 50 to 60 to furnish a chamber. It is desirable, that the sum should be 60. If any thing remains, it will be appropriated to other articles of furniture. The whole amount can be given in money, though it is recommended, that the clothing for the bed, the towels, a pair of pillows, and an under-bed-tick should be furnished in the articles, and the remainder in money. In making out the estimate, nothing has been allowed for bedding but plain, durable articles. Good judgment will teach what we mean by, this, and also how much bedding will be needed in our coldest New England weather. When we have been asked for directions, however, on this subject, we have said with regard to quantity, two pairs of sheets and pillow cases, four towels, pair of blankets, comforter and bedquilt—and with regard to quality, common cotton (unbleached and whitened) for sheets, a little finer for pillow cases, colored cotton, or cheap calico for comforter, cheap calico, durable colors for bedquilt, any kind of blankets, a little worn, if more convenient, as in that case, some lady may give a pair of blankets or two ladies, each a blanket.

Besides the clothing for the bed, the towels, a pair of pillows, and an under-bed-tick, the sum to be given in money should not be less than 35 or 40. Donations may be forwarded to Dea. Daniel Safford, No. 3. Beacon Street.

7

Circular to the Young Ladies

1837

Circular to the young ladies who are to be members of the Mount Holyoke Female Seminary.

The effort to procure furniture for this institution has been at a very trying season. On this account it is with the utmost difficulty that it can be ready for the reception of scholars the present Autumn. The furniture will consist of two parts—that for the young ladies chambers and the furniture for all other parts of the establishment. The amount necessary for each is far from being yet completed. When money is given for a chamber it is with the understanding that the surplus is to be devoted to the dining room, or some other part of the common furniture. There will however be but very little aid from this source. In some instances nothing is given in bedding for a chamber but the estimated amount is furnished in money With the extreme difficulty of procuring money, it is very desirable that the bedding for such chambers should be given by other individuals, perhaps in other towns, who cannot so easily give money that there may be more surplus for other furniture This no doubt could be done could there be time to attend to it. Where a part only of the bedding is given the deficiency might be supplied in a similar manner. In some places where an effort is making to furnish each chamber the whole may not be made out before the commencement of school and yet it will be very desirable that the room should be occupied. To meet these cases and many more and to aid in bringing the institution into operation in November before all the means for the furniture can be raised the friends of the Seminary might render very important assistance by giving the use of some articles of furniture for a few months, or a year, many no doubt would do this most cheerfully even at a personal sacrifice were it not for the difficulty of transporting and retransporting. Perhaps the young ladies who are to be members of this Seminary can render some aid in this particular, as they could bring with them extra baggage with their own. Each young lady to whom this circular is sent is requested to make an immediate inquiry and canvass the benevolent ladies of her acquaintance and ascertain whether she could borrow in behalf of the Seminary, and bring with her, the following articles or a part of them—two pair of sheets, and pillow cases, two towels, two blankets, a comforter, bedquilt, underbedtick, pair of pillows, and either two silver tea spoons, or one silver table spoon. An early reply is requested stating how many of these articles can be obtained if necessary; as the number of scholars to be received may depend somewhat on the reply to this. Some young ladies may find it more convenient to bring a greater number of some articles and none of others. If so it is desirable that it should be definitely stated. If any young lady should find it convenient to bring a greater number of pillows and spoons than is specified they would be particularly acceptable as it will be most difficult to procure these articles. The reply may be directed to Miss Mary Lyon South Hadley. Each young lady may expect a letter a short time before the school opens stating whether all the articles mentioned in her reply to this will be needed. The articles which are lent should be marked with the owners name and the young ladies to whom they are committed will be responsible for their careful usage and safe return.

If any young lady who has engaged a place in the Seminary should fail of attending, it is important that information should be communicated as early as possible as many applicants must be refused.

8

Prospectus of Mount Holyoke Female Seminary

1837

This institution, located at South Hadley, Mass., will probably be ready for the reception of scholars, early next autumn. The time of opening the school, will soon be fixed, and then public notice will be given.

TRUSTEES AND TEACHERS.

The Board of Trustees consists of the following gentlemen:—Rev. Heman Humphrey, D. D., president of Amherst college; Rev. Edward Hitchcock, professor in Amherst college; Rev. Roswell Hawks (permanent agent); Rev. Joseph D. Condit, of South Hadley; Rev. William Tyler and William Bowdoin, Esq., of South Hadley Canal; David Choate, Esq., of Essex; Dea. Andrew W. Porter, of Monson; Mr. Joseph Avery, of Conway, and Dea. Daniel Safford, of Boston. Miss Mary Lyon, formerly connected with the Ipswich Female Seminary, will be Principal, and Miss Eunice Caldwell, Principal of the Wheaton Female Seminary, at Norton, Assistant Principal. They will be aided by other well-qualified teachers.

COURSE OF STUDY, ETC.

There will be an extensive and systematic English course of study, essentially the same as that adopted in the Ipswich Female Seminary. The regular classes will be denominated Junior, Middle, and Senior. The studies of each class are designed for one year, though the pupils will be advanced from class to class, according to their progress, and not according to the time spent in the institution. Individuals may in some cases, devote half of their time to branches not included in the regular course, (Latin, for instance,) and occupy two years in completing the studies of one class.

The classes below the Senior class have not the same denomination as in the Ipswich Female Seminary, but the difference is merely nominal.

The following is an outline of the regular course of study in that institution, as annexed to the last catalogue.

PRIMARY STUDIES.

Written Arithmetic,	Adams's.
Algebra,	Bailey's and Day's.
English Grammar,	Murray's.
Modern and Ancient Geography,	Woodbridge's Universal Geography and Atlas, and Worcester's Ancient Atlas.
History of the United States,	Goodrich's.
Modern and Ancient History,	Worcester's Elements of History, with Grimshaw's France and Goldsmith's England, Greece and Rome.
Botany commenced,	Phelp's.
Improvement of the Mind,	Watt's.
Rhetoric commenced,	Newman's.

STUDIES OF THE JUNIOR CLASS.

English Grammar continued,	Murray's.
Rhetoric concluded,	Whateley's.
Human Physiology,	Hayward's.
Euclid's Geometry,	Simson's and Playfair's.
Botany concluded,	Beck's.
Natural Philosophy,	Olmstead's.
Chemistry,	Beck's.
Astronomy,	Wilkins's.
Intellectual Philosophy,	Abercrombie's.
Philosophy of Natural History,	Smellie's.

STUDIES OF THE SENIOR CLASS.

Some of the preceding studies reviewed and continued.

Outline of Geology,	Mather's.
Ecclesiastical History,	Marsh's is preferred.
Logic,	Whateley's.
Natural Theology,	Paley's.
Moral Philosophy,	Wayland's.
Analogy of Natural and Revealed Religion to the Constitution and Course of Nature,	Butler's.
Evidences of Christianity,	Alexander's.

In this seminary, the studies of the Junior class will principally be embraced in the preceding list of "primary studies," and the Middle class will correspond essentially with the preceding "Junior class."

PREPARATORY STUDIES.

The requisites for entering the Junior class, will be an acquaintance with the general principles of English Grammar, a good knowledge of Modern Geography, History of the United States, Watts on the Mind, Colburn's First Lessons, and the *whole* of Adams's New Arithmetic, or what would be equivalent in Written Arithmetic. It is very important that all, on entering the seminary, should be prepared for admission to the Junior class. In extraordinary cases, however, individuals may be received the first year, though they should be deficient in some parts of the preparatory course. It is desirable that those who cannot continue members of the seminary more than one or two years, should, in addition to the preparatory studies, advance as far as may be in the regular course, before they enter.

CLASSIFICATION OF THE PUPILS.

In recitations, the regular classes will not be kept distinct, but member of different classes will recite together, as their necessities may require.

Pupils will be admitted to the regular classes only on careful examination. The regular time for admission to the Junior class will be at the commencement of the year, and the regular time for advancing the pupils from one class to another will be at the close of the year. Those, who, on entering the seminary, are candidates for admission to an advanced standing, will be examined and admitted at any time, as shall be convenient.

Those, who, on entering the seminary, are found to be somewhat deficient in the preparatory studies, will be allowed a short time for reviewing, before being examined or for admission to the regular classes. On this account, it is very important that they bring with them such books as they have previously studied. It is also recommended, that those who are to become members of the seminary at its commencement, should previously devote as much time as they can to study, especially to reviewing.

None can be admitted to the Junior class, without passing a good examination on the preparatory studies, whatever may be their knowledge of other branches. But individuals may be admitted to the Middle and Senior classes, by passing a good examination on the preparatory studies, and on such branches of the regular course, as shall be equivalent to a full preparation. At the close of the year, all who are prepared, will receive a testimonial of having completed the regular course of study in the seminary.

TERM BILLS.

There will be two terms in a year of 20 weeks each, or four quarters of 10 weeks each.

The expenses of board and tuition will be settled by fair experiment. It would be difficult now to fix on any permanent price; especially considering the present fluctuating state of the market, and the Trustees will venture to pledge only for one quarter at a time, till they shall have had opportunity to ascertain at what it can be placed. But as the institution is designed principally for the benefit of those preparing to be teachers, every effort will be made to reduce the expenses as low as possible, without injuring the character of the institution. It is confidently believed, that they can be placed so much below those in our best female seminaries, which have received no public aid, as shall in this particular alone, reward all the efforts that have been made in behalf of the institution.

The Trustees have, however, for the first quarter, decided to place board, exclusive of fuel and lights, at $13, and tuition at $3, making the regular bill of board and tuition for the quarter of 10 weeks, $16.

The bills are to be paid in advance, and no deduction will be made for a short absence at the commencement, close, or in any part of the quarter. In case of a protracted absence, the board may be paid by the week, and not by the quarter, though the charge will be higher in proportion, probably about the usual price of board elsewhere.

It is believed, that by requiring payment in advance, and deducting nothing for a short absence, the interests of the institution will be promoted. It will have a tendency to prevent irregularity in entering and leaving the school, thus producing with ease a very important result, which otherwise might not be obtained without great care and effort on the part of the teachers, Plans, which are suited by their own unaided influence, to secure regularity to the system adopted in the seminary, will tend to perpetuate the prosperity of the institution, and to secure it from being materially interrupted by the necessary changes of teachers. It is ever to be remembered, that the lives and continued usefulness of teachers are but temporary at best, and always precarious. This truth will be kept in view in the formation of all the plans of this seminary. Much care will be taken to adopt and settle principles, which may be permanent, and to form and mature a system of operations, which may essentially outlive those, to whose care it is at first committed.

The term bills, as fixed for the first quarter, are very low, considering the present price of provisions, and the increased price of board and tuition elsewhere. It may be found on experiment, that they must be somewhat raised to meet the real expenses. If so, it is believed that the reasonable expectations of the donors to this seminary will still be realized. Those who have contributed to the funds of this institution for the purpose of preparing the daughters of our land for usefulness, and of raising up teachers for the good of our country, have anticipated a reduction of expenses. As far as any definite views have been presented, the expectation has been encouraged, that the regular bills for board and tuition would be from one-third to one-half less than in other large female seminaries generally, and on comparison, it will be seen that for the first quarter, they do not vary much from one-half the amount. The expectations of the public will therefore be fully realized, though the bills for board and tuition should hereafter be somewhat increased.

DOMESTIC DEPARTMENT.

This department will be under the superintendence of a lady, qualified for the undertaking. All the members of the school will aid to some extent in the domestic labors of the family. The portion of time thus occupied, will be so small, that it will not retard their progress in study, but will rather facilitate it by the invigorating influence of a little daily exercise of the best kind.

The division of labor will be very systematic, giving to each young lady not much change or variety in a term, and enabling her to perform her part in a proper manner, without solicitude. To each one will be assigned that in which she has been well versed at home, and no one will expect to receive instruction in any thing, with which she is entirely unacquainted. It is no part of the design of this seminary to teach young ladies domestic work. This branch of education is exceedingly important, but a literary institution is not the place to gain it. Home is the proper place for the daughters of our country to be taught on this subject; and the mother is the appropriate teacher. Some may inquire, "What then can be the design of this arrangement?" We reply, that the family work must be performed—that it is difficult to find hired domestics, and to retain them any considerable time, when they are found—and that young ladies engaged in study suffer much in their vigor and intellectual energy, and in their future health, for the want of exercise. The construction of the building, and the family arrangements are to be such, as will render it convenient and suitable for the members of the school to take exercise in the domestic department, thus receiving benefit themselves, and conferring a benefit on others. Daughters of well-bred families in New England have independence enough to engage in any business, which will promote their best interests, and the best interests of those around them, and for such families this institution is designed, whatever may be their circumstances in other respects.

This feature of the institution will not relieve mothers from the responsibility of giving their daughters a thorough domestic education, but it will rather throw before those who are seeking for them, the privileges of this seminary, additional motives to be faithful in this important duty. And do not many in New England need some additional motive on this subject? What mechanic would hazard his reputation by sending out a regularly taught apprentice, who should be as unskillful in his business as many daughters are in domestic pursuits, when their mothers send them forth to preside in their own families, and to guide their own households? Is it not a reflection on both mother and daughter, when the daughter is not so educated, that she can perform with skill and cheerfulness any domestic labor, which it is suitable for her mother to perform?

The plan for the domestic department is an experiment—but one, respecting which there are sanguine hopes of success. That the experiment may be a fair one, it is regarded as of great importance, that the plan should be executed on the principle of entire equality—that the labor should be performed as a gratuitous service, that all should participate; and that none should be received into the institution, who are entirely unacquainted with domestic pursuits, or who cannot cheerfully cooperate with others in carrying out this part of the system.

APPLICATIONS FOR ADMISSION.

As the number is to be limited, in deciding the cases of applicants, some reference will be had to age, attainments, and objects in view. It is particularly desirable, that those who have been engaged in teaching, should have the opportunity to improve their education, if they desire it. To secure a place for such, it may be necessary to decline receiving some other desirable applicants.

Except in extraordinary cases, none will be admitted under the age of sixteen. The teachers and the pupils will constitute one family, and none will be received to board in other families.

Applications for admission may be made to Miss Mary Lyon, directed, before the first of July, to Boston, care of Dea. Daniel Safford, and after that time, to South Hadley, Mass. It may be necessary to delay the answer a short time, but a decisive reply may in every case be expected within six weeks after the application is received, and perhaps sooner, if it is particularly requested by the applicant.

Relative to each applicant, it is desirable, that some information should be communicated respecting her age, her attainments, especially in the branches required for entering the Junior class, the books she has studied, the state of her health, her domestic education, and domestic habits, and whether she has been engaged in teaching, and how long; whether it is her personal wish to become a member of the institution, or a mere acquiescence in the wishes of her friends; the probable length of time she will continue a member of the institution, and whether the first application is for one year, or only one term.

If any one should be prevented from attending after having made an engagement, information should be communicated as soon as possible, so that the place may be given to another. It is very important, that every individual should be present the first day.

The Bible lessons will commence with the New Testament. Pupils are requested to bring a Commentary on the Gospels and a Concordance, if they own them; also any common school books which they possess. Every one should be supplied with a Bible, an English Dictionary, and a Modern Atlas.

In behalf of the Trustees,
J. D. CONDIT, Secretary
South Hadley, Mass. May 1, 1837.

9

First Annual Catalogue
Of the
Officers and Members
Of the
Mount Holyoke Female Seminary

South Hadley, Mass.

1837-8

TRUSTEES

Rev. William Tyler, President
Rev. Joseph D. Condit, Secretary
Rev. Heman Humphrey, D.D.
Rev. Edward Hitchcock
Rev. Roswell Hawks
William Bowdoin, Esq.
David Choate, Esq.
Dea. Andrew W. Porter
Mr. Joseph Avery
Dea. Daniel Safford

TEACHERS

Miss Mary Lyon, Principal
Miss Eunice Caldwell, Associate Principal
Miss Mary W. Smith, Teacher
Miss Amanda A. Hodgman, Teacher
Miss Abigail Moore, Assistant Pupil
Miss Persis C. Woods, Assistant Pupil
Miss Susan Reed, Assistant Pupil

PUPILS

SENIOR CLASS

Martha A. Abbott,	Framingham.
Sarah Brigham,	Grafton.
Abigail Moore,	Fredonia, N. Y.
Persis C. Woods,	Enfield.

Senior Class 4

MIDDLE CLASS

Sarah A. Adams,	Hopkinton.
Julia Adams,	Hopkinton.
Sarah B. Adams,	Franklin.
Hannah O. Bailey,	Amesbury.
Lucia L. Bass,	Colebrook, Ct.
Abigail Bigelow,	Winchendon.
Hannah Brigham,	Grafton.
Lucy A. Brigham,	Grafton.
Catharine W. Bridgman,	Belchertown.
Sarah H. Browne,	Templeton.
Eliza Cambell,	Acworth, N. H.
Sarah E. Clarke,	Granby.
Cordelia Dickinson,	Amherst.

P. Augusta Ely,	Lyme, Ct.
Nancy S. Everett,	Wrentham.
Mary A. Gillett,	Sarah Hadley Falls.
Marion A. Hawks,	South Hadley.
Maria Howe,	Marlboro'.
Helen Humphrey,	Southwick.
Catharine S. Leach,	Pittsford, Vt.
Martha A. Leach,	Pittsford, Vt.
Almira W. Lothrop,	Easton.
Elizabeth Mann,	Boston.
H. Aurelia Matson,	Ithaca, N. Y.
Bethiah A. Miller,	Heath.
Susan Reed,	Heath.
Louisa T. Richardson,	Harford, Pa.
Prudence Richardson,	Dracut.
Mary E. Smith,	Amherst.
Sarah A. Stuart,	Pittsford, Vt.
Harriet N. Thomson,	Heath.
Sarah H. Torrey,	North Bridgewater.
Sarah E. Walker,	Belchertown.
Mary C. Whitman,	East Bridgewater.

Middle Class 34

JUNIOR CLASS*

Theresa T. Arms,	Deerfield.
Frances M. Atwood,	Nashua, N.H.
Mary Avery,	Conway.
Elizabeth K. Baldwin,	Ashfield.
Lucy Barnard,	Woburn.
Emma L. Bliss,	Springfield.
Anna E. Bosworth,	Bristol, R. I.
Laura G. Bowdoin.,	South Hadley Falls.
Lydia Bradstreet,	Danvers.
Mary Bridgman,	Northampton.
Cornelia A. Brigham,	Grafton.
Elizabeth Bucklen,	Ludlow.

Elizabeth G. Bull,	Danbury, Ct.
Ursula Bull,	Danbury, Ct.
Mary Burr,	Norfolk, Ct.
Caroline Burr,	Norfolk, Ct.
Mary A. Caldwell,	Ipswich.
Abigail A. Chandler,	Saxton's River, Vt.
Mary W. Chapin,	Somers, Ct.
Mary A. Chase,	Leominster.
Zillah D. Chenery,	Holden.
Sophia A. Clapp,	Belchertown.
Eliza M. Day,	South Hadley Falls.
Clara Dwight,	Belchertown.
Serena Field,	North Bridgewater.
Eliza S. Forbes,	Westboro'.
Elizabeth S. Gates,	Ashby.
Elizabeth H. Goodale,	Marlboro'.
Lucy T. Goodale,	Marlboro'.
Sarah H. Grout,	Hawley.
Mary C. Haskell,	Hardwick.
Elizabeth S. Hawks,	South Hadley.
Philena N. Hawks,	Charlemont.
Rachel Hathaway,	Freetown.
Helen A. Henry,	Amherst.
Frances M. Hitchcock,	Pittsford, Vt.
Harriet B. Hollister,	Manchester, Vt.
Julia Hyde,	Wayland.
Eliza Judd,	South Hadley.
Sarah A. Mather,	Northampton.
Persis F. Maynard,	Princeton, N. J.
Mary S. Nash,	South Hadley.
Hannah Ordway,	Amesbury.
Louisa. F. Packard,	North Bridgewater.
Eliza L. Packard,	Monson.
Harriet S. Park,	Orange, N. J.
Eleanor Penfield,	Pittsford, Vt.
Sarah Platt,	Bethel, Ct.

Jerusha Pomeroy,	Stonington, Ct.
Harriet Rice,	Charlemont.
Catherine F. Sawin,	Sherburne.
Harriot B. Savage,	Sharon.
Wealthy H. Shepard,	Buckland.
Mary H. Shumway,	Oxford.
Zeviah L. Shumway,	Oxford.
Martha Smith,	Northampton.
Maria Smith,	South Hadley.
Elizabeth P. Smith,	South Hadley.
Miranda A. Smith,	Hatfield.
Abigail N. Spaulding,	Honesdale, Pa.
Julia Spencer,	Hinsdale.
Helen M. Thomson,	Heath.
Sarah M. Thomson,	Monson.
Eliza Ann Tirrill,	Boston.
Catharine D. Torrey,	Killingly, Ct.
Sophronia H. Topping,	Bridgehampton, N. Y.
Margaret Tufts,	New Haven, Ct.
Elizabeth. S. Tyler,	Attleborough.
Harriet Wheeler,	Hardwick.

Junior Class 69

*There is a great diversity of attainments among the members of this class. None have been admitted to the class without passing a thorough examination on *all* the preparatory studies, but several have *this year* been under the necessity of completing the preparation after entering the Seminary, and will not be able during the year to finish the Junior studies. Others on entering the Seminary were considerably in advance of the class, but not fully prepared to enter the Middle class.

UNCLASSED

Abby M. Bosworth,	Bristol, R. I.
Joanna M. Coggeshall,	Bristol, R. I.
Mary E. Hayes,	Cincinnati, O.

Martha A. Smead,	Greenfield.
Eliza Spencer,	Hinsdale.
Emeline Sweasey,	Newark, N. J.
Ann M. Sutherland,	Bath, N. H.
Rebecca B. Trask,	Lincoln.
Mary E. Tyler,	Haddam, Ct.

Unclassed 9

SUMMARY

Senior Class,	4
Middle Class,	34
Junior Class,	69
Unclassed,	9
Total	116*

Winter Term 77—Summer Term 89

*The first term a few were admitted for only one quarter. The names of such are not inserted in the Catalogue.

APPENDIX

Course of Study and Instruction

There is an extensive and systematic English course of study pursued in the Seminary in three regular classes, denominated Junior, Middle and Senior. The studies of each class are designed for one year, though the pupils will be advanced from class to class according to their progress, and not according to the time spent in the Institution. In some cases, individuals may devote a part of their time to branches not included in the regular course, (Latin for instance) and occupy a longer period in completing the studies of one class.

Preparatory Studies

The requisites for entering the Junior class are, an acquaintance with the general principles of English Grammar, a good knowledge of Modern Geography, History of the United State, Watts on the Mind, Colburn's First Lessons, and the *whole* of Adams's New Arithmetic, or what would be equivalent in Written Arithmetic. These branches are to be required of candidates for admission to the Seminary.

Studies of the Junior Class

English Grammar, Ancient Geography, Ancient and Modern History, Sullivan's Political Class Book, Botany, Newman's Rhetoric, Euclid, Human Physiology.

Studies of the Middle Class

English Grammar continued, Algebra, Botany continued, Natural Philosophy, Smellie's Philosophy of Natural History, Intellectual Philosophy.

Studies of the Senior Class

Chemistry, Astronomy, Geology, Ecclesiastical History, Evidences of Christianity, Whately's Logic, Whately's Rhetoric, Moral Philosophy, Natural Theology, Butler's Analogy.

The above is the course, as pursued in the Seminary the present year. To the studies of the Senior class, there will probably be added, hereafter, two or three branches, and something will be taken from the present list, and added to those of the two preceding classes. On this account, it will be more important, that the preparation to enter the Junior class should be full and thorough.

Classification of Pupils

None can be admitted to the Junior class without passing a good examination on all the *preparatory studies*, whatever may be their attainments in other branches. But individuals may be admitted to the Middle and Senior classes, by passing a good examination on the preparatory studies, and on such branches of the regular course as shall be equivalent to a full preparation.

The commencement of the year is the regular time for admitting pupils to the Junior class, and for advancing them from one class to another. Those, however, who on entering the Seminary are candidates for admission to the Middle or Senior class, may need some time for review and examination, before their true standing can be determined. Of such, an advance in studies will be required, corresponding with the time which shall have transpired before they are admitted. To those who desire it, a few days will be allowed for reviewing the preparatory studies before examination. It is desirable that young ladies bring with them such books as they have studied.

In recitations, the regular classes are not kept distinct, but members of different classes recite together as their necessities require.

Text Books

The following are the principal used in the Seminary. Murray's Grammar and Exercises, Worcester's Elements of History, with Goldsmith's England, Greece and Rome, and Grimshaw's France, Simson's Euclid, or Playfair's (old edition) Sullivan's Political Class Book, Newman's Rhetoric, Hayward's Physiology, Day's Algebra, Olmstead's Natural Philosophy, Smellie's Philosophy of Natural History, Beck's Chemistry, Beck's Botany, Wilkins' Astronomy, Alexander's Evidences of Christianity, Marsh's Ecclesiastical History, Whately's Logic, Whately's Rhetoric, Paley's Natural Theology, Wayland's Moral Philosophy, Butler's Analogy.

As books and stationary can be had at the Seminary on very low terms, young ladies need not purchase them elsewhere. They are requested, however, to bring with them any of the preceding list of Text Books, which they may own—also a Bible, an English Dictionary, and if they own them, a Concordance, a Commentary on the Bible, Village Hymns, Watt's Psalms and Hymns, and some collection of sacred music, Parker's Progressive Exercises in Reading, books containing selections in poetry and prose for improvement in reading, a Modern Atlas, an Ancient Atlas, Burritt's Celestial Atlas, standard works on Poetry, especially Pope's Essay on Man, and Milton's Paradise Lost.

Terms and Vacations

During the year, 40 weeks are embraced in term time, and 12 vacations. The ensuing year will be divided into three terms. The first and second will be 13 weeks each, and the third 14. Most of the time embraced in vacations will be at the close of the year, which will accommodate many of the pupils who are a great distance from home. There will be a short recess at the close of the first and second term, but not sufficient to allow the pupils to visit their friends, unless they are in the immediate vicinity.

Terms of Admission

The regular time for the admission of pupils is at the commencement of the year. Except in extraordinary cases, none will be received for a part of the year. When exceptions are made on this point, it will generally be in favor of those who have been previously members of the Seminary, and who in their studies, are in advance of their classes. It would be much better, however, that in such cases they should remain the whole year, and devote the surplus time to branches not strictly required in the course. When there is any such absence, it is recommended, that it should be in the Middle year, as it is very important, that no one should be absent a single week during the Senior year.

None are considered admissible to the Institution unless they have completed their sixteenth year, and are acquainted with the preparatory studies. It is recommended, that young ladies review the preparatory studies before entering, especially the principles of Arithmetic, and the more intricate questions in the latter part of Adams's New Arithmetic. It is desirable that those, who cannot continue members of the Seminary more than one or two years, should in addition to the preparatory studies, advance as far as possible in the regular course before they enter.

Family Accommodations

All the teachers and pupils board in the establishment. None are received to board elsewhere. Whenever convenient it is recommended that the young ladies engage their own roommates. In cases where this is not convenient, the teachers will make every effort, to place those together of congenial tastes and habits. The family and school are so organized, that they form constituent parts of the same whole, each advancing the interests of the other, and both uniting to promote the improvement, comfort, and happiness of the household. Every thing relative to the division and improvement of time, to giving and receiving instruction, and to social intercourse, partakes much more of the freedom and simplicity of the family circle, than of the common restrictive rules of the school system.

Moral and Religious Influence

The institution has been given to the community as the results of benevolent efforts. That it would be decidedly religious in its influence has been the expectation of its friends. The location of the Seminary, and all the surrounding circumstances are favorable to such an influence. A very large proportion of the pupils are professors of religion.

Domestic Department

All the members of the school aid to some extent in the domestic labors of the family. The portion of time thus occupied, is so small that it does not retard their progress in study, but rather facilities it by the invigorating influence of a little regular daily exercise of the best kind. The division of labor is very systematic, giving to each young lady not much change or variety in a term, and enabling her to perform her part in a proper manner without solicitate. In ordinary cases, to each one is assigned that in which she has been well trained at home. No one will expect to receive instruction in any thing, with which she is entirely unacquainted. It is no part of the design of this

Seminary to teach young ladies domestic work. This branch of education is exceedingly important, but a literary institution is not the place to gain it. Home is the proper place for the daughters of our country to be taught on this subject; and the mother is the appropriate teacher. Some may inquire, "What then can be the design of this arrangement?" It may be replied, that the family work must be performed—that it is difficult to find hired domestics, and to retain them any considerable time, when they are found—and that young ladies engaged in study suffer much in their vigor and intellectual energy, and in their future health for the want of exercise. The construction of the building and the family arrangements are such, as render it convenient and suitable for the members of the school to take exercise in the domestic department, thus receiving a benefit themselves, and conferring a benefit on others. Daughters of well bred families in New England have independence enough to engage in any business, which will promote their own best interests, and the best interests of those around them, and for such families this institution is designed, whatever may be their circumstances in other respects.

This feature of the institution will not relieve mothers from the responsibility of giving their daughters a thorough domestic education, but it will rather throw before those who are seeking for them the privileges of this Seminary, additional motives to be faithful in this important duty.

Term Bills

Board exclusive of fuel and lights, will be $16 a term, and tuition $4, making the bills for the year $60. The regular bills for each term ($20) are to be paid in advance, and no deduction will be made for a short absence, either at the commencement or close, or during any part of the term. In case of a necessary protracted absence, the board can be paid by the week, and not by term, though the charge in such a case will be higher in proportion—about the usual price of board elsewhere.

Applications

Applications for admission may be made to Miss Mary Lyon, South Hadley, Mass.

In making a selection from the applicants, reference is had to age, attainments, maturity of character, and time of application. Relative to each applicant, it is desirable that facts should be stated respecting her age, attainments, general character and habits. The present year will close on Thursday, Aug. 23, and the ensuing year will commence Wednesday Oct. 3. The vacation at the close of the present year is shortened, that the opening of school may be earlier in the season.

Notice to Pupils Already Engaged

If any whose application has been accepted should find that they have misunderstood terms of reception, and cannot now comply with them, they are requested to give the information as early as possible, that their places may be given to others.

Where it is convenient, each young lady is requested to bring with her towels for her own use, one pair of sheets and pillow cases for her bed, and one table spoon and one tea spoon.

The plans of the institution make it exceedingly important, that every member of the school should be present the first day, and if possible as early as Tuesday evening.

Stages

A daily stage from Hartford to Brattleboro' and from Brattleboro' to Hartford passes South Hadley. Young ladies from the west, by passing the night at Springfield, will find a stage in the morning for South Hadley, and from Northampton they can take an early stage to Hadley, where they will find another stage for South Hadley. Those from the east can pass the night at Springfield, Hadley, or Amherst, where they will find a morning stage for South Hadley. By taking a private conveyance at Belchertown, they can arrive the same evening and avoid the travel of several miles. A private carriage will be sent from South Hadley to meet the stage on its arrival at Belchertown for such young ladies, as will write seasonably (directed to Miss Lyon) making the request, and stating definitely what day they will be there. South Hadley is about six miles from Northampton. Young ladies who arrive at Northampton from the west, may find it more pleasant to come on directly in the evening, than to spend the night, and take a more indirect route by stage in the morning. By writing seasonably as directed above, they can secure a private carriage, to meet them on their arrival at Northampton.

Note—The opening of the school the ensuing year will not be advertised in the papers. Those who receive this are therefore requested to circulate it among their friends, who may be desirous of gaining information relative to the admission of pupils.

10

Female Education

JUNE 1839

Female Education, Tendencies Of The Principles Embraced, And The System Adopted In The Mount Holyoke Female Seminary.

The founders of this Seminary have an important object in view. They are endeavoring to furnish an institution, which shall exert an unequivocal influence in rendering female education a handmaid to the gospel, and an efficient auxiliary in the great work of renovating the world. It is desirable that the friends of this enterprise should examine the principles of the institution, and observe its results and its tendencies. It is hoped, that they will find reason to rejoice that they have not labored in vain. They have commenced a great work, which, if worthy to be commenced, is worthy to be carried forward. They will have much occasion still for patient and persevering effort. While the friends of this seminary rejoice in its prosperity, let them not look on the work as already achieved. They may rejoice in the *kind* of influence it is beginning to exert, but not in the *degree*. They must remember, that it is still a little one—an infant of less than two years. And when they shall have finished the work of building, and the original plan shall have been completed, its immediate influence will scarcely be seen on this great moral world. But it is the kind of its influence, and the natural *tendencies* of its principles, which, if any thing, must give it importance. Let its friends trace the natural results of maturing the principles here adopted, and of carrying them out in hundreds of other schools throughout the country. Then let them return and inquire, whether this seminary is worthy to be completed for the encouragement of all, who shall hereafter devise liberal things in behalf of female education; or whether the work shall stop where it is, and remain a monument of the inability and discouragement of its friends. The institution *must* live; but whether its influence shall be extended, and its principles disseminated, is yet to be determined. Much depends upon the promptness, with which the present wants of the institution are met. The buds of promise are now flattering, and give delightful encouragement of abundant fruit. But they are tender, and can be easily blasted by untimely frosts.

It may not be inappropriate here to mention a few facts, for those who are unacquainted with this institution.

1. The funds are raised, and the seminary founded on principles of public benevolence. It is designed to meet public, rather than private wants. It invites none to enlist in its behalf on principles of self-interest. It promises no peculiar reward or favors to its donors; but it does promise to use the means that are furnished, in the most economical and profitable manner, for the good of the cause, whose interests it is pledged to support. The efforts for raising funds have all been made during the late pecuniary embarrassments. But the success has been such as to give interesting evidence, that there is in the community a principle of benevolence, which can be drawn forth in behalf of education more powerfully than any principle of personal, private, or local interest.

2. In the system adopted in this school, the real wants of the community have been regarded. Its design is to promote the best interests of the public, rather than to secure the greatest amount of patronage. Efforts are made to furnish the best possible school, and not to secure the greatest number of scholars. It has adopted a regular system, to which it strictly adheres. It is open for the reception of all who can meet its requisitions. In the early stages of the enterprise, some of its friends, who admired its principles,

doubted the expediency of endeavoring to introduce them. They feared, that scholars could not be procured without greater latitude in the principles adopted, and in the terms of admission. But the result shows, that it is still safer to seek *wisdom*, rather than *riches*. The school has not only been full from the commencement, but hundreds have been refused for the want of room, and it is doubtful whether a happier company of youth can any where be found, than is embraced in this family circle.

3. This institution is established in South Hadley, Mass. The scenery in the valley of the Connecticut needs no praise. The salubrity of the air of South Hadley, and the sweetness of its little village, with its hills, and valleys, and streams, are well known in the vicinity.

The enterprise of founding this seminary was commenced nearly five years ago. More than three years were occupied in preparing the way, in raising the funds, and in erecting the building now occupied. It was ready for the reception of scholars, November 8, 1837.

4. The original plan was to provide for 200. Only the first building has yet been erected. This can accommodate only 90. Though it is a noble edifice, and well adapted to its end, it is but a beginning. Full one-half of the funds must yet be raised. In order to finish the plan, at least $20,000 more will be needed for the buildings, besides perhaps $5,000, or more, for furniture, library and apparatus.

5. The current expenses of the institution are defrayed by the regular bills of board and tuition. There are no funds to sustain the school. The guardians of this seminary have asked of the community only the means to provide the necessary accommodations. They are pledged to use the means committed to them according to the best of their ability. The friends of education are invited to examine their work, and judge whether they have been faithful to their trust, and whether it is safe and wise to commit still more to their disposal. Let them see what a home they have furnished for the young ladies, and what means of instruction and improvement are enjoyed, with an annual charge for board and tuition, exclusive of fuel and lights, of only $60.

What college has done more in proportion to the money, which has been raised in its behalf? Shall not the guardians of this seminary, then, have the privilege of going forward with their work?

6. The institution embraces the principles of permanency. It is placed on a firm legal basis. It is encumbered with no private claims, nor local obligations. It has the same elements of perpetuity which are embraced in our colleges.

7. It has adopted a thorough, extensive, and systematic course of study, occupying at present three years, and it aims at a very high standard of intellectual culture. It does not provide for the earlier stages of education, as it does not receive any under sixteen years of age, and definite qualifications are requisite for admission. It proposes to take young ladies, when qualified in age and attainments, and carry them through the regular course. Those, however, who particularly desire it, are received for one year.

8. The teachers and pupils, without a single exception, constitute one family. This plan is found greatly to promote an economical division of time, and to aid in forming and executing a regular system.

9. The domestic work of the family is performed by the members of the seminary. This is divided equally among the young ladies, giving to each a little daily exercise. This department is under the general direction of the Principal, and the time of one lady is devoted to definite superintendence. There has not been a hired domestic in the family since its organization, but it is believed, that its domestic standard will not suffer in comparison with that of most well regulated families. The success of this department has exceeded the anticipations of its most sanguine friends.

TENDENCIES

Means of education are to be valued more according to their natural tendencies, and their legitimate influence, than according to their immediate results. The favorable influence which this institution has a tendency to exert, is of two kinds—first, on its members, and secondly, on the cause of education.

ON ITS MEMBERS

This seminary is specific in its character, and of course does not provide for the entire education of a young lady. Such a provision may be found expedient in foreign countries, where all systems can be brought under the rigid rules of monarchy, without being subject to the continual encroachments and changes, necessarily resulting from a free government. But in our country it is doubted whether female seminaries generally can attain a high standard of excellence, till they become more specific, and less mixed in their character. Who does not value the precedence which our New England colleges have in this respect over those in our new settlements? The mutual aid which specific schools render to each other, while each confines itself to its own appropriate sphere, is productive of more beneficial results, than where each one attempts to do the whole. The nursery, the primary school, the academy, the college and the theological seminary, should each perform only its appropriate part in the educating of a minister; but their combined influence should be directed to the same great end. Thus while this seminary is designed only to conduct the education after the age of sixteen, it seeks to cooperate with all other means which are to unite in educating the female, from the cradle to womanhood.

The period of childhood, and of the earlier part of youth, is a most important portion of existence. It is then that most of the essential habits for life are formed, and such impressions on the mind and heart are made, as shall be interwoven with the very texture of the soul. But when this is past, another succeeds of scarcely less importance. It is a period when all the precepts, example, and salutary influence of early years may be embodied into general rules of duty—when principles are to be adopted for life, and when character is to receive almost its last and final impression. This is the period over which this institution seeks in various ways, to cast a powerful and decided influence—an influence, which shall extend through this life, and through the ceaseless ages of eternity.

1. *Religious culture.*

This lies at the foundation of that female character, which the founders of this seminary have contemplated. Without this, their efforts would entirely fail of their design. This institution has been built for the Lord, that it might be peculiarly his own. It has been solemnly and publicly dedicated to his service. It has been embalmed by prayer in many hearts, and consecrated around many a family altar. The donors and benefactors of this institution, with its trustees and teachers, have felt a united obligation to seek, in behalf of this beloved seminary, "first the kingdom of God and his righteousness." Endeavors have been made to raise the funds, and to lay the whole foundation on Christian principles—to organize a school and form a family, that from day to day might illustrate the precepts and spirit of the gospel. Public worship, the Bible lesson, and other appropriate duties of the Sabbath; a regular observance of secret devotion, suitable attention to religious instruction and social prayer meetings, and the maintaining of a consistent Christian deportment, are considered the most important objects of regard, for both teachers and scholars. The friends of this seminary have sought that this might be a spot where souls shall be born of God; and where much shall be done for maturing and elevating Christian character. The smiles of Providence, and the influences of the Holy Spirit have encouraged them to hope, that their desires will not be in vain.

2. *Cultivation of benevolence.*

This is implied in the last particular, but it needs special care in a lady's education. While many of the present active generation are fixed in their habits, and will never rise above the standard of benevolence already adopted, the eye of hope rests with anxious solicitude on the next generation. But who shall take all the little ones, and by precept, and still more by example, enforce on them the sentiments of benevolence, and, aided by the Holy Spirit, train them up from their infancy for the service of the Redeemer? Is there not here an appropriate sphere for the efforts of woman, through whose moulding hands all our children and youth must inevitably pass?

How important then is it, that the education of a female should be conducted on strictly benevolent principles; and how infinitely important, that this spirit should be the presiding genius in every female school. Should it not be so incorporated with its nature, and so wrought into its very existence, that it cannot prosper without it? Such a school the friends of this seminary have sought to furnish. They would have the spirit of benevolence manifest in all its principles, and in the manner of conferring its privileges—in the mutual duties it requires of its members, and in the claims it makes on them to devote their future lives to doing good.

3. *Intellectual culture.*

This trait of character is of inestimable value to a lady who desires to be useful. A thorough and well balanced intellectual education, will be to her a valuable auxiliary in every department of duty.

This seminary has peculiar advantages for gaining a high intellectual standard. The age will give to the pupils as a whole, greater mental power, and the attainments required for admission, will secure to the institution a higher standard of scholarship. The plan of receiving none for less than a year will contribute greatly to systematic and thorough intellectual culture, and the moderate expenses of the institution will doubtless lead many a father to expend more on the education of a daughter here, than he would think advisable at any other school, because it will carry her through a regular course of study. These and other circumstances have combined in rendering it practicable to adopt a high standard even in the present infant state of the seminary. But there is still much room for advance; and from the character of the institution, and the facilities it possesses, it is encouraged to aim still higher and higher. It is believed, too, that the more elevated the standard adopted in the seminary, the more valuable will be the attainments of all, even of those who do not go through the regular course.

4. *Physical culture.*

The value of health to a lady is inestimable. Her appropriate duties are so numerous and varied, and so constant in their demands, and so imperious in the moment of their calls, as will render this treasure to her above price. How difficult is it for her to perform all her duties faithfully and successfully, unless she possesses at all times a calm mind, an even temper, a cheerful heart and a happy face. But a feeble system, and a nervous frame are often the direct antagonists of these indispensable traits in a lady's character. A gentleman may possibly live and do some good without much health; but what can a lady do, unless she takes the attitude of an invalid, and seeks to do good, principally by patience and submission? If a gentleman cannot do his work in one hour, he may perhaps do it in another; but a lady's duties often allow of no compromise in hours. If a gentleman is annoyed and vexed with the nervousness of his feeble frame, he may perhaps use it to some advantage, as he attempts to move the world by his pen, or by his voice. Though such a use will probably be to the shortening of his days, yet he may do something while he does live. But a lady cannot make such a use of this infirmity in her influence over her children and family—an influence which must be at all times under the control of gentleness and equanimity. Much has been said on this subject, but enough has not been *done* in our systems of education, to promote the health of young ladies. This is an object of special regard in this seminary.

The time is all regularly and systematically divided. The hours for rising and retiring are early. The food is plain and simple, but well prepared, and from the best materials. No article of second quality of the kind is ever purchased for the family, and no standard of cooking is allowed, but that of doing every thing as well as it can be done. The day is so divided that the lessons can be well learned, and ample time allowed for sleep; the hour for exercise in the domestic department can be secured without interruption, and a half hour in the morning and evening for secret devotion, also half an hour for vocal music, and twenty minutes for calisthenics. Besides, there are the leisure hours, in which much is done of sewing, knitting, and ornamental needle work; and much is enjoyed in social intercourse, in walking, and in botanical excursions. This institution presupposes a good degree of health, and correct habits. But little can be done in this seminary or any other, for those whose constitution is already impaired, or whose physical habits, up to the age of sixteen, are particularly defective. This institution professes to make no remarkable physical renovations. But it is believed, that a young lady, who is fitted for the system, and who can voluntarily and cheerfully adopt it as her own, will find this place favorable for preserving unimpaired the health she brings with her, and for promoting and establishing the good physical habits already acquired.

5. Social and domestic character.

The excellence of the female character in this respect, consists principally, in a preparation to be happy herself in her social and domestic relations, and to make all others happy around her. All her duties, of whatever kind, are in an important sense, social and domestic. They are retired and private, and not public, like those of the other sex. Whatever she does beyond her own family, should be but another application and illustration of social and domestic excellence. She may occupy the place of an important teacher; but her most vigorous labors should be modest and unobtrusive. She may go on a foreign mission; but she will there find a retired spot, where, away from the public gaze, she may wear out, or lay down a valuable life. She may promote the interests of the Sabbath school, or be an angel of mercy to the poor and afflicted—she may seek in various ways to increase the spirit of benevolence, and the zeal for the cause of missions, and she may labor for the salvation of souls. But her work is to be done by the whisper of her still and gentle voice, by the silent step of her unwearied feet, and by the power of her uniform and consistent example.

The following elements should be embraced in the social and domestic character of a lady.

(a.) *Economy.* Economy consists in providing well at little comparative expense. It necessarily implies good judgment and good taste. It can be equally manifested in the tasteful decorations of a palace, and in the simple comforts of a cottage. Suppose all ladies possessed this in a high degree, how much more would be found in families, of comfort and convenience—of taste and refinement—of education and improvement—of charity and good works.

This institution, it is well known, is distinguished for its economical features. Economy, however, is not adopted principally for its own sake, but as a means of education—as a mode of producing favorable effects on character, and of preparing young ladies for the duties of life. The great object is to make the school really better. An economical character is to be formed by precept, by practice, and by example. Example has great effect, not only in furnishing a model for imitation, but also in proving that economy is practicable, which is one of the most essential requisites for success. Let a young lady spend two or three years, on intimate terms, in a family distinguished for a judicious and consistent illustration of this principle, and the effects cannot be lost. Suppose it to be a minister's family. He dwells among a people, who do not abound in the riches of this world. His salary is small, and his family numerous, but he has a treasure in his wife. Of her it might be emphatically said, "The heart of her husband doth safely trust in her, so that he shall have no need of *spoil.*" He always finds his house in order, his children neatly dressed, his table simply, but invitingly spread, and his sweet *home* an abode of kindness and hospitality. In all good works, and in every deed of charity, he is able to be an example to his flock, and at the close of the year, he has no debt weighing down his spirits.

Such a family, substantially, the founders of this seminary would seek to furnish as an example to its members. The bills of board are very low, and yet they supply the means of sustaining a family enjoying all necessary comforts and conveniences, and supporting a style of taste and refinement, equal to the more genteel families in our common country towns. This is produced by no extraordinary means. It is the natural result of the system. It might be easily attained in any other seminary, founded on the same principles, adopting the same system, and observing the same rules for the admission of pupils.

(b.) *A suitable feeling of independence.* There are two kinds of dependence, very unlike in their nature, but both inconsistent with the highest degree of domestic bliss. To one of these, ladies in cities and large towns are more particularly subject; but it is an evil, from which ladies in the country are not wholly exempt. It is a feeling of dependence on the will of servants. Every lady should be so educated, as far as it can be done, that she will feel able to take care of herself, and if need be, of a family, whatever may be her situation in life, and whatever her station in society. Otherwise, if she remains in these United States, she may be rendered unhappy by constantly feeling that her daily comforts are at the control of her servants, who in such cases are often unfaithful, unreasonable, and dissatisfied. The withering effects of family perplexities on the social character, is well known to every observer of domestic life. On the other hand, how much happiness often results from a suitable feeling of independence. A lady in one of our large cities, who is distinguished for having faithful servants, considers the secret as lying in her feeling of independence. If one, in a fit of caprice, proposes leaving her, she has only to say, "You may go today. If need be, I can take care of my own family, until your place is supplied."

Against this kind of dependence, this institution seeks to exert its decided influence. The whole aspect of the family, and all the plans of the school are suited to cultivate habits entirely the reverse. In the domestic independence of the household, all have an interest. The daily hour for these duties returns to each at the appointed time, and no one inquires, whether it can be omitted or transferred to another. No one receives any pecuniary reward for her services, and no one seeks with her money, to deprive herself of the privilege of sharing in the freedom, simplicity, and independence of her *home*.

There is another kind of independence, entirely different in its nature, but equally essential to a high degree of domestic happiness. This is the result of economy already considered. It is the power of bringing personal and family expenses, fairly and easily within the means enjoyed. The whole system adopted in this seminary is designed to give a living illustration of the principle by which this power is to be gained. This ability will be of immense value in active life. It will prepare one to sustain the reverses of fortune with submission, or to meet the claims of hospitality and charity with promptness. This kind of independence might be to the great cause of benevolence, like an overflowing fountain, whose streams will never fail.

(c.) *Skill and expedition in household duties.* Let a young lady despise this branch of the duties of woman, and she despises the appointments of the Author of her existence. The laws of God, made known by nature and by Providence, and also by the Bible, enjoin these duties on the sex, and she cannot violate them with impunity. Let her have occasion to preside at the head of her own family and table, and she may despair of enjoying herself, or of giving to others the highest degree of domestic happiness. Does she seek to do good by teaching? The time we hope is not far distant, when no mother will commit her daughters to the influence of such a teacher. Does she seek to do good in the Sabbath school? How can she enforce all the duties to God and man in their due proportion, while she contemns one of the most obvious laws of her nature. Would she endeavor to show the poor and the ignorant how to find the comforts of life? How can she teach what she has never learned? Does she become the wife of a missionary? How does her heart sink within her, as her desponding husband strives in vain to avoid the evils resulting from her inefficiency.

This institution is not designed to conduct this branch of a young lady's education. It would not take this privilege from the mother. But it does seek to preserve the good habits already acquired, and to make a favorable impression with regard to the value of system, promptness and fidelity in this branch of the duties of woman.

(d.) *An obliging disposition.* This is of special importance in forming a lovely, social and domestic character. Young ladies at school, with all the conveniences and comforts which they should have, and with all the benefits of system which they should enjoy, can have but little opportunity for self-denial. This little should be used to the best advantage. To bring every such opportunity to bear on the character, has been a leading object in all the plans of this institution, in the organization of the school, and especially in the arrangements of the family. As the domestic work is done entirely by the young ladies, the varied and mutual duties of the day, furnish many little opportunities for the manifestation of a generous, obliging and self-denying spirit, the influence of which, we trust, will be felt through life. "He that is faithful in the least, is faithful also in much," is a motto for the daily guidance of this household.

(e.) *A spirit of gratitude and a sense of obligation.* Domestic life is little else but a continued scene of conferring and receiving favors. How much of happiness depends on their being conferred with the manifest evidence of a willing heart, and on their being received with suitable tokens of gratitude. These two lovely traits go hand in hand, not often to be separated. The formation of a character that can be grateful, is an object of special importance in a lady's education. Parents should seek to give to their daughters privileges, and especially the means of education in a manner suited to lead them to realize that they are favors for which gratitude is due. When a daughter is sent abroad to school, circumstances should be thrown around her, favorable to the cultivation of the same spirit. Otherwise she may begin to say to herself, "My father pays amply for all I receive, and why should I be grateful? The obligation is rather on the part of my teachers and the guardians of the school for patronage received." But the spirit of ingratitude stops not in its progress. The next ravages may be on filial piety. She may begin to look on the privileges she enjoys as hers by right of inheritance, allowing but little occasion for gratitude to parents. What hope is there that such a heart will be led by the goodness of God to repentance, or that it will delight to follow Him, "who though he was rich, yet for our sakes became poor."

To a spirit of ingratitude, the genius of this institution is specially opposed. On entering this seminary, young ladies can scarcely avoid feeling, that they are sharing the fruits of benevolent efforts—that they are enjoying privileges, which they cannot purchase—that they owe a debt of gratitude to the founders, which gold and silver can never cancel, and which can be met, only by a useful Christian life.

These are some of the influences which this institution has a tendency to exert on its members.

The principles of the system carried out and extended would also have a favorable influence.

ON THE CAUSE OF EDUCATION

1. In furnishing a supply of female teachers

Teaching is really the business of almost every useful woman. If there are any, to whom this does not apply, they may be considered exceptions to a general rule. Of course, no female is well educated, who has not all the acquisitions, necessary for a good teacher. The most essential qualifications are thorough mental culture, a well balanced character, a benevolent heart, an ability to communicate knowledge and apply it to practice, an acquaintance with human nature, and the power of controlling the minds of others. And are not these the qualifications which every lady needs, in order to be useful, whether she teaches a regular school or not? One important means then of supplying teachers for regular schools, is to increase the number of well educated ladies. This institution will have a favorable bearing on such an object.

But it is not enough, that a great number of ladies are well educated. They must also have benevolence enough to engage in teaching, when other duties will allow, and when their labors are needed. Female teachers should not expect to be fully compensated for their services, unless it be by kindness and gratitude. If this is a benevolent work, why should the more wealthy exclude themselves from the privilege? The prospect of being prepared to teach has a favorable effect on the improvement of a young lady. And why may not every one have this object in view? Those who have the proper qualifications and the willing heart, will find occasion to do good by teaching.

But let there be ever so large a number of ladies thoroughly educated, and ever so many willing to teach, there cannot be a supply, while they refuse to take the care of common schools. There are situations for teachers, which are so pleasant and improving as to require but little sacrifice. There is, however, a large field, which must be occupied, and which will furnish ample opportunities for the exercise of benevolence. Most of the schools for children, and all those in the more uninviting spots in every town must be conducted by females, or not at all. Perhaps one cause of a deficiency of well qualified female teachers is, a practice in many places of addressing too exclusively their pecuniary interests. The reward which has been given them in this respect has not been too great, but there has been too much dependence upon it as a means of securing their services. There are many other chords in female hearts, which will vibrate much more tenderly and powerfully than this. There is a large and increasing number of educated ladies, who will make the best of teachers, but who can be allured much more by respectful attention, by kindness and gratitude, by suitable school-rooms, and apparatus, and other facilities for rendering their labors pleasant and successful, than they can by the prospect of a pecuniary reward. Let sufficient efforts be made to secure the services of this class of teachers, and every department of female and common education will experience the beneficial results.

The spirit of this seminary is suited not only to increase the number of educated ladies, but to enforce on them the obligation to use their talents for the good of others, especially in teaching. It is hoped it may also lead them to be more willing to take any school, and in any place where their services are most needed.

2. *In promoting the prosperity of common schools.*

Among the great mass of the people, throughout the country, this class of schools must be of more interest than all others. All higher institutions will have an influence on these fountains of learning. That of colleges will be more indirect and remote, and that of academies and female seminaries, more direct and immediate.

The academy and common school should mutually aid each other, and each should confine itself to its own appropriate business. Whoever will devise means, by which reading, spelling, arithmetic, geography and grammar shall receive as thorough attention in common schools as they deserve, and whoever will throw inducements before the older female scholars to remain in them longer and attend thoroughly to these branches, as an example to others, will do much to elevate their standard. Such an influence this seminary seeks to exert.

To enter the Junior Class, nothing is needed but that thorough course, which should be pursued in every common school. But many, who have been a long time at an academy, cannot be received for the want of suitable qualifications.

3. *In counteracting certain errors, which have prevailed to some extent in female education.*

First Error. Tasking the mind too early with severe mental discipline. The evils of this course are beginning to be felt by careful observers of the human mind, and of human character. When the effort is attended with the greatest success, there is generally the greatest injury. This is sometimes done in order to finish the child's education, before her time seems of much value. This is not *economy* of time, but *avarice*, which will bring with it its own punishment. It is like a man's borrowing money to become rich on such terms, that in a few years the principal and interest will render him a bankrupt. If a full list of facts could be collected on ruined constitutions, on nervous excitability, sadness without a reason, religious depression, and the first appearances of monomania, with their causes and attendant circumstances, it is believed, that it would form an alarming chapter on this subject. But sometimes the mind utterly refuses this unnatural taxation, and the effects then are not so disastrous. But in such cases, it often proves forever fatal to high intellectual cultivation, so that the child, instead of becoming a prodigy, as was expected, never attains even to mediocrity. Such repulsive associations may be formed with the title-page and aspect of every text-book, as will render every future lesson a task rather than a delight. The most discouraging field which any teacher was ever called to cultivate, is the mind of a young lady who has been studying all her days, and has gone over most of the natural and moral sciences without any valuable improvement, until she is tired of school, tired of books, and tired almost of life. As this institution proposes to conduct young ladies through a regular intellectual course, after the age of sixteen, its influence will be against this error.

Second Error. Deferring some parts of education till too late a period. This error is the cause of permanent defects of character, and of a great loss of time to those, who attempt to acquire at *a later period*, what should have been gained in childhood. Among the things neglected till *too late a period* are the manners, the cultivation of the voice, including singing, pronunciation and all the characteristics of good reading—gaining skill and expedition in the common necessary mechanical operations, such as sewing, knitting, writing and drawing, and acquiring, by daily practice, a knowledge and a love of domestic pursuits. To these might be added some things, which depend almost entirely on the memory, such as spelling; and others, which are suited to lay the foundation of a literary taste, such as a judicious course of reading, practice in composition, &c. Those, who are to attend to instrumental music, the ornamental branches, and the pronunciation of foreign languages, must commence early. Many other branches should also receive some attention; but, if necessary, they may be deferred to a later age without great loss. As this seminary asks for three years of a young lady's time, after she is sixteen, to be devoted principally to the severer studies, it will tend indirectly to counteract this error. It may lead mothers to fear that there will not be time for all, unless the appropriate parts of early education are commenced more seasonably.

Third Error. Placing daughters too young in a boarding-school or large seminary. A common boarding-school is not a suitable place for a little girl. She needs the little home of her childhood, or one like it. Direct individual attention, such as can be given by no one who has the care of many, is the necessary means of forming her character, of cultivating her manners, of developing her affections, and of nurturing all that is lovely and of good report. She wants the uninterrupted sympathies of a mother's heart. She needs a constant and gentle hand, leading her singly along in the path of safety and improvement. If her mother cannot give her all the personal attention she should receive, or if she is removed from her by death, let some friend or benefactress take her place, but let it not be a lady with the care of boarders, nor a teacher, who must give equal attention to many others. Perhaps the evils of a boarding-house are most unfavorable on her character, just as she is entering her teens. Who can guide this self-sufficient age but the mother, who has gained a permanent place in her affections, and a decided influence over her life. Who but the mother, who first taught her to obey, can lay on her the necessary restrictions without exposing her to form the unlovely trait of character, gained by complaining of those, whom she should love and respect, and who deserve her gratitude. The separate pecuniary interest of young ladies as boarders, and of those who have the care of them, is sometimes the occasion of suspicions and opinions, very unfavorable on social character at this most unreasonable and injudicious age of life. How often has a daughter who has been accustomed to more elevated views and habits at home, been led to stoop low enough to make the food on the table the subject of conversation and complaint in her social intercourse with her companions, and to charge the real or supposed evils to mercenary motives. Who has not reflected with deep admiration on the divine wisdom and goodness manifested in the family organization as it relates to this principle? It gives but one pecuniary interest to the united head, around which the members cluster like branches of the same olive-tree. From this scene of social and domestic singleness of heart, the daughter should not be removed till she has strength to sustain the change.

Simply putting a little girl in a large seminary during the day is less injurious; but this practice is attended with serious evils, with really no redeeming advantages. It is not the place to give to the mind, the heart, nor the manners, the best means of cultivation. A little family-like school, with a single, affectionate, faithful teacher, will be far better for her, till she has acquired discretion and prudence, a permanent modesty and propriety of manners, and the elements of studious habits, and of correct scholarship.

The influence of this seminary is of course against the error here mentioned.

4. *In giving just views of the advantages of large female seminaries.*

Such institutions furnish peculiar privileges, which cannot be secured by smaller schools; but in most cases, they have not been able to produce their legitimate results. They have often suffered for the want of accommodations and other facilities for successful operation, from their temporary and unsettled existence, from their want of system, and sometimes from too public a location, and too public an aspect in their features. Their efforts also to accommodate all ages and all classes, often prevent their having any fixed or determinate character. This institution seeks to avoid all these evils, and to develop the real advantages of a large seminary.

In order that a lady may have the most thorough education, she should spend a number of years in close intellectual application, after her mental powers have acquired sufficient strength, and her physical system sufficient maturity, and after she has all the necessary preparation. This must be during the best part of her life, when every year is worth more than can be estimated in gold and silver. Facilities for success should be given her, which will be an ample reward for the sacrifice of so much time. She should have the benefits of a systematic course, and should pursue studies in their natural order, while she has the privilege of reciting in a class of a suitable number, and of similar improvement to her own. Whoever has undertaken to organize a school, has had abundant evidence that all these points cannot be gained where the number is not large. This seminary is able now to secure all these advantages in some degree, but not so perfectly as it will, when the two hundred can be received. What is now done is effected by a great effort of the teachers, and a great loss of time, to which they will not then be subject. Library and apparatus, such as cannot be found in little schools, are as necessary for females pursuing a thorough course of study, as for the other sex. Perhaps experiments and illustrations are more important for them, as they have a less number of years for the pursuit, and as their time must be more occupied with other things.

The influence of a large seminary on the social character, is also important. The very discipline necessary to preserve little girls from exposure to injury, and to cultivate the principles of virtue and loveliness, is attended with some necessary evils, which will need a pruning hand at a maturer age. Not the least prominent of these, is a narrowness of soul, giving her limited views of others. She is in danger of feeling that her mother and her sisters are of more importance in the scale of being than all the rest of the world—that her *home* is the centre of the universe, and the *standard* by which every thing is to be tried. If she belongs to a plain country family, she looks on the wealthy in cities and large villages as proud, extravagant, and haughty if she has been confined to the city or large village, she looks on every daughter of the hills and valleys as outlandish and vulgar. This illiberality must be corrected at a proper season, or the social character will be essentially defective. To effect this, but few means can be used, which are suitable for females. Perhaps there is no one, at the same time so powerful and appropriate, and so attainable by all, as the influence of a large female seminary, established in a retired country village, uniting so much of refinement and elevation with so much of plainness, simplicity and economy, as will render it an attractive point for the most promising candidates for usefulness, from all parts of the country, and from all classes of the community.

The spirit of monopolizing privileges is to some extent the effect of giving to a little girl, all that individual care and affectionate attention, which her cultivation demands. A large seminary, and more especially a large family, have a tendency to remove this. The young lady needs to feel herself a member of a large community, where the interests of others are to be sought equally with her own. She needs to learn by practice as well as by principle, that individual accommodations and private interests are to be sacrificed for the public good; and she needs to know from experience, that those who make such a sacrifice, will receive an ample reward in the improvement of the community, among whom they are to dwell. This institution is designed to secure to its members the advantages of a large seminary and a large family, and to avoid all their prominent evils.

5. In giving the claims of large female seminaries an acknowledged place among the other objects of public beneficence.

The claims of those for the other sex were admitted two hundred years ago; and the colleges, academies, and theological seminaries, all over the land, show that the wise and the good have not been weary in well doing. The general system of education which is adopted in all colleges, with its regulating influence on academies, and every branch of male education, proves the wisdom of this course. But it has not been so with those for females. This bond of interest and cooperation is not found here, and the legitimate results are every where felt. Who could hope for any general system in female education, or any permanency in our female seminaries? Might we not rather expect that they would sometimes be under the control of the mercantile principle, so suitable in its application to commercial business, but so withering in its effects as the controlling power over education or religion? How ridiculous would be the attempt to found colleges in the manner that some female seminaries have been founded. Suppose a gentleman, having a large family depending on him for support, finds his health not sufficient for the duties of his profession. Casting his eye around, he looks on the office of a president of a college, as affording more ample means, and a more pleasant and respectable situation for his family than any other he can command. But a new college must be founded to furnish him the place. He selects a large village in New England, or at the West, or at the South, as may best favor the accomplishment of his object, and where he can find buildings which he can buy or rent on some conditions, though they may be far from being adapted to such an end. He purchases his apparatus, or has none, and procures professors on his own responsibility. Thus prepared, he commences, making his charge to the students such as will meet the rent of buildings, furniture and apparatus, and the salaries of his professors, besides furnishing a handsome support to his own family. What could such a college do to encourage thorough and systematic education in our country? But this is scarcely a caricature of the manner in which some female seminaries have been founded. And where the benevolent principle has existed, it has been confined to individuals, as if the trustees of a college should depend upon the generosity of the president to furnish the students gratuitously with all their facilities for improvement, instead of obtaining them by public benevolence.

We cannot hope for a state of things essentially better, till the principle is admitted, that female seminaries designed for the public benefit, must be founded by the hand of public benevolence, and be subject to the rules enjoined by such benevolence. Let this principle be fully admitted, and let it have sufficient time to produce its natural effects, and it will be productive of more important results than can be easily estimated. Then our large seminaries may be permanent, with all the mutual responsibility and cooperation which the principle of permanency produces. Then, if "the teacher makes the school," there will be a school which will find the teacher. Then each public seminary may be a central point, around which several smaller and more private schools may cluster, and to which they may look for influence, for guidance, and for a supply of teachers. There will then be laid a broad and sure foundation for system, improvement, and elevation in female education. May we not hope, that this state of things is not far distant? Has not every friend of education observed with peculiar interest the change that is taking place in public sentiment on this subject? What more is now needed to produce entire conviction of duty, and entire confidence of success, but the united and decided action of the most intelligent and benevolent friends of this cause?

Perhaps the influence which this seminary exerts in this respect, will be more important in its results, than all its other influence. It has scattered some seeds in the hearts of those who have given it aid which will not be lost. But such seed needs to be scattered more abundantly, and to spring up, and grow, and bear fruit. And may we not expect this will be the case? Are there not those who will lend to this cause all the aid that it needs? Females cannot with propriety plead for their own comforts, but there are those, who will not on this account neglect them. They cannot ask for their own bread, but there are those who will ask it for them. Have not the friends of education another blessing to bestow, though they have already done so liberally in behalf of their own sex? And are there not many who will remember this cause, as they come around the mercy seat of Him, whose is the silver and the gold, and the cattle on a thousand hills? "Except the Lord build the house, they labor in vain that build it: except the Lord keep the city, the watchmen waketh but in vain."

South Hadley, Mass., June, 1839.
Donations to this seminary may be forwarded to Rev. ROSWELL HAWKS, South Hadley, or to Dea. DANIEL SAFFORD, Boston.

11

Preparation for Admission

SEPTEMBER 1840

Candidates for admission should be very careful and thorough in their preparation. There has been some deficiency in understanding the required qualifications, though these qualifications have been better understood from year to year. On account of this deficiency, and on account of the infant state of the Seminary, some indulgence has hitherto been allowed to those unprepared. In some cases, their examination has been delayed, and they have been admitted to the Junior Class after the usual time. Such a course should be discontinued as soon as it can be done consistently, as it is a disadvantage to the young ladies themselves, as well as to the Institution.

Probably it would be better for most individuals to leave the Seminary, and delay attendance another year, rather than to be much behind their Class. As the plans and principles of the Institution are now so well understood, probably any indulgence hereafter relative to preparation will be unnecessary and inexpedient. Any Candidate for the coming year therefore, who is not confident about her preparation, is requested to look at the Catalogue again. If she still remains doubtful whether she is prepared to pass a prompt and thorough examination on all the preparatory studies, especially on the more difficult parts of Arithmetic, she is requested to consult her last teacher, or some one well acquainted with her scholarship and attainments. If the evidence of her preparation is found to be unsatisfactory to those qualified to judge, it would be better for her to withdraw the application now, than to hazard the necessity of leaving the Institution after having entered. If any wish to withdraw their application, it should be done as soon as possible, as a delay will occasion great inconvenience.

This communication will be sent to those, whose preparation is known to be good, as well as to those, of whom but little evidence has yet been received. Individuals who are themselves prepared to pass a good examination, can exert a favorable influence over other candidates. It is recommended to all, who wish to be received one year from this Autumn, to devote as much of the intervening time as possible to the study of Latin. In this branch as well as in every other, a little done thoroughly is better than much done superficially. Any thing which a young lady has studied, but in which she cannot pass a good examination, will be regarded as of but little value in estimating her standing.

Those designing to be admitted to an advanced standing should carefully review all the studies of the regular course with which they consider themselves acquainted, that they may be ready to pass a good examination on entering the Seminary.

It is very desirable, that the request in the Catalogue relative to a few articles of furniture, should not be overlooked.

12

Report of the Teachers

DATE UNKNOWN, POSSIBLY 1839

The second year now closes. We have much for gratitude to a Providence that has kindly watched over us and given us so much prosperity in our infant state. We have occasion for gratitude also to those benevolent friends who have furnished the means of doing all that we have done, and of enjoying all that we enjoy in this place. Next to pleasing our God, our highest ambition is to merit and receive the candid approbation of those who have built this home, and given all that is contained in it. We would encourage them not only to finish this building and give us the needed furniture, and add to our library, our apparatus etc. but we would encourage them to do much more for the education of our sex.

In reviewing the two past years we can see great improvement, and considerable progress towards the maturing of system. In conscientious faithfulness, and the manifestation of a noble and generous spirit, our first pupils can never be excelled. The cheerfulness with which they met the inconveniences of a building not entirely finished, and of incomplete furniture, and of immature system or rather no system at all, will ever be remembered with the liveliest interest. Their progress in study and improvement notwithstanding these inconveniences will ever be a worthy example under our care. But on the whole, the school has been much better the past year than the first. There has been more maturity of plans, and much less of interruption in the system adopted. The cooperation of teachers, pupils and friends in executing our system is essential to success. The whole year is embraced in a single plan, no part of which can be supplied by any other part. A succession of winters could not give to a young lady all the privileges of the seminary without the corresponding summers. Every pupil should be here the first day, and never be absent from a single exercise during the whole year. Those who return home or visit friends, in the vicinity during vacations, and the little recesses should return in time to prepare the first lesson thoroughly, instead of arriving just to meet the class, all in confusion with the fatigue of a morning ride, and with a lesson half learned. The promptness in all these respects has been much more perfect than last year. All of us, both teachers and pupils have better understood the importance of it and their united efforts have not been in vain. We have been much gratified that the cooperation of parents and friends has also been more perfect than the last year.

No week in the Year can be lost, no day in the week, and no part of the day without making a chasm which cannot be easily supplied. There is no recreation day or holiday except Saturday. The daily study hours are regular and definite, and should not be interrupted. Two or three hours each evening closing at 7 or 8 according to the season of the year, are devoted to recreation, and on these hours study should never be allowed to encroach. It seems much better understood, that young ladies who would make the greatest improvement, must confine their visits and calls to Saturday and recreation hours. It is also seen to be more important, that friends in the vicinity should confine their calls to the same hours, and those at a distance too far, as it can be done conveniently.

III
A MISSIONARY OFFERING

A Missionary Offering,

or

Christian Sympathy, Personal Responsibility, and the Present Crisis in Foreign Missions.

PREFACE

This little "Missionary Offering," as will be perceived, has a particular reference to the present crisis in Foreign Missions. But the general sentiments will apply equally to the subject of Missions at any other time, and to the calls of benevolence from every other department in the great work of renovating the world. In its application, it has also a special reference to charitable contributions. But whatever, in the sentiments, shall serve as a motive in the matter of raising funds, will be alike so in every other branch of Christian effort, and self-denial.

There is a single object, which this little book would fain serve, though, in so great a cause, it be unworthy to give a cup of cold water, or to stoop down, and unloose the latchet of a shoe. This object is the salvation of immortal souls ready to perish, and the glory of Him, who gave his life a ransom for sin.

The friends of the writer, for whom this little work has been prepared, may not receive it, till the present exigency in Foreign Missions shall be past, and its place supplied by some other appeal more urgent, perhaps, and more affecting to a tender conscience, and to an enlightened Christian sympathy. But this will be a matter of small consequence. To whomsoever, it would be worth reading in 1843, it will be worth reading at any other time, while souls can be found on the earth, who are far from a knowledge of the truth, and who know not the joys of salvation. The subjects of the second chapter are earnestly recommended to the solemn and devout consideration of all the friends of the writer, who may take up this little book—not according to this feeble development, but as they are exhibited by God in all their solemn and momentous realities.

Without the power of these affecting truths, it would be better to lay aside this small offering, than to spend time in the perusal. Without their influence on the mind, it contains only a collection of unmeaning words, or at best, only a few useless, ineffective thoughts. But it is earnestly desired, and fervently and humbly implored, that these truths may be interwoven, as it were, with the very fibers of the soul, and incorporated with the deepest feelings of the heart, and carried along, and applied in the perusal of every page.

CHAPTER I
CHRISTIAN SYMPATHY— PERSONAL RESPONSIBILITY— MISSIONARY CIRCULAR— AMERICAN BOARD OF FOREIGN MISSIONS

In the great work of converting the world to God, Christian Sympathy, and a just and solemn conviction of Personal Responsibility, are the two grand effective powers of the human soul. Their influence on the mind must be united to be effectual. In urging us forward in the path of duty, they are like companions and fellow-laborers, the one suggests, the other executes. The one is like a living, glowing, energetic soul; the other is like the embodying of that soul in a visible, active and efficient form.

Sympathy is a powerful and important principle of human nature. In its use and adaptation, the children of this world have been wise in their generation. The statesman, the lawyer, the poet, the musician, the devotee of Paganism, the follower of the false prophet, and the worshipper of the beast and his image, have known, and used, and felt its power.

But has the follower of Jesus, the soldier of the cross, been equally wise in his generation? No one has such a scope for sympathy as he has, and nowhere can it accomplish such wonders, as in the hands of the devoted servant of Christ. His is a noble sympathy. It never becomes insipid by repetition; on review, it never appears unworthy of himself. This world, with all its regions of reality, and of fiction too, can furnish no such field, as is spread out before the Christian's sympathizing spirit. The joys of the New Jerusalem, the wailings of the bottomless pit, the dying groans of the Lamb of God, all gather around his heart, and enter into the deepest fountains of his soul.

The sympathy of the Christian is not left to wear itself out by its own perpetual corrodings. It is not shut up to become loathsome and stagnant for the want of fresh air. No. It can flow forth in living streams of active benevolence, fertilizing many a barren plain, till it mingles in the great ocean of love, and thence it can return to refresh the soul. The Providence of God is opening to the Christian every where, a way, a high way, a way of holiness, in which his willing feet can run, as on the wings of the wind, carrying the tidings of salvation to the remotest ends of the earth.

The great work of converting the world to God, can never be fully accomplished without the most strenuous and self-denying efforts, of which man is capable. If the powers of depravity would remain stationary—if each succeeding generation would be content with the measure of iniquity practised by their fathers, the case would be somewhat different. But Christianity has now much to do to overtake the powers of darkness in their rapid flight, and to place herself side by side, in even combat for final victory. She may make positive and cheering progress in her course, and yet gain no relative advance on the enemy. In view of the two great contending powers as they now stand, can an intelligent faith look up to God, and ask that the kingdoms of this world may be given to Christ, by an instrumental effort, which is feeble, partial and changeable? Are not, self-denying labors here required, which can be prompted by nothing less than the strongest powers of the human soul? The principles of mere philosophy and justice, in their influence over the human mind, are not sufficient to meet the necessities of the case. Their propelling power can never carry to all the inhabitants of earth, that salvation, the basis of which was laid in tears of blood, and in groans of the tenderest compassion. The sympathies of our nature, sanctified, and turned into the channel of the gospel, will be essential for this work. The aid of Christian sympathy in converting the world, was appointed of God in infinite wisdom, and in condescending love. This wonderful principle of the human soul, under the influence of grace, presents, in its powers, capabilities and relations, a glorious specimen of the handiwork of the Author of our salvation.

Christian sympathy, as a means of converting the world,

may embrace sympathy with the sufferings of Christ and sympathy with our race in view of their future condition, just as it will be, either in heaven, or in hell. But this power of the soul will not spring up spontaneously, neither is it found in the natural heart. The foundation must be laid, and the work carried forward by the influence of the Holy Ghost. But the Holy Spirit will never so set aside the Divine plan, and so dishonor the Godhead, as to accomplish such a work in the heart without the skillful and diligent use of means.

Every means, natural, social and moral, should be employed for its growth and maturity. The work of cultivating Christian sympathy should be commenced in the earliest years of childhood, and it should be carried on, till the days on earth are finished, and the soul is released to go home and dwell forever in a world of infinite sympathy—of infinite fellowship—of infinite love.

But Christian sympathy can never live, and thrive, and endure, unless it be carried out into real life by a just and solemn conviction of personal responsibility. It must be a conviction, which rests down on the soul itself with such an overwhelming power, with such an absorbing influence, that it leaves but little time, or strength, or desire, to apply duty to others—to the church—to the public. It takes away the asperity of censure. It softens the words of reproof. And yet, as it beams forth in the life, it often comes home to the hearts of others with a power indescribable and irresistible. It often speaks not, but in silence, it looks on the deficiencies of others, as the Saviour looked on Peter.

This conviction of responsibility in the work of saving souls, will apply duty to the heart with a skilful hand. It will divide out to the understanding, and to the conscience, like a workman that needeth not to be ashamed. It will not be partial in judging between the interests of self, and the eternal interests of others. It will constrain the soul to adopt and practise the following sentiments of Howard— "Our superfluities should be given up for the convenience of others—our conveniences should give way to others' necessities—our necessities should give way to the extremities of others." Are not these the sentiments, which must be adopted and practised to bring the whole world to a knowledge of the truth? Are they not sentiments contained in the second great command of the law, and in the golden rule? In the great work of saving souls from death, let us then first give up our superfluities. When that is done, if the Providence of God still calls, let us next give up our conveniences. When we have done that, if souls are still left unsaved and unenlightened, and if the door is still kept open by Divine Providence, inviting us to enter, let us last of all give up our necessities to the infinite extremities of immortal beings.

Thoughts like these were hovering around my mind last Monday evening, as we assembled in our village church for the missionary concert. Our beloved pastor announced to us, that he had a letter from the Missionary House at Boston. The simple fact thrilled through my heart. I remembered the letter, of Sept. 1841, and I remembered how its contents weighed down my soul, and followed me by night and by day. I remembered too the fatal scenes of 1837. I had from time to time watched the progress, of the missionary receipts. I had wept and prayed over our disappointed hopes. But I had not brought the subject before my mind distinctly in all its solemn and trying realities. But as the letter was opening to be read in our ears, the veil seemed lifted from mine eyes, and the sad decline in the missionary receipts, with all its dreadful consequences, passed in rapid review before my imagination. My weak and trembling heart almost shrunk from hearing the contents of the letter. I well knew that a Circular to the churches from this source, was no unmeaning sound. I well knew that it was a messenger of painful tidings. I knew that both wisdom and discretion had done their utmost to avoid such a resort. No messenger from this source ever comes to us, except from burdened souls and bleeding hearts. It comes only to tell us of plain and solemn facts—of dangers, of necessities, such as the world knows not of—of an approaching crisis in the kingdom of Christ, such as is never known among the affairs of men,—among the kingdoms of this world. But I folded my arms to listen to the letter. I expected no warm appeal—I expected no glow of the imagination, such as we sometimes meet from the pen of those who have just put on the harness. But I did expect solid facts—facts, which through the understanding, the judgment and the conscience, can find their way into the deepest fountains of the soul. In this I was not disappointed. I listened as for my life, to every line. I returned from the concert. I retired to rest, but not to sleep. The contents of the letter, the present state of the missionary funds, the dreadful condition of the perishing heathen, the last command of our dear Redeemer, his dying groans in the garden and on the cross, all passed in rapid review before me. The subject, in its various bearings, spread itself out before my mind with an unwonted vividness and expansion.

I took a survey of *Modern Missions*. What a sublime spectacle. I glanced over the history of the American Board of Commissioners for Foreign Missions—the glory of our country, —the corner stone of all our voluntary benevolent associations. I love to go back in its history more than thirty years. I love to look at its origin, and from that point, I love to wander along the way, and linger as I pass, till I arrive at our present position. Though I was but a child, I love even now the very *thought* that I can remember even the beginnings of this great and glorious enterprize. I beheld the infant rocked in its cradle, but I knew not why it was born, or wherefore it was there. I saw it grow and advance, and I have seen it become a man, endowed with wisdom and understanding, giving laws to other minds, and directions to other powers. I well remember the time, when the names of Mills and his associates first began to fall on my ear. I remember the thoughts of my young heart, when the subject of Foreign Missions first began to find its way into the family circle, and was spoken of as one of the marvellous things of the age. A marvellous thing it has indeed proved, and it will furnish an abundant reward to every one, who will trace its history, and follow it in its growth. Here I have found one of my richest fields of thought, of meditation, and of feeling.

Our country's grand scene of the sublime in nature, must be seen to be felt, must be known to be loved and revered. There is an outer court, and there is an inner temple. Many assemble in the outer court, but only here and there one will tarry long enough, to find his way into the inner temple. The traveller, who stops a day *to rest and visit Niagara*, knows naught of the communings of that spirit, which spends week after week in beholding and admiring the ever increasing wonders of that hallowed spot, till his eyes see a greatness and a glory in the falling waters, which no other eyes have ever seen.

Niagara, with all its simplicity, never tires, never satiates, never satisfies. The devoted lover of its scenes asks only to behold the same things over and over again. Day by day, he finds a growing admiration of every view he takes, from the smaller cascade, which leaps from rock to rock, as if fearful to make one fatal plunge, to its broadest mass of many waters, which with wild speed, and with a voice as of mighty thunderings, rush down the awful height. Thus it is with every view which we can take of the principal Foreign Missionary Society of our country, — our nation's grand feature of the morally sublime. The more we see and the more we know, the more we admire, and the more we love. In whatever aspect we behold it, it grows on contemplation, whether it be of its principles, of its history, of the men whom God has raised up to guide in its counsels, and carry forward its work at home, or of those, who have taken their lives in their hand, and gone forth, voluntary exiles "from their country, from their kindred, and from their father's house." The passing traveller, who occasionally glances at the doings of the American Board, and year by year, or month by month, casts in his pittance into its treasury, knows naught of the communings of one, whose heart lives and glows in all its interests—whose life, whose property, whose influence, whose all is pledged for its support.

If I am permitted to enjoy but one more scene of nature's sublimity, I will not ask to behold the wonders of other lands, and of other climes, I will only ask to taste once more of the delights of our own Niagara's scenes. So if I am permitted to behold but one more public scene of moral sublimity, let that be another annual meeting of the American Board. I ask not to visit the splendid halls of the old world, and listen to the eloquence of those master minds, whose praise is in all the earth, from the equator to the poles. Whatever may be those sublime delights, *I* only ask to witness again the simple, the modest, the unpretending grandeur of one of the annual sessions of the American Board. Let me again behold those kindred spirits, from all parts of the country, and from all departments of business, assembling with one accord, in one place, that they may consult together, and transact business in behalf of this great cause. Day after day, let me listen to their deliberations, till my thoughts gain an unwonted strength, and my heart an unwonted refreshing. How chastened are the public addresses. Each speaker seems to feel that his theme needs no ornament, no eloquence, no aggrandizement. Each trembles to speak on such an occasion, before such an audience, and on such a subject; and fears to add a single sentence, after he has given us his last thought.

Who can ever forget the last meeting at Norwich in Connecticut? What a place for comparing this transitory life with the two worlds, to one of which we are all hastening. It has justly been called a little heaven on earth. But to me, it seemed more like a scene on a vast platform, raised over that "great gulf fixed," which no one can pass, if he would. On the right was the world of glory, and on the left, the world of despair. At one time, our attention was directed to the right, and there was but a step between us and heaven, and we sung with new delight,

"Why was I made to hear thy voice,
And enter while there's room
When thousands make a wretched choice,
And rather starve than come?"

At another time, our attention was directed to the left, and we beheld the deep gulf of despair yawning beneath our feet, and an innumerable company of immortal beings crowded together, and plunging over its awful brink. Who that was there, can ever again be absorbed in the things of the world, or can ever again seek to please himself? Who that was there, can ever again forget that cause for which Christ suffered and died?

The American Board, what a subject! Who does not admire its chapter in our American history? Who does not love to review its scenes, and commune with its spirit? The admirer of great principles, rather than of single facts, and immediate results, can here find a rich field for thought and investigation, and an ample scope for his largest desires, and for his greatest efforts. He, whose soul is formed to be touched by the immediate wants and woes of our race, can here find enough to reach the deepest fountains of his heart, while he strives to snatch the perishing heathen from the devouring elements, and while he hastens to give a piece of bread, and a cup of water to those, who are famishing with hunger, and dying with thirst. The lover of Bible scenes, and of Bible principles, can here find copious illustrations in this great providential work of the Divine Hand. He, who in all places, and under all circumstances, is determined not to know anything, save Jesus Christ, and him crucified, may thank God, that in these last days, he has given such an illustration, and such an application of the doctrines of the cross. Who among us, in the growth of his mind, and in the development of his heart, does not feel himself indebted to the American Board? Who that knows what it is to have an expanding and deepening Christian sympathy in his bosom, and an increasing and strengthening conviction of personal obligation resting on his soul, does not in this, feel himself indebted to the American Board? And who can bear the thought of one retrograde step in all its movements? Who would not sooner give of his last mite, and divide his last loaf? Though the barrel of meal be ever so low, and the cruise of oil ever so far spent, who will not run, and first make a little cake for this servant of the Lord?

CHAPTER II

FELLOWSHIP WITH CHRIST'S SUFFERINGS—VIEW OF THE WORLD OF DESPAIR—VIEW OF HEAVEN

As I mused on these things, the spirit of meditation came over me, and I was led away to visit the three great scenes of Christian sympathy. My first scene was that of the Saviour's life, sufferings and death. I wandered over the plains of Judea, silently I walked in the cold garden, and I stood by the fatal cross. I seemed to hear the Saviour's voice, calling to us in accents of melting tenderness; "Go ye into all the world, and preach the gospel to every creature." "The servant is not greater than his Lord." "Come follow me; walk in my footsteps, and we will be glorified together." The sympathy between the infinite Son of God, and his unworthy followers, appeared to me wonderful indeed, casting a glorious light over the whole subject of Missions, and receiving back in return, a living illustration, a living epistle, known and read of all men. What remarkable expressions do we find in the sacred volume on this subject. None but an infinite mind could conceive such thoughts, and none but an infinite pen would dare to write them. "He was tempted in all points like as we are." "He can be touched with the feeling of our infirmities."—"The captain of our salvation is made perfect through sufferings."—"He learned obedience by the things which he suffered."—"Himself being tempted, he is able to succor them that are tempted." His is not a sympathy, which simply pities, and feels for us. It is a sympathy, which knows by experience, how to partake in our every cup of joy, and in our every cup of sorrow. But this is not all. He not only suffers with us, and for us, but he even invites and accepts our sympathy in his behalf. Here is the preeminent glory of all this subject. We are permitted to labor with him, and for him,—to suffer with him and for him,—to be partakers in his reward—to share in the joy that was set before him, for which he endured the cross, despising the shame. We are said to be crucified with Christ—to be partakers of his sufferings; to weep with him; to rejoice with him; to reign with him. He is not ashamed to call us brethren—brethren in labors—brethren in sufferings—brethren in gathering in the rich harvest of immortal souls. We are to be conformed to his image, that he may be the first-born among many brethren. —We are to be heirs of God, and joint heirs with Christ, if so be that we suffer with him. Who could conceive of condescension like this? Is not a life of suffering for Christ's sake a great privilege? Is it not surrounded by an unparalleled halo of glory? Well might the Apostle seek to know the fellowship of Christ's sufferings, being made conformable to his death.

But what is this fellowship with Christ's sufferings, I inquired? What is that life, which consists "in always bearing about in the body, the dying of the Lord Jesus, that the life also of Jesus might be made manifest?" My heart exclaimed, Lord teach me thus to manifest the life of Jesus; Lord teach me to live more as he lived—to feel more as he felt—to labor more as he labored—to deny myself more as he denied himself—to pray more as he prayed—to agonize over a lost and dying world, more as he agonized. But again I inquired, what is it to know the fellowship of Christ's sufferings? Is it to take it patiently, when we are buffeted for our faults? Is it to submit patiently to those afflictive dispensations of Providence; which we cannot escape? No. All this is a duty, and it shall not lose its reward. But it is not a peculiar fellowship with Christ's sufferings. Is it to choose suffering for its own sake? No. This would be only will worship, which profiteth nothing. Does it consist in boldly and courageously refuting error? No. Whatever may, or may not be acceptable with God in this, it can have no peculiar communion with the sufferings of Him, whose tender spirit knew no abatement of its sorrows from revengeful feelings, from resistful words, or from opposing conduct—of Him, "who when he was reviled, reviled not again, when he suffered, he threatened not"—of Him, who "was led as a Lamb to the slaughter, and as a sheep before her shearers is dumb, so he opened not his mouth." As I reflected on this subject, three circumstances recurred to my mind as important in characterizing this class of sorrows. Other sufferings of the Christian will, doubtless, be accepted of God, though they may not possess all the distinguishing characteristics, which marked the sufferings of our Saviour. The three circumstances which presented themselves to my mind were the following.

In the first place, the life of the one who suffers, must be consecrated to the great work of saving souls, for which Christ lived, and suffered, and died. In the next place, only those sufferings of his, which are essential parts of his work, can be admitted into this holy communion. In the life of our blessed Redeemer, there was no needless expenditure of suffering. Each sorrow of his, bore a symmetrical relation to the whole great work of giving his life a ransom for sin. Such must be the life of his follower, who would know the fellowship of his sufferings. Not a pain, not a sorrow of his, embraced and endured for Christ's sake, must be such as could fall to the ground, without marring the symmetry of his Christ-like life. In the last place, his sufferings must be voluntary, or such as could be avoided, simply by giving up his work, or a part of it. The sufferings of Christ were all voluntary. Of his own will, he forsook the riches of more than ten thousand worlds, and was numbered among the poorest of men. Of his own will, he submitted to cruel mockings, and scourgings, and ignominy, and death, even the death of the cross. At any moment, he could have summoned more than twelve legions of angels to rescue him from his enemies. Nay more, he could have lifted his own almighty arm for his deliverance. He could have saved himself. He could have come down from the cross. That same power, which had so often bound up the bleeding hearts of others, he could have put forth to assuage his own grief. But this he would not do. Not one jot or tittle of his unparalleled sufferings would he allow to fail. All must be fulfilled. He would bear the weight of the divine stroke in all the depths of his tender spirit, and with a grief unassuaged, and with a heart uncomforted, unsustained.

So the sufferings of Christ's follower, which are admitted into a holy fellowship with his own sufferings, must be voluntary, or such as he could escape, simply by turning aside from the footsteps of his blessed Redeemer. The martyr, who refuses offered pardon, rather than to renounce the doctrines of the cross, may be a partaker of Christ's sufferings. The man, who in obedience to the calls of Providence, will voluntarily become poor for the salvation of men, may hold communion with the sorrows of Him, who, "though he was rich, yet for our sakes became poor, that we through his poverty, might be rich." He who will labor more, give more, and deny himself more, to save immortal souls from death, than to gain the greatest earthly good, may partake of the sufferings of Him, "who had not where to lay his head," and whose meat and whose drink it was to do the will of his heavenly Father. He who will use the best of his time, the most powerful energies of his mind, and the greatest strength of his heart, in weeping over, praying over, and agonizing over immortal souls just ready to perish, may hold communion with Him, who found in the cold mountain, a time, and a place for his prayers, —with Him, who "prayed more earnestly," and whose "soul was exceeding sorrowful, even unto death." Who that loves his precious Bible, and is allowed to hold sweet communion with his dear Redeemer, will not consider it a great privilege to suffer for his sake? With what an honor was the converted Saul invested, when the Lord said of him, "He is a chosen vessel." "I will make him to know how great things he must suffer for my name's sake." But this holy fellowship with the sufferings of Christ will not be urged on any one, whose unwilling heart would fain be rid of the cumbrous load. Here are sorrows, which none will be compelled to know, which no heart will be required to endure. This holy privilege is reserved for those, who can "rejoice that they are made partakers of Christ's sufferings, that when his glory shall be revealed, they may be glad also with exceeding joy."

This holy fellowship with Christ's sufferings contains the very vital blood of all the missionary enterprise. Who then can ever look for this work to be carried forward by self-denial, which is not felt? Who can anticipate its onward, and ever onward progress only as it is watered by tears, by sacrifices, and by self-denials, which will be sorely felt? Where one can be found in danger of doing less hereafter, because he is doing so much at the present time, can we not find a hundred who will do less tomorrow, because they are not doing enough today, to taste of that fellowship with the sufferings of Christ?

As I left the dying scene of our dear Redeemer, I seemed to hear his voice in overwhelming tones of bleeding love, saying, "My followers, my dearest friends, will ye know the fellowship of my sufferings?—will ye be conformable unto my death?—or will ye crucify to yourselves the Son of God afresh, and put him to an open shame?"

But I was led on to another, and a very different scene. It was a scene on the borders of the world of despair,—a scene casting, to my mind, a glare of lurid light over the whole missionary enterprise, and urging the Christian on with unexampled speed to unknown and untold sacrifices and sufferings for its sake. Necessity seemed laid upon me to take a nearer view of the finally lost than I ever had done. I *had* turned to those fearful passages in my Bible. I had followed the criminal as near the place of execution as I dared approach. But as the flames began to flash in my face, and as the groans of despair began to fall on my ear, my affrighted spirit started back, and fled away from the dreadful sight. But now I felt that I must take a nearer view of the second death than I ever had done. Without such a view, I feared that I should not weigh things in a just balance—that I should not rid the skirts of my garments of the blood of souls—that I should not use as I ought, each hour of my passing days, and spend as I should, each dollar which comes under my control. Without such a view, I feared that I should not understand as I might, and love and adore as I ought, that infinite price paid for the ransom of the soul.

I asked God for strength to meet the dreadful scene. I approached nearer and nearer to the awful brink of the bottomless pit, and I trembled at every step. I arrived at its very edge, and the foundations seemed to crumble beneath my feet. I stooped over to take a view of the dreadful place, and the yawning gulf seemed to open wide its mouth to receive my fainting spirit. I beheld the worm that never dies, and the fire that never is quenched. I heard the unutterable groans of the forever lost, and I saw the smoke of their torment, which ascendeth up forever and ever. Who can endure this, I exclaimed, a single year? —a single day?—a single hour? But, O forever and ever! O eternity of misery! what is it? Many have told us what it is not, but who can tell us what it is.

I have read of the horrors of war. The mere outline has chilled the blood in my veins, but the details I have never dared to survey. I have beheld at a distance the fires of persecution. The horrors of the inquisition, the tortures of the rack, and the terrors of that death, which wears out life by mere agony of distress, but into the secrets of such scenes, I have never dared to enter. But the living realities of all this, a hundred times told, would be nothing compared with the second death. The Bible seems to labor to find fearful words and terrific figures, by which to describe the dreadful truth. Human ingenuity has been exhausted in finding comparisons and delineations to tell us what it is not, but no one has attempted to tell us what it is. One comparison more flashed on my affrighted imagination. It came from the regions of war, of bloodshed, of cruelty and death. It came from the regions of faggots, of racks and inquisitorial horrors. It was drawn from those very scenes, at which my heart has ever recoiled with indescribable dread, and therefore, it seemed to my agonizing spirit, a fit semblance of hell, or rather a fit semblance of what it is not. The supposition was as follows.

A timid, sensitive female, who ventures not to set foot on a worm, is endued with a life of thousands and tens of thousands of years, and she is ever to continue the same human being that she now is, with all her present susceptibilities, and all her present feelings of horror at the sight of cruelty and distress. This sensitive creature is confined to an immovable spot, where she is to behold with her own eyes, all the miseries of the whole race of man, in all their length and breadth, and in all their living realities. She is compelled to hear, one by one, every groan, and witness every scene of distress among the inhabitants of earth from Adam to the present time. She enters on her dreadful existence. Day by day her soul shrinks more and more from the sight of instruments of torture, and her fainting spirit becomes more and more alive to the anguish of cries, and of groans, and of horrid features, and to the agonies of death. But all this is nothing, compared with the miseries of the forever lost. All this is nothing, compared with the dreadful realities, which are now meeting the eye of many a timid female in that world of ruin.

Ages on ages roll on, and none but this wretched being knows with what agonizing slowness they pass away. But all this is nothing, compared with a hopeless eternity. The years will wear away. The end will come. Yes. I cast my eye onward through an untold series of ages, and I behold her just passing through the last suffering scene. Her trembling spirit, worn out with agony, and now fainting under the prospect of a speedy release, is on the eve of its everlasting flight. Just at this moment, another messenger of vengeance comes, bearing the heart-rending intelligence, that another and a more dreadful portion of misery and death is yet to fill her cup of anguish. This timid, this sensitive, this wretched being, is now herself to become the suffering victim of all which her eyes have beheld—she is destined to live over, one by one, every wretched life, and die every cruel death, at the sight of which her heart has been torn asunder a thousand times. What frightful images, what horrors of the imagination now chase her affrighted spirit! But there is no escape. Her shrinking soul, exhausted by indescribable terror and by agonizing sympathy, must now yield to the dreadful sentence. But all this is not hell. No. Let the permission now be given to the most timid and sensitive creature in that world of woe, to exchange her prison house of despair for a miserable existence like this, and that moment a ray of hope would find its way into her dismal abode. Dreadful as the prospect would be, and infinitely more dreadful as would be the reality, it would not be hell. However severe the agony might be, and however insupportable to her sad spirit, the repetition might become, and however slow the myriads on myriads of ages might roll away, it would not be forever and ever. The seal of hopeless despair would not be fixed on her condemnation. O eternity of ruin! what is it? Who can bear a view of the depths of despair? O who can bear to know by experience its dreadful realities?

Again I stooped over, and again I took a lower and a deeper view of the abode of the forever lost; and I exclaimed, can this be the eternal home of a human being? Must his misery be forever? Will there be no end? Is there no escape? Cannot a way be devised for his release? And I heard a voice from heaven, replying to my troubled soul, and to my struggling spirit, "Be still and know that I am God." It is forever. But it is right—it is just. The finally lost thou canst not pluck from the devouring flames. They might have been saved, but it is now too late. Forever and ever is their dreadful portion. But there are those who can be saved. Send forth all thine agonizing sympathy in their behalf. Fly to their relief. Soon they will be past hope. Soon they will plunge down the awful precipice. Soon they will be numbered with the lost—the forever lost.

The price of their redemption has been paid. The Holy Spirit has been given. But one thing more of all the counsels of heaven is wanting to secure their salvation—to make sure their eternal safety. This one thing is the voluntary instrumentality of man. For the want of this, millions and millions during the last eighteen centuries, have gone down to everlasting death. Why, O why, I inquired, are the chariot wheels delayed so long for this feeble, this worthless work of man? And again I heard a voice from heaven, saying unto me, "Be still and know that I am God." This instrumentality was appointed in the counsels of heaven, and that is enough. Not one jot or tittle of it shall fall to the ground. Sooner shall another eighteen centuries pass by, and all the teeming millions of each succeeding generation go down to everlasting death.

Again I stooped over to take another view of the world of ruin, and my agonizing spirit seemed to descend lower still into the depths of eternal despair. What a view did I there take of the importance of the missionary enterprize! What a view did I then have of the bleeding Lamb of God, groaning, agonizing and dying to save a lost and ruined world from hopeless despair! How did my heart at that moment, cling to that "hope, which is an anchor to the soul, both sure and steadfast, and which entereth to that within the veil." But, O the forever lost! They know nothing of this precious hope. Those teeming millions just ready to perish, know nothing of this precious hope. Who that knows aught of its worth—who that has ever stood on the borders of that world of endless woe, will not strive with all his might to save a fellow immortal from the anguish of the second death? Who, in such a work, will count his life dear unto him? Who will call aught that he has his own?

As I took my last lingering look of that dreadful place, the words of the Saviour came home to my heart with indescribable power, "Love thy neighbor as thyself." "Whatsoever ye would that men should do to you, do ye even so to them." "Freely ye have received, freely give."

I was led on to another scene. It was a scene at the gate of heaven, casting a sweet and glorious light over the whole subject of Missions.

There I beheld a "great multitude, which no man could number, of all nations, and kindreds, and people, and tongues, stand before the throne." And one said to me, "These are they which came out of great tribulation, and have washed their robes and made them white in the blood of the Lamb." Then I heard the Saviour's voice, that sweetest music of the heavenly world, saying, These are my followers—these are my dearest friends. They have known of the fellowship of my sufferings, they shall now be partakers of my joy. "Where I am there shall they be also, that they may behold my glory." And I heard that new song, which no man could learn, but those "who follow the Lamb whithersoever he goeth." And as they sung, "worthy art thou for thou hast redeemed us to God by thy blood," my heart responded,

"My willing soul would stay
In such a place as this,

And sit and sing herself away
To everlasting bliss."

But O the forever lost, I again exclaimed! Never, O never will they unite in that new song. Never will they hear the Saviour's blessed voice. Never will they sit under the banner of his love. O the millions ready to perish! Must they be shut out forever from the New Jerusalem? Must they be banished forever from the Saviour's blissful presence? O who will not give his all, to save them from eternal death, and raise to eternal glory?

Here I stopped a moment to reflect on the three great scenes over which I had passed. How solemn the contemplation! What a view did I then take of the gratifications, the comforts, and even the necessities of this life, compared with the eternal interests of immortal souls.

CHAPTER III

VIEW OF PERSONAL RESPONSIBILITY—SCENE OF THE JUDGMENT—SCENE AT THE MISSIONARY HOUSE

But I was led away to mingle in other scenes, and to receive other impressions. First I passed on to mingle in the busy scenes of our own Christian land. And the veil was lifted from mine eyes, and I saw things as they are seen by Him, with whom "one day is as a thousand years, and a thousand years as one day." Spread out before me, was a solemn and awful view of personal responsibility. There I beheld the momentous results, both near and remote, both visible and invisible, of all human events. Each blow that was struck, however gentle it might seem, sent a thrill of joy, or of horror, throughout the universe, as it raised an immortal soul to eternal glory, or sunk it to endless perdition. There I beheld, too, the Divine Hand, making certain the destiny of every human deed, whether it took hold on the gate of heaven, or stretched forth its fatal grasp to the lowest depths of endless despair. There were made manifest the folly and the delusion of those, who are ever striving to secure for some of their steps, a middle path between the service of Christ, and the service of his enemy. That vast field of neutral ground, in human affairs, so long, and so carefully maintained, was all divided out between the two great contending powers of eternal life, and of eternal death. There it was seen that each one's life must be given for the salvation of men, or be devoted to their eternal destruction. Every thing about me seemed written all over with the Saviour's words, "He that is not for me, is against me, and he that gathereth not with me, scattereth abroad." The vast and solemn spectacle spread out before my vision, seemed like an immense "harp of a thousand strings," ever vibrating with the least touch of the hand, with the least breath of the lips, whose every note continued to wander onward, and onward, and ceased not, till it mingled in the songs of the New Jerusalem, or till it waked up a deep tone of wailing in the bottomless pit. O who can play with a careless, heedless hand on the chords of such a harp! Who does not tremble to live, to walk, to speak, in such a world as this? How distressing is the mere apprehension of having by accident administered a fatal cup of poison to a fellow-being! How unavailing would be the consoling words, that the same hand in a hundred other cases, had given bread to the hungry, and water to the thirsty, and clothing to the destitute! But infinitely more distressing is the almost certainty of having by neglect, or self-indulgence, destroyed a never dying soul in eternal misery! My heart exclaimed, Let the past of my life suffice in the work of death,—henceforth let me live only for the salvation of men. I looked up to the God of my salvation, and cried, Lord, grant that I may never again spend ought of my time or of my possessions without seeking guidance and direction from above—grant that I may never again spend ought of earth's treasures on myself, without the united approval of the word of God, the providence of God, and the Spirit of God.

But time hastened me away, and I passed on to another scene. It was the scene of the judgment. There I beheld the Son of man seated on his throne of glory, and all the holy angels with him. And I beheld the books as they were opened, "and the dead were to be judged out of those things which were written in the books, according to their works." First came an unfolding of the scenes of time, and after that was to be the judgment, and the final sentence. And I beheld a balance lifted high. It was a balance of time, in which had been weighed most of the offerings cast into the treasury of the Lord. It was a false balance, named "human discretion," with deceitful weights, brought there to be examined, judged and condemned. It was a balance for the thoughtful and considerate, not for those who *weigh* not their doings. It was a balance, by which immortal beings had been weighed and sold, —not for trifles, but for gratifications, innocent, useful, laudable, when not compared with the deathless soul. The whole of earth's scenes passed in rapid review before me. I saw provinces, kingdoms, and empires; houses, lands, and merchandize, cast into the ponderous scales, and made to outweigh an innumerable company of human beings, destined to live for ever and ever. I passed along over eighteen centuries, and I saw the countless myriads of earth's teeming inhabitants, cast into the scales, one by one, and as the price of each was found, he was sold over to eternal bondage in the prison-house of despair.

At length the spring of 1843 opened on my vision. It was a season of great struggle. It was a trying time for the missionary cause—a trying time for benevolent hearts, for tender consciences. The darkness of former ages had passed away. Money had received a new and inestimable value. The price of blood had been found. The worth of a dollar had been estimated. The pieces of silver, for which a soul on heathen shore could be bought or sold, had been calculated with almost numerical exactness. The perishing heathen had been brought, and put down at every man's door, and how could the bread of life be refused? The American Board had undertaken a great work, and the Christians of our country had pledged, that it should be carried through. The pledge for this year was far from being redeemed, and but a few weeks more were allowed for its redemption. Minds were not all blinded. Hearts were not all cold. Many a sigh, many a falling tear, plainly told that the wants of the heathen were not forgotten, and that the pledge to the American Board was still remembered. But—the times were hard. Money was scarce. And the spring was just the time when money was most needed. This was the common season for building and rebuilding, for enlarging, for replenishing, for repairing, for purchasing; and all this could not be done without money. The great purchases of former days, no Christian asked now to make. The superfluities and luxuries of other times, no one asked now to enjoy. But then there were the comforts, the conveniences, and the necessaries of life. Must these be given up? We had heard of such sacrifices for Christ's sake in other days, and in other lands. But we had not supposed, that such things could ever be known in our free, our fruitful, our rich, our glorious country. We had not looked for a return of those "hard times," which tried men's souls in the iron furnace of poverty. We had not expected a call for the Paul-like, or rather the Christ-like sacrifices of those severe and cruel days.

I saw a fearful struggle of conscience, carried forward in many a bosom over the comforts, the conveniences, and even the necessaries of life. Then came the old and the young, the rich and the poor, the learned and the unlearned, laden down with the treasures of earth of every name and description. They came to find a way to retain their needed stones, and to seek relief from a troubled conscience, as the heathen were turned over to everlasting death. All were cast into the great balance, each outweighing a deathless soul, and consigning it over to eternal ruin. Among others came the delicate female, bringing her various possessions, adapted to her age and condition, and as each article seemed to sign the death warrant of an immortal being, her hand trembled, her spirit fainted, and she could be revived only by the comforting word, that necessity, respectability and deference to superiors, required all this. Oh that deceitful balance for those tender consciences of 1843! Had it not been for her fatal decisions, what wonders would have been wrought even in those hard times!—what a multitude of souls would have been saved through the self denying zeal of those anxious, inquiring spirits. The call of Missions would have been met, and far more than met. The American Board would have been made to shine "forth as the morning, fair as the moon, clear as the sun, and terrible as an army with banners." Nay more, we should have seen all the seven planets in the moral system for converting the world, with all their attending satellites, urged forward in their own orbits with an unexampled velocity. But O that fatal balance of human discretion!—how unsafe to be trusted when the destiny of immortal souls is at stake.

The review went forward. At length the examination of the scenes and doings of time was over, and then came the judgment. And I saw another balance lifted high. On its polished front was engraved, "Love the Lord thy God with all thine heart. Love thy neighbor as thyself." This was the balance of eternal truth and justice, by which are weighed, all other scales, and all other weights, and all the principles, and all the deeds of the children of men. There by the decisions of this revealer of truth, it was found, that the responsibility of the church, so much inculcated and enforced, so much admired and loved, had often been only a creature of the imagination, while personal responsibility coming directly home to self, which had been so much neglected, overlooked and resisted, had ever been a most fearful and solemn reality. There it was proved "that there is a way which seemeth right unto a man, but the end thereof are the ways of death." And I beheld the speechless agony of those, in whose garments was found the blood of souls. There I saw many a face gather blackness, and I heard many a despairing cry; Lord, when did I destroy the souls of the heathen? And the reply was, Inasmuch as thou didst not save them, "thou art weighed in the balances, and art found wanting." And I beheld too the unspeakable joy of those, who received the approving sentence, "Well done, good and faithful servant." Then it was made manifest, that the system of rewards, built on the firm foundation of grace, is as real, as impartial, and as much according to the deeds done in the body, as could be any system of boasted morality. Then I heard a voice saying, what shall it profit a man, if he gain the whole world, and destroy an immortal soul?—What shall it profit a Christian father, though by his wisdom and foresight, he shall provide well for his own household, if he refuse the bread of life to the perishing heathen?—What shall it profit a Christian mother, though by her industry and discretion, she shall clothe all "her household in scarlet, in silk and in purple," if she refuse the robe of Christ's righteousness to the destitute heathen? But as I heard the last and awful sentence, "Depart ye cursed," I turned away, and came back, again to mingle in the doings and events of time.

My next scene was in the city of the Pilgrims, in a solemn council chamber, whose door, and whose posts were written all over with the Saviour's last and great command, "Go ye into all the world, and preach the gospel to every creature." It was a momentous scene. Paleness and anxiety sat on all faces. Fatal decisions were that day to be made. The members of that council had not that day convened to examine, judge and condemn a fellow man, and to commit him over to the hand of the executioner. No. They had met to sign the death warrant of immortal beings, and to consign them over to the agonies of the second death. Mercy seemed to cry, Stay thine hand, spare the stroke; but justice cried, The will of the people must be done. The will of the people has been done for eighteen centuries in sending millions of millions to endless despair. The will of the people shall still be done, for that is the decree of heaven. The decisions of the American churches must be executed; the will of the individual members of these churches shall be done; what they are sowing they shall reap, and they shall have their reward.

In the midst of this trying scene, I did rejoice, though with agony of spirit, that God had raised up men, who would stand by the principles of eternal justice—that hitherto he had given them strength for every trying hour. I prayed, that he would still sustain them by his almighty arm—that he would ever keep them from turning aside to the right hand, or to the left. Though every missionary station should be clad in mourning, and every missionary heart be filled with anguish, I could pray, that they might ever preserve the vital principle from the fatal ravages of an accumulating debt. Who that is saved from sitting in such a council, and from passing such decisions, shall think it too much to give of his money, or even of the bread from his table?

But I waited not the result. I could not hear the final sentence? As I passed away, my heart exclaimed, Must this be? Must these waiting prisoners of hope be sentenced to that dreadful, that hopeless, that eternal prison of despair? Cannot one hundred thousand dollars be raised at once, and sent to the spot, before the fatal mandate shall have gone forth through the length and breadth of this wide world? Is there no hope? Where are the marks of poverty which justify such a conclusion? Famine has not laid his grasping hand on our gnawing vitals? Pestilence is not walking through our streets, destroying the stay and the staff—the husband and the father, and the widow's only son. War is not abroad in the midst of us, seizing upon our young men, and taking away our possessions—clothing our fields with barrenness, and filling our shops and our counting rooms with desolation. Have we not all food to eat and to spare, and raiment to put on? If money is scarce, shall not our wants be made to be few? If the times are hard, shall we not manifest that we believe it, by living on coarser fare, and by clothing ourselves in a coarser apparrel? If the community, if the church as such, can resist this call, are not individuals to be found who will meet it in all its urgent claims? Is there not power sufficient in personal responsibility, resting on the hearts of a few individuals to accomplish the work? Cannot a few be found who can rejoice to be made partakers of Christ's sufferings for such a cause as this, and at such a time as this?

CHAPTER IV
THE GOD COVETOUSNESS BECOMING AN ADVOCATE FOR FOREIGN MISSIONS—LABORS OF COVETOUSNESS

But I heard the footsteps of an enemy in the camp—of a deceitful foe, who had found his way into the very heart of the community. It was the idolatry of the Christian dispensation. It was the god of this world, named by the Holy Ghost, "Covetousness." He was clad in a beautiful robe of symmetrical proportions; he was well skilled in the philosophy and logic of this world, and his words were smoother than oil. By vain philosophy, by smooth words, and fair speeches, he was able to blind the minds of many, that they should believe a lie, and he attempted even to cast a mist over the moral vision of some of the Solomons of our day. He could transform himself into an angel of light, and he could put on every garb, from that of Milton's cherub youth, to that of the highest, and boldest archangel before the throne. He was a friend of every cause, and he could become an agent of every enterprise. He now appeared as an advocate for Foreign Missions. There was a call for special effort, and he came to proffer his assistance in carrying it forward. His grand point, to be gained in behalf of the cause, was to subvert personal responsibility, and substitute in its stead, the responsibility of the church, and the responsibility of a neighbor. Whether he employed the words of truth or falsehood, it was all alike to him, provided his end could be attained. In war, his secret lay in the ambush. In this case, his policy was to divide, and draw off the attention, and disperse responsibility. He presented a crafty mixture of truth and falsehood, of valuable principles, and subjects of mere speculation. He furnished such a variety of subjects for thought, and topics for conversation, that few had any time for serious reflection on duty, on the worth of the soul, and on the realities of a coming retribution.

I beheld this advocate, as he went forward with his labors. His public appeals in behalf of Missions were warm and spirited. His censures on the apathy of the church, were loud and vociferous. He made an eloquent speech on the extravagances and luxuries of the age, and on the vast imports and expenditures of the nation. He entered into a labored and exact calculation of the ability and resources of the church. He proved to the entire satisfaction of his hearers, that there was wealth enough in the country, —that the work could all be accomplished without the least self denial of a single individual. Just look, he said, at the vast amount worse than thrown away on our Congress, on our State Legislatures, and on our Navy, and in every other department of government. Just look at the sums expended annually on the articles of rum, wine, and brandy—of tea, sugar, and coffee—of silks, laces, and ribbons, and of a thousand other things, a mere fraction of which, would sustain the whole cause of Missions.

Missions, he remarked, must be sustained; but then the burden should not all be laid on a few, while so many were left to do nothing. People must be reasonable; no one could do more than he was able to do. A man could not give what he did not possess. The willing hearted must take care about committing themselves. If they assumed a burden, others would let them bear it.

With every other observer of human events, he was aware, he said, that there must ever be a falling off somewhere of the Missionary receipts—that among the subscriptions of one year, there must be many failures the next—some from deaths, some from great losses, and some from apostacy. He believed too, that it was the imperious duty of the *church* to make up such deficiencies. But then he would not have all the burden sustained by those, who had already done much more than their proportion. There were many abundantly able, who had never done any thing for the cause. Such ought now to come forward liberally, and make up for past remissness in duty. He could point to a hardy farmer of three score years and ten, who once in his life gave a fourpence to a missionary, because he was going to Jerusalem. That man could give five thousand dollars better than not. The deed would only relieve him of a part of his insupportable burden of possessions. He believed, that some missionary agent, by spending time enough, and strength enough, might possibly convince that man, and make him give his five thousand. In case of failure, there would be the satisfaction of having tried.

This friend of Missions was a great admirer of Providence. Help would be raised up from some quarter. He believed, that the cause was safe in the hands of Providence. There, he said, were those princely possessions. How easy would it be for God to convert the owners, and bring their willing offerings into the treasury of the Lord. Then *there* was that rich merchant, for whose conversion, his wife had been praying for twenty years. How easy would it be for God to answer those prayers, and open wide that man's heart, and hands in behalf of Missions. Besides, *there* were all the converts of the past year. We might safely calculate on their aid in this time of necessity. He had been observing the leadings of Providence, and he had the greatest confidence, that the pledge to Missions would be fully redeemed before the financial year should close. He did not think that any one need be anxious about it, or that any one would have occasion to bear any heavy burden in carrying it through.

Our advocate for Missions had great versatility of genius, and great fluency of speech. With the greatest facility, he could change his position to meet all circumstances of time and place. At one time, I saw him walking through the streets of the city, descanting on the ability of the *country* to meet the present exigency. The pressure was not felt there as it was in the city. It was true, that the farmer could not realize as much money in exchange for his produce; but on the other hand, he did not now need as much. When the scales were turned, and he became the buyer instead of the seller, all was made even and equal again. At another time, I saw him pleading the cause before the owners of a manufacturing establishment. He was as decided as ever, that the present necessities of the missionary cause must be met. But he thought, that all extra effort should be made by those best able to do it. He was very eloquent in exhibiting the felicity of the merchant's condition, compared with that of the manufacturer, who could not now, with his utmost skill, keep his capital good. He talked wisely about the tariff, and many a kindred subject, all proving that it plainly belonged to the merchant, rather than to the manufacturer, to make extra effort. Again, I saw him riding over the hills, and through the valleys of the country, declaiming against the extravagance of city life, and city style. Here was the grand obstacle to the progress of Missions. The wealth of the city was sufficient to accomplish any thing, and every thing. Let the people there just give up their extravagance, and live as they do in the country, and there would be no more lack of funds for benevolent objects. He knew a good man in Boston, who in addition to his liberal regular donations, had just given one thousand dollars extra, to meet the present necessities of the missionary cause. He knew too, that this thousand dollars had cost him great self-denial, great effort, and great care. With the approbation of his wife and daughters, they were to relinquish their usual summer journey. Besides this, his early watch and care, his increased labors and assiduity in his business, and his anxious midnight thoughts, which the farmer knows not of, all testified, that it was no easy matter for him to make out that thousand dollars. But notwithstanding all this, he could now just exchange his house for another, and sell off his carpets and mirrors, and then he would be able to give another thousand without the least difficulty.

  At one time, I saw this same advocate for Missions come into an assembly composed entirely of men, who were discussing this subject. There he was very eloquent in praise of female sympathy, female piety, and female benevolence. Woman, he said, was last at the cross, and first at the sepulchre, and she had ever been first in every good work. There was scarcely a female in the land, who was not now either knitting or sewing for the cause. Woman was fruitful in invention; what she undertook, she always accomplished. While the Board had so many warm hearted, faithful friends, there was nothing to fear. Man had only to go forward in the even tenor of his way, and give about as he had done. All that was extra, he might safely commit over to the industry, the ingenuity, and the benevolence of the other sex.

Again I saw him seated in a circle of females. They were relating, one by one, the various difficulties in their missionary efforts, and comparing their condition with the more easy lot of the other sex, who had all the money under their own control. With all their toils, and all their self-denying zeal, the little sum, which they could raise, would avail nothing in so great an enterprise. It was a serious question, whether it would not be wise to give up their efforts, and commit the whole work over to the other sex. Just at that moment, he proffered his kind advice. He should not favor so rash a step as was last proposed. The cause of Missions needed female sympathy, and female prayers. It would be well to sustain their sewing societies, and to endeavor to keep up an interest. Woman ought in some way to do a *little* —just enough to open her heart, and secure her prayers. But no one ought to look to her to meet extra calls. He thought it the height of folly and injustice, to make such efforts, as were made in some places, to beg money of women and children, who had nothing of their own, and who were entirely dependent on their husbands, and fathers. The cause of Missions must be sustained—the present necessities must be met. But this was the appropriate work of men. A man at the head of his own business, knew far better what he could do, than did his wife and daughters. Besides, if he did not do his duty, they were not responsible for it.

In all his various positions, he was but too successful in his delusive wiles. The imploring voice of benevolence was often neglected and turned aside, while the words of this enemy in the camp, found ready access to the attentive mind, and to be the willing heart. O where, I exclaimed, is the remembrance of the Saviour's dying love? O where is the remembrance of that eternity, where all the inhabitants of earth will soon find their everlasting and unchangeable home? O where is the remembrance of that day of final account, where together the tempters and the tempted, will meet their trying and solemn sentence from their righteous judges?

CHAPTER V

LABORS OF COVETOUSNESS CONTINUED—
CONVENTION OF THE LABORING
AND UNEDUCATED CLASSES—
RECOLLECTIONS OF A
LITTLE MOUNTAIN HOME

But the labors of this enemy in the garb of a friend still went on. I next met him in a large promiscuous assembly of both sexes of the avowed friends of Missions. The discussions of the day were to be closed by a subscription in behalf of the cause. It was a professed convention of the laboring and uneducated classes. The invitations given out to attend this convention, had, however, been rather partial. The managers had designedly left out some, lest their influence and example should cast more light, than their eyes were then prepared to endure. Among those passed by in these invitations, were the intelligent and generous farmer, the liberal and benevolent mechanic, and the widow with her two mites—and many others of kindred spirit, found on the hills, in the valleys, and between the granite rocks of New England, and scattered over the fertile fields of the Empire State, and of the Great Valley, and dispersed over the extended plains of every other State and Territory of the Union. These were "nature's noblemen," made nobler still by the spirit and power of the gospel; and no wonder, that they were excluded from a convention of men, who had always feared the influence of the nobility. In dress and manners, there was a great dissimilarity in this audience, and yet there were important principles of sympathy and union. Our advocate made no set speech in this assembly. His remarks were all colloquial and desultory. He gave some gentle hints against learning, and learned men. He made some remarks of doubtful meaning about the salaries of ministers, and their power over the people, and about the payment of agents. He introduced some ambiguous insinuations concerning the management of the missionary enterprise, and the mode of expending money on some of the stations. He spoke of donations to this cause, as a kind of favor conferred on its officers, and on the ministers of the gospel, who were most active in its service. He seemed to regard the duty of carrying forward the missionary enterprise, as particularly belonging to this class of men, forgetting the condemnation of the unprofitable servant, who hid his one talent in the earth.

But the discussions were soon over, and then our advocate begged the privilege of carrying around the subscription paper, that he might facilitate the work, and advise and comfort his friends. He first came to a sturdy farmer, whose possessions amounted to about one hundred acres. I did not expect as much of him, as I should of a liberal minded man, to say nothing of benevolence. But as he was a professor of religion, he cannot, I said, do less on this occasion, than twenty-five cents to an acre, so we shall be sure of twenty-five dollars. But really it fell so much below, that I should blush to mention the sum.

He next came to a professedly poor man, whose estate consisted of a half acre of land, and a little cottage. He had been whispering over the matter with his wife, and as the paper came along, he put down seventy-five cents, adding that a poor man had enough to do to take care of himself. It was well known, however, that that poor man and his wife allowed themselves many a luxury, which was not found on the table of their more self-denying pastor.

I next saw the paper passing into the hands of a young man of athletic form, and noble countenance, who must, thought I, possess that liberal heart, so often found in young men of that appearance. But his downcast look plainly told of regrets for the past, which were revolving in his breast. He wished, that he could be liberal on this occasion. Poor man, he had lost so many days from his work during the last winter by sleigh rides and parties, and he had been so generous with all, especially to the other sex, that he had been able to lay aside but little for this important occasion. But a sudden lifting up of his head, and a sparkling of his eye, revealed the desires of his heart, and the noble purposes, which were forming in his soul. He gave strong indications, that there was a spirit within, which needed only encouragement and sympathy, to burst forth into all its cheering and comforting influence. In a moment, he seemed to come to himself. He remembered his covenant obligations. He remembered that Saviour, whom he professed to love, and to follow. I heard him whisper a vow, that when another sleigh-riding winter should come, he would remember, and lay aside for the cause of Missions. Though he viewed it as noble indeed, to be generous in the things of this life, he then felt, that it was far more noble, and far more glorious, to be generous in the cause of Christ, and for the salvation of souls.

He soon came with his paper to a lady of very gay attire, with her daughter by her side. She wrote down a figure three. Stop, said I, involuntarily, the lady, by mistake, has omitted the cypher at the right hand, for surely, thought I, if she has the least taste for the beauty of proportions, to say nothing more, she cannot, allow a sum less than thirty dollars to stand beside her rich apparel. But I found myself mistaken to my great embarrassment, and I enquired into her history. She was a widow, and supported herself and daughter by her needle. But many a one in like circumstances, with her skilful needle, would have been a Dorcas indeed, dexterously using it in its most delightful work of making coats and garments for the needy. But the sequel of her story was told in her dress, and that of her daughter. She early took a strange fancy, that to bring her daughter forward in the world, was the grand end of life. To this she sacrificed her all. From month to month, she spent all her earnings in striving to prove herself equal in one thing at least to her more affluent neighbor, like a silly dove, who begged, that she might exchange her own beautiful, and well-fitted wings for those of the peacock, in which she could neither walk nor fly. The mystery was now all explained, and the awkward position of the small sum of three dollars, beside that rich attire, was made plain and intelligible.

The paper passed on to another female of about twenty years of age. In dress, she did not fall much below the one just described. But I had learned to distrust appearances, and I waited to know her history. She was the eldest daughter of a Green Mountain farmer, who lived on a moderate scale, but who, in true independent simplicity, was very willing to support his own daughters at home. There she might have lived in a neat and simple style, enjoying the country school, and the village library. There she might have lived to fan the flame on their little missionary altar, to throw the increasing power of her influence over all the younger children, and to surround the hearts of her kind parents with her cheering words and affectionate smiles. But when she was about sixteen, the daughter of a far poorer neighbor returned from our principal manufacturing village, dressed out in silks and laces, and bringing such a report of the fairyland, that her young heart could not resist the inducement of becoming her companion. So she forsook her beautiful "mountain home," and all its rural sweets, and left behind her all those warm and loving hearts, that she might know the luxury of that "outward adorning of plaiting the hair, of wearing of gold, and of putting on of apparel." What an immense sacrifice did she make at the shrine of vanity. No wonder, that she could offer up at the same shrine, the missionary spirit, which her good mother had been endeavoring to kindle in her bosom. No wonder, that she was able to lay aside but little in her missionary purse for this important occasion. Whatever may be laudable for others less favored, who, thought I, can ever be made willing to exchange a beautiful mountain home, and an ample sphere of domestic usefulness, and domestic happiness for a more lucrative situation within the walls of a manufactory?

As I cast my eye on the dress and appearance of the last two, I was strongly reminded by contrast of another widow, whom I knew and loved forty years ago, and of her "mountain home." She was not rich in the treasures of earth. Her little farm was surely not more to her in providing for her seven, than was that skilful needle in providing for the one. But want, at that "mountain home," was made to walk so fairly, and so gracefully within that little circle of means, that she had always room enough, and to spare to a more restricted neighbor. I can now see that loved widow, just as I did in the days of my childhood. She is a little less than forty years of age, and her complexion is as fair, and her forehead as noble, and as lofty as on her bridal day. Now she is in that sweet little garden, which needs only to be seen to be loved. Now she is surveying the work of the hired man, and her little son, on that wild romantic little farm, made one would think more to feast the soul, than to feed the body. But almost always she was to be found busy, both early and late, amid her household cares, and amid the culture of the olive plants around her table. In that little domain, nothing was left to take its own way. Every thing was made to yield to her faithful and diligent hand. It was no mistake of that good-hearted neighbor, who came in one day, begging the privilege of setting a plant of rare virtues in a corner of her garden, because, as he said, *there* it could never die. The roses, the pinks, and the peonies, those old fashioned flowers, which keep time with Old Hundred, could no where grow so fresh, and so sweet as in that little garden. And no where else have I ever seen wild strawberries, in such profusion and richness, as were gathered into those little baskets. Never were rareripes so large and so yellow, and never were peaches so delicious and so fair, as grew on the trees of that little farm. The apples too, contrived to ripen before all others, so as to meet in sweet fellowship with peaches and plums, to entertain the aunts and the cousins.

  I can now see that little mountain home with its sweet little rivulet, finding its way among rocks, and cliffs, and hillocks, and deep craggy dells. Then just beyond the precincts of that family domain, was that "top of the hill," crowned by its high rolling rock, ever inviting the enterprise of each aspiring heart. Every one was amply repaid, who would climb that steep hill, and ascend that high rock. There might be seen the far-off mountains in all their grandeur, and the deep valleys, and widely extended plains, and more than all, that little village below, containing only a very few white houses, but more than those young eyes had ever yet seen. But sweetest of all, through a mile or more, to that village church, was that wild winding way, traversed each Sabbath morning by that little group, while the family pony gave the mother her horseback ride. There, too, in winter, was that little sleigh, packed so snugly, and gliding so gently, over that same winding way, to that same little church.

At that little mountain home, every want was promptly and abundantly met by the bounties of summer, and by the providence for winter. The autumnal stores, so nicely sorted and arranged, always travelled hand in hand through the long winter, like the barrel of meal and the cruise of oil. The apples came out fresh in the spring, and the maple sugar, that most important grocery of that little neighborhood, was never known to fail, till the warm sun on the sparkling snow, gave delightful indications, that sugar days were near. When gathered around that simple table, no one desired a richer supply than was furnished by the hand of that dear mother. The simple school day dress too, so neat and so clean, was amply sufficient in view of those young minds, while the rare gift of the Sunday suit, kept expressly for the occasion, formed an important era in the life of the possessor, and was remembered with grateful smiles for many days to come. The children of that household, thus abundantly supplied, never thought of being dependent or depressed. They felt, that their father had laid up for them a rich store in grateful hearts, and among the treasures which will never decay, and that their mother, who was considered in all that little neighborhood, a sort of presiding angel of good works, was continually adding to those stores. I can now remember just the appearance of that woman, who had a numerous household to clothe, as she said one day, how is it, that the widow can do more for me than any one else?

But I remember the sorrows, as well as the joys, and the labors of that loved widow, that dearest friend of my young heart. On the twenty-first of last December, about noon, the days of forty long years were just numbered and finished, since death came to that "mountain home," and took away that affectionate husband, that kindest of fathers. That dying scene in that retired "north room" of that little dwelling, I can never forget.

How mournful was the contrast between that clear mid-day sun and those sorrowing hearts, those bursting sighs, and those flowing tears. Those last faltering words, "My dear children—what shall I say to you, my children—God bless you, my children," have not yet died away on my ear. Then came the funeral, which gathered all that little neighborhood around that mourning circle. Gently was it whispered by one and another, "We have all lost a friend—the peacemaker is gone." How deep were those weeds of mourning shrouding that family. Even the plaintive tones of the little one, but just able to lisp her father's name, were oft and long repeated by kind hearted neighbors. Then came that first cold winter of widowhood. How mournfully did that cheerful fire blaze on the domestic hearth, as they gathered around that bereaved family altar. What child of that household could ever forget those extraordinary prayers of that sorrowing mother for the salvation of her fatherless children, as they were offered up day by day through all that long, cold winter? Before that mourning day came, the eldest, while yet a little girl, professed to love the God of her fathers. As the remaining six were gathered into the kingdom one by one, all before they had passed the years of their youth, that mother failed not to refer to her own agonizing prayers, during that first winter of her widowhood. But that mother is gone, and most of the seven are gone. Together they are gathered home to their peaceful rest. Only a remnant remains to talk of that sweet "mountain home," of that bereaving December, of that afflicted family altar, and of those never-to-be-forgotten prayers.

How sweet did I find it, once more to commune with the days of my childhood—once more to linger around the dearest scenes of that loved spot, long since laid up among the cherished jewels of memory's most sacred casket. There, at that "mountain home," growing on the perennial stalk of great principles, I thought I could see, even through a veil of forty years, the buddings of sentiments, of customs, and of habits, which, if spread over the country, and fanned by the gentle breezes of intelligence, of influence, and of Christian sympathy, might produce a rich and abundant harvest for the treasury of the Lord. In the vast work of converting the world to the aid of that great mass of the community, to whom wealth can never come, for there has not been wealth enough created, to suffice one in a hundred of all their number. O that simplicity, and taste, and intelligence, and influence, might all lend their aid in fitting them for their great work. In this vast field, a mighty tree of power, has struck deep its roots, and its rising and extending branches, are rapidly spreading over all the land. In watering its roots and in nourishing it in its growth, how momentous is the responsibility of every one, to whom God has given a controlling mind, a controlling heart, or a controlling position. In such a place, who does not tremble, as, in the encouragement of principles and customs, he beholds his own example, extending downward and upward, till it reaches the minutest fibres of the lowest roots, and the smallest twigs of the topmost boughs. Among the many thousand customs and fashions, which are introduced year by year, from which all may select, what Christian of piety, and of intelligent influence, cannot, and will not resist every one at variance with taste, with comfort, with propriety, and with Christian liberality? I would that the true spirit of gospel sympathy, and of gospel benevolence, as exhibited in the life and example of our blessed Redeemer, and as enjoined so frequently, and so tenderly on his followers, might be rocked in every cradle of maternal affection, and dandled on every knee of a father's love. I would that it might live in the smiles of the nursery, and find a place of controlling power around every family table, and around every family altar. I would that it might be the motto, and the reward, and the presiding genius in every school room in the land, and that it might be present in every domestic scene, and in every social circle. I would that it might form the silken cords of enduring friendship, and the strong bands, uniting the hearts, the hands, and the lives of neighbors, of communities, and of the whole nation.

CHAPTER VI

LABORS OF COVETOUSNESS CONTINUED— HIS SPEECH BEFORE A LITERARY ASSEMBLY—REPLY OF DISINTERESTED BENEVOLENCE

But in my journeys and travels, I continued to hear the sound of the footsteps, and to witness the labors of Covetousness. I met him at a great meeting, which he had long been expecting, and for which he had long been preparing. It was convened by special invitation in the most spacious hall in the country. Both sexes were there, though the proportion of females was very small. It was composed of those powers, which bear rule over the dominions of mind—of those spirits, whose business it is to commune with minds, and with hearts, instead of holding perpetual communings with dollars, and with cents, and with eating, and drinking, and putting on of apparel. Of this class, however, invitations were extended only to the professed friends of Missions. It was a great missionary meeting for the investigation of duty. Ministers of the gospel, officers and agents of our benevolent associations, professors in our colleges and theological seminaries, editors of our various periodical publications, and the makers of our books, composed a large part of the audience. Besides, there were many from the departments of law and medicine, and not a few of civilians of the day, and of the rulers over the land. Then there was a mixed class, who by some means, came to share in the reign over the vast realm of mind. Some of this class obtained this right by hereditary decent, some by personal merit, and some by the favor of friends. Last, but not least, was a great body of teachers of youth of both sexes. As might be expected, some of the wives of the gentlemen came in under the wing of their husbands, and occasionally a mother in Israel was admitted too, as she entered, leaning on the gentle arm of an affectionate son in the gospel. It was an august assembly, though not exactly splendid or magnificent. Our advocate had a written address for this occasion. He had laid out all his strength to meet the demands of his audience. His whole discourse was so learned, and his composition so beautifully finished, that I found it difficult to remember much of it, and I shall find it still more difficult to relate it. I shall only attempt to gather up a few of the leading thoughts, leaving behind all the learning, and all the beauties of style.

In a truly philosophic manner, he laid the foundation of his subject in a collection of facts. He was careful to adhere strictly to truth in all his statements; as the experience of those present would readily detect any error. In this part of his discourse, his grand object was to exhibit the vast indebtedness of the world to the members of his audience. The honored gentlemen present, whose office it was to rule over the dominions of mind, had sacrificed time, money, strength, ease, and all for the good of mankind, who often knew not, or cared not for all their self denying zeal, and for all their unwearied and unrequited labors. He could scarcely put his finger on a man of wealth, he said, in all that vast assembly; and yet who had power more than they, to monopolize wealth, if they were disposed so to do?

He gave a very just and accurate description of the minister's life, all illustrating the grand argument of his discourse, that the world was vastly indebted to the honored members of his audience. Just look, he said, at his limited salary, proverbial throughout the whole generous world. If possessions are found in his hands, every one knows, that they are of hereditary descent. And what are his labors, his toils, and his self-denying zeal in return? A minister, who expects others to know, or appreciate his labors and toils, cannot, he remarked, have been long in the field. Who knows or cares for that exhaustion of mind, which bids defiance to sleep, as he has just finished his second long sermon for the Sabbath? What man ever takes time to multiply the pastoral calls at his own house, by the number of families under the care of his beloved minister, that he may know how to meet him with a smile, inquiring how he could come so soon again, instead of reproving him for staying away so long? What man, that spends one or two long hours in his pastor's study, talking about anything, and every thing, but the matter in hand, thinks of inquiring how sermons could be written, if every man in the church should take the same liberty? Who thinks any sympathy due to his pastor for chaining his mind away from his sermon for a whole half day, to examine and recommend the teachers for the coming season? Who thinks of casting a compassionate look on his minister, as he sits in the chair of state, as the inspector and examiner of the school? He strives with untold effort to put on the cheerful smile, and to assume the sparkling eye, which the importance of the occasion demands. But who knows aught of that exhaustion, which is now weighing down his spirits, enough to forbid an animated look under the most powerful blaze of eloquence? What two men, who shall choose to enter into a quarrel, and bring it into the church, knows aught of the vast expenditure of settling it by a council, which shall consume the precious time of all the ministers in the region for a whole week? With such a life of toil, and with such a salary, who could ever expect that a clergyman would put his hand into his own purse to meet the calls of charity? But what was the fact? He could prove from unquestioned statistics, that for the last thirty years, no class of men had given as much for the cause of benevolence in proportion to their income, as had the ministers of the gospel. From all these facts, there was an inference, he said, of vast importance—an inference convincing in its power, just in its claims, and imperious in its demands. From this inference, he believed not one in the hearing of his voice, would be able to escape. But for this, he should refer his audience to another part of the discourse, where he should present the conclusion of the whole argument.

  He next drew a picture of the teacher's life. Many he allowed had entered this office from unworthy motives, and without suitable qualifications, who deserved not the name, or the place. But as none but *real* teachers had been invited to this meeting, his audience would understand how to make application of his remarks. He rejoiced, that so many noble souls were that day present, who had condescended to withstand the under-bidding of many an ignoramus, and to keep their stations, still honoring and blessing the world. He gave a true and graphic description of their toils, their labors, and their self denying zeal, and of the mere apology for a salary, which was sometimes offered them, and above all of their liberal hearts, and liberal hands in the cause of benevolence. The application as before, was reserved for another part of the discourse.

He next proceeded to various other departments in the wide dominions of power over mind, setting forth the value of their labors in behalf of an ungrateful world. Some of these stations, he was aware, had been entered from unworthy and lucrative motives, but he believed, that in such cases, the occupants usually found very soon, that they had quite mistaken their calling. He did not fear giving offence in this remark, as none of that description had been invited to this meeting. Still, he kept closely in the path of truth, and I never was more strongly impressed with the fact, that in every department, learning, influence, and power over mind, can be used to great advantage in the cause of benevolence.

He finished the first part of his subject, and then proceeded to the application and the conclusion. In this part of his address, he had but one leading thought, but this he so enlarged, applied and illustrated, that it occupied more than half his discourse. His grand inference was announced in the following words; "Justice and equality require, that the members of this assembly should now do less, inasmuch as they have ever done vastly more than their proportion." His great object was to discourage them from a continued and increasing course of self-denying action in the cause of benevolence, especially in the department of raising funds. They were called upon, he said, by all the facts, just adduced, to consider their doings, and to retrace their steps. Self respect, and the dignity of their station demanded this. Due regard to their own happiness, and to the happiness of their families required it. To what would that august body soon come, if they should go on, advancing in their unjust and unequal system of benevolence, as they had been doing for a few years past? To what a state of meanness too, would all the rest of the world be reduced, not having enough left them even to foster the spirit of generosity? How long would this honorable body be able to stand up before the world as wise men—as men worthy to bear rule over the dominions of mind? They would soon prove themselves to be among "the foolish things of the world," and among "the weak things of the world," and among "the base things of the world," and among "the things which are despised." They would soon prove themselves to be of all men the most foolish, and of all men "the most miserable." He considered it ridiculous indeed, that those men, who had already done much more than their proportion, should continue to do more and more, just as if they had not discernment enough, to know what belonged to themselves, and what belonged to others.

During all the first part of his discourse, there was the most profound attention. His statements, all true to life, met a ready response from his audience. The universal smile of approbation, passing over that vast assembly, often seemed like the waving leaves of a mighty forest. But on the first announcement of his grand inference, the scene was changed. Some still smiled with approbation, as his words still found a response in their hearts. Others smiled with contempt, and others with pity, while some sat in breathless agony, as if they were beholding the martyrdom of their dearest friends, for whom they had given their lives, and their all.

As he took his seat, a few beckoned a reply from their modest, but warm hearted friend, "Disinterested Benevolence," who was seated in a retired part of the hall. As he rose from his seat his unassuming manners, strongly reminded me of a distinguished friend of the missionary cause. In his appearance, he gave no certain proof, that he even belonged to the literary world, and yet there was nothing about him, which would render it improbable that he might be the most learned man in the country. He bore just those non-distinctive marks, which not unfrequently characterize men, whose expansion of mind, and largeness of heart, seem to carry them far above all other minds, and all other hearts. He commenced with a low voice, seeming to invite us to listen, but as he proceeded, it increased to a melodious fullness and sweetness, which must have charmed the ear, though it had delivered words in an unknown tongue.

He should detain the audience, he said, but a few moments. He had no set speech to make. He never assumed the attitude of an opponent. He could not wear that armor, any more than David could a coat of mail. He should not have risen on this occasion, and before this audience, except in behalf of a few of his warm, and most devoted friends, whose principles, and course of life had at least been called in question.

He disagreed, he said, with the last speaker, only on one point. But that one point was of infinite importance, lying at the very foundation of the gospel. The difference of opinion between us, he remarked, must rest on this simple question; Is the gospel a system of justice, of merit, and of reward? —or is it a system of mercy, and of grace? If the former, then may we begin to talk of going back, of standing still, of doing less, because we have done so much. But if the latter be true, if the gospel is really a system of grace, of favor to the guilty, of mercy to the undeserving, then there is no place to stand still, no place to return back. Freely we have received, freely we must give. How much shall we give? How much have we received? How freely shall we give? How freely have we received? Shall we give our richest treasures? We have received the richest treasure of the heavenly world, even the only begotten Son, who was in the bosom of the Father.

He objected, as he had said before, only to the *inference* of the discourse. He, was happy to admit, that it contained a collection of important and valuable facts. He could testify to all, which had been said on the vast indebtedness of the world to his respected audience. Nay more, there were those present, who had done far more than words could express. He had the honor of being their personal friend. He knew their history. He did not appeal to statistics, for statistics would not tell one half of the truth. If he should attempt to tell one half which he knew of them, his veracity would be called in question. He would, that modesty would allow him, but this once, to speak—that she would allow him, but this once, to present those dear friends to this audience by their names, and by their works. We should hear no more of being weary in well-doing—no more of going back—no more of standing still—no more of doing less, that others may do their part.

He could, if he might, point to a beloved brother in the gospel ministry, who had long been able uniformly to say, in heart and in life, "I will very gladly spend and be spent for you, though the more abundantly I love you, the less I be loved." He could point to another of kindred spirit. He had oftener listened with great interest to his urgent appeals, and to his imploring entreaties in behalf of the great enterprise for the world's conversion. All of his flock, from the oldest to the youngest, felt that he was a living epistle of all, for which he was striving in their behalf. He had often seen the spirit of praying to be excused, put to shame in his presence, and the voice of cavilling, compelled to be silent. To his beloved church, he had need only to say, "Those things, which ye have both learned, and received, and heard, and seen in *me*, do." He could point, he said, to a teacher, whose labors, and cares, and self-denying zeal, he should not attempt to relate, and in the division of whose salary, the part ever found for the treasury of the Lord, he should not undertake to specify. He could point, too, to an aged mother in Israel, under whose hospitable banner he had often sat with great delight. He had known what it was to be neglected, and despised, and to be trodden in the dust, and to be left wounded, and bleeding, and helpless. Then it was, that this dear friend of his heart came to his relief, and with her own hand, bound up his wounds, pouring in oil and wine, and then took him to her own house. He had been hungry, and she had given him meat, thirsty, and she had given him drink, a stranger, and she had taken him in, naked, and she had clothed him, sick and in prison, and she had visited him. He could point, also, to a younger friend, who was fast following in the same footsteps. Her husband, a minister of the gospel, and a dear friend of his, had, according to the practice of some wise men, committed to her care and discretion, the disposal of his salary, and all the family purse. He had been an eye witness, he said, of her stewardship. He had seen her intelligence and superior education, her refinement and taste, all put in requisition, in providing, on the one hand, for the comfort of her household, and on the other for the treasury of the Lord. This very morning, he beheld those grateful tears of tenderest affection, in return for a generous purse, brought forward for this occasion. Her husband then felt, that truly his confidence had not been misplaced, and that he had "obtained favor of the Lord."

But modesty, he said, would not allow him to proceed. But this morning's call on those dear friends—or those blessed spirits, he could never forget. He found them at their devotions. The fire was glowing on their missionary altar. They came from that altar to this meeting. They brought the missionary cause on their hearts, with all its present wants. They brought, too, all their personal responsibility, weighing down their spirits. He could now see them scattered through this vast assembly, as they were bowing their heads, beneath the oppressive load. One word like going back, like standing still, like being satisfied with present attainments in the missionary work, was like a barbed arrow to their bleeding hearts. He would not throw that barbed arrow. He would, that he might bind up those bleeding hearts. He would, that he might pour into them the oil of consolation. He would administer that sweetest cordial, encouragement to go on in their self-denying work. He would have them run the race, and gain the prize. He would have them fight the good fight, and finish their course, and obtain the crown. He would not stop them in their onward path. He would not stay them in their upward flight.

It had been said, that the members of his audience had done more than other men. That was indeed true. But well might those men, who were appointed to *rule* over the dominions of mind, become more able, and more willing, to spend and be spent in its service, than were other men. Well might those dear friends of his, labor more, and give more to save *souls* from death, than did any other individuals, for they knew more of its worth.

Well might they deny themselves more to extend the triumphs of the cross, for they could behold glories in the great work of redemption, which other eyes had never seen. Well might they do more to light up the lamp of hope in benighted minds than others could, for they knew more of that precious hope, which is like an anchor to the soul. Well might they labor more to lead the lost and perishing to the foot of the cross, for they knew more of the sweetness of pardoning mercy, and of the unspeakable preciousness of the dying love of Christ. He believed, that in the great and self-denying work of saving a lost and guilty world, it was emphatically true, that "unto every one that hath shall be given, and he shall have abundance, but from him that hath not, shall be taken away even that which he hath."

As I left this assembly, my heart was filled with gratitude, that so much of the savor of life was found in the pathway of human knowledge, and in the walks of science and literature. Here I have long seen a precious bud of promise, comforting the heart, sustaining the spirits, and encouraging hope in the darkest hour. I would, that the time might speedily be hastened, when the little leaven, which is scarcely yet visible to many eyes, may spread and increase, till the whole shall be leavened. I would, that the feeblest among them might become as David, and the house of David, as the angel of the Lord.

CHAPTER VII

LABORS OF COVETOUSNESS CONTINUED—HIS NEWSPAPER ARTICLE —HIS PERSONAL ADVICE TO FRIENDS

But the labors of Covetousness were not yet finished. I next met with a long newspaper article from his pen. He commenced by remarking, that he could not close his labors in behalf of this cause, without giving his decided testimony in favor of public, rather than of private and individual conscience—in favor of public, rather than of private and personal responsibility.

In his view, there would be vastly more dignity and magnificence in some great plan, which could be applied to the whole church, than in that personal and individual self denial and effort, by which Missions had hitherto been sustained. After travelling through the whole country, he was satisfied, that want of union was the grand obstacle to the success of Missions. Nothing could be done effectually, while the church was so divided about the mode of doing it. He brought forward a wise plan for meeting the whole case, and for reconciling all parties. It was to make out an exact estimate, and assign to each church member his exact proportion. There would be a difficulty in estimating the value of each man's property, and there would be great danger of equivocation, as was often the case in collecting the minister's salary. To meet this difficulty, and to save time and trouble, he proposed to make an estimate on individuals, without distinction of circumstances. It would be so small a sum for each, that it could be made out without difficulty. He entered into an exact calculation of the number of cents, that each must give, to raise the hundred thousand dollars now needed by the American Board of Missions. This could be done by every one. The poorest woman in the church, he said, could spin it out in a few days.

To make the system more sure and perfect in its operations, he would add one more feature. It was this. He would in some way clothe the church with power to collect this benevolent tax of her members. This could be done. The Mother Church had done it, and so could we.

It might take some time to introduce this system universally, but its benefits as a guide to conscience, could at once be realized. By its estimate, a man might know, when he had done his duty, and if others would not do their part, he could not be held responsible.

In favor of his plan, he brought forward the following arguments.

    1. It could be adapted to human nature. In matters of duty, he believed, that human nature must be consulted. We must take the world as we find it, and not as we

would make it. If we would bring men up to their duty, we must bring the standard of duty down to their views. He had no belief in an attempt to convert the world by the supernatural power of love to Christ, and self denial for his sake. He believed, that it must be done on the principles of human nature, just as the Church of Rome had made her conquests. His plan could be made to meet the claims of human nature. If the general standard of benevolence now adopted, was found to be too high for human nature, it could be reduced, and each department could regulate its operations by its means.

2. It would adapt itself to the peculiar views of the different classes of the community. Its claims on wealth would be so trifling, that it must satisfy that class. This was a great point gained. Nothing could be carried forward, without the example of the rich and honorable. He had always noticed, that men of wealth were very much pleased with that proof of the ability of the church, which was made out from the small average sum now given by each of her members. The good effects of such statements could be seen, not only in elevating the public conscience, but also in soothing the private conscience of the rich. In his own important plan, he must confess himself indebted to hints, drawn from such statements, (though the good men, the authors of those estimates, deserved no more credit for his inferences, than did the gospel deserve blame, for being made a savor of death unto death.) On the whole, his system must have the unfailing approbation of all in the ranks of wealth. As to the poorer classes, it would meet them on entirely another principle. These classes had always been ready to expend more than they could afford, to purchase an equality with the rich, and no doubt they would be ready to do it in this case.

3. It would promote "Systematic Charity." He could apply important principles with as much facility, as Satan could quote Scripture. This important principle, he would carry much farther, than any of its advocates would allow. By it, he would satisfy the conscience of every one,

who would give systematically, let the amount be ever so small.

4. It would remove anxiety and doubt. By the present system of raising funds, an insupportable load of suspense, of anxiety, and of fear, was laid on all the active and devoted friends of Missions. It was severely felt by the officers of the Board, and through them, by every sympathizing friend throughout the country. The constant excitement, which had been going on for a few years, relative to the funds of the American Board, could not be endured much longer. He was aware, that the laborers in Christ's vineyard had ever been obliged to bear just such a load of suspense, of fear, and of anxious doubt, often having no other resource but simple reliance on an unseen hand for support. Not an inch of ground had been gained, or kept, without constant struggle. Great effort and great self-denial to meet distressing emergencies in the kingdom of Christ, had seemed to be the principal business of followers of Jesus, from the great Apostle to the Gentiles, down to the self-denying friends of Modern Missions. But we could not continue to bear this burden. Better would it be, to return to the bosom of the Mother Church, and submit to her less oppressive yoke.

5. It would relieve from the self-denial of voluntary contributions. These constant calls from various benevolent objects were insupportable. He was aware, that some strict adherents to Bible phraseology, even now believed, that the followers of Christ must still take up the cross— must still come out of great tribulation—that if sympathy with Christ's sufferings did not now require them to give their bodies to be burned, it might, by the calls of Providence, require them to make the living sacrifice, of giving their goods to feed the souls of the perishing heathen. But he could not agree with such fanatics. With other learned men, he believed in a very liberal interpretation and application of the doctrines of the Bible, and above all, of its duties. Times of persecution, of tribulation, and of bearing the cross, must be confined to the days of the apostles and martyrs. They could not apply to this enlightened, this glori-

ous age of the world. The world must be converted, if ever, "on flowery beds of ease." The promised millennium of holiness and joy, was delightful indeed, but a millennium of *rest and ease*, had never yet been described in all its glory—not even in the Bible.

In concluding his newspaper article, he confessed, that his opinions had undergone some change. On a superficial view of this subject, he had considered it very important, that the present necessities of the Board should be met—that the deficiencies in the receipts should be made up, before the financial year should close. But on a more thorough investigation of the whole subject, he did not regard it as a matter of much consequence. Indeed, it might be seen hereafter, that God had a wise use to make of a failure. Perhaps the American Board had taken a higher standard than she could maintain. Perhaps she could not secure to herself, a more honorable retreat, than now, just to recall our missionaries, and use her scanty funds in paying their passage home, to disband those precious schools, and send the children back to Paganism, to give up those tender lambs to be devoured by the enemy, and to deliver up those souls, brought almost to the gate of heaven, to an eternity of hopeless despair.

These were his public addresses, and this the substance of his newspaper article. But the graces of this advocate of Missions shone most in the family circle. As a personal friend, he was most known, and best loved. He could instruct, and he could advise; he could comfort, and he could console. I saw him meet one of an inquiring spirit, seeking to know his whole duty in making an extra donation. I heard him whisper in his ear, "Be prudent, be discreet, give not too much at this time, lest there should be a reaction, or a falling off at another." I saw him meet another tender conscience, about deciding to send one hundred dollars as an extra offering to Missions. I heard him whisper a kind word in that man's ear, reminding him that others should do their proportion; and I beheld him smile with fiendish delight, as that hundred dollars was reduced down to five, the remaining ninety and five being assigned over to neighbors, who knew not, or cared not for this great emergency. I saw him meet a father, who had made his missionary donation equal to that of the last year, but whose conscience could not be satisfied without doing something more. Into his ear, I heard him whisper the comforting excuse, that he was educating his son. I witnessed the soothing power of his influence over the tender conscience of another father, as he reminded him, that he was educating his daughters.

I saw him meet another man of active, and engaging manners, and of enterprising spirit. He passed among his neighbors as a rich man, though his wealth lay more in paper and ink, and in lands, treasured up for future generations, than in valuable possessions. His troubled conscience was pleading for the treasury of the Lord. Into his ear, I heard him whisper a lesson of foresight in behalf of the cause of Missions. Many, he said, from the impulse of the moment, would take care for the present, but only here and there one, by forethought and far-reaching views, would look out for coming days. He advised him to withhold the needed relief from the destitute and the perishing, a few years longer, and then, from under his magic hand, his multiplied wealth might be poured into the treasury of the Lord in the richest profusion. I next saw him meet another man a little past the meridian of life, who had walked in the same path just recommended to the last. For many years he strove to become rich, that he might be the greatest missionary donor in the country. But that luxury he never found. In this thing, a retributive Providence had long since said concerning him, "Take from him the pound, and give it to him, that hath ten pounds." Into that man's ear, I heard him whisper a lesson of justice. He could not do any thing now, and be just to his creditors, especially as this was the only point, where he could retrench, without endangering the standing of his family.

Into one ear of warm hearted benevolence, I heard him whisper a word in behalf of the slave. His sympathy, however, in behalf of a brother in adversity, and in behalf of those choice spirits, who approach so near the great pattern of love, that they can "remember them that are in bonds, as bound with them," was not more sincere, than was the newly made friendship between Herod and Pilate. In the presence of such spirits, he ventured not a direct attack, and an open avowal of his sentiments. But he well understood the great and true maxim, that union is strength. He well knew, that a house divided against itself cannot stand. Among the few rare spirits, that were ready to give up themselves, and their all, for the conversion of the world, he would fain, for conscience sake, throw in some plausible occasion for strife, that if possible, he might "separate chief friends." Having done this, the way would be prepared for a bolder step, and a more successful assault. Into the other ear of warm hearted benevolence, I heard him whisper a word in behalf of Home Missions, revealing the wise thought, that after all, the first and most important work to be done, was to convert our own country, and then we should have money enough, and men enough too, to convert the world—not that he cared for Home Missions any more than Judas did for the poor, when he grudged the very anointing for the tomb of Him, whom he was about to betray. Think ye, that Christ could forget the poor, whom he came to bless? No sooner can the devoted friends of the American Board forget the precious cause of Home Missions.

These were his labors, and this his success in the single department of raising funds. But his favorite, and more glorious field of operation was that of furnishing men for the work. By his public speeches, any one would suppose, that all the world must at once go on a Mission; but, for the private conscience, he always found some very peculiar, some very urgent reason, why each should be excused. His powerful and eloquent addresses in our colleges, and theological seminaries, and academies, and his personal advice, and consoling words to one and another in our halls of science—his travels over the country, and his whisperings in the ear of a father, of a mother, of a brother, and of a sister, I have not time to relate. Neither does he need my feeble testimony to prove his success. The painful truth, admitted by the officers of the Board at the close of the last year, that scarcely five men stood pledged to its immediate service, speaks volumes on the power of his influence over the minds, the consciences, and the hearts of our young men.

As I here stopped a moment to reflect on my reverie, a suggestion was whispered in my ear, of writing a sketch of my travels, and of the labors of this Advocate for Missions, for the benefit of my friends. But why, I replied, should I be foolish enough to listen to such a suggestion, when a hundred able tongues, and a hundred able pens, have been lifting their warning voices against the power of "Mammon," and against the delusive wiles of "Covetousness, the Sin of the Church?" Besides, if the pen of a ready writer should, but this once, be given me, that I might describe things as they are, and delineate in true characters, the footsteps of Covetousness, which lead immortal souls down to the chambers of death, what would it avail? Who would listen to my words of urgent necessity, of anxious entreaty, and imploring love? Some of my friends might see their own face in the glass, and smile at the sight. Others might see that of a neighbor, and be amused at the resemblance. Together they might commend the truth of the similitude, and praise the skillfulness of the performance, and so much the more, as it came from the hand of a friend, whom they loved. But possibly one might be found, who silently and thoughtfully would consider the subject, and make solemn and faithful self-application. Possibly one might be led to renewed diligence in turning away from the delusive charms of the enemy, to follow the footsteps of wisdom, of mercy, and of infinite love. If so, I should feel myself repaid a thousand fold for my feeble endeavors, and for my seeming presumption.

CHAPTER VIII

POWER OF PERSONAL RESPONSIBILITY IN BEHALF OF MISSIONS —CASES OF SELF-DENYING BENEVOLENCE

I turned away from the footsteps of Covetousness to mingle in other, and far different scenes. A brighter vision came over my waking dream. I heard a voice, saying, "Who is this uncircumcised Philistine, that he should defy the armies of the living God?" "Fear not." "I have reserved to me seven thousand, that have not bowed the knee to Baal." To them, it shall now be given to know of the fellowship of Christ's sufferings. To them shall be given the honor, and the reward of a victory in behalf of Missions. Mine eyes were then opened, and I beheld here and there a stripling David, clad in the armor of Personal Responsibility, with sling in hand, and a pebble from the brook, running to meet the enemy. The precious number was few indeed, but they were scattered throughout the land, from Maine to Georgia, and from the Atlantic to the Pacific. They were found about equally in the city, and in the country, among the high and the low, among the rich and the poor, among the learned and the unlearned, among ministers and their people. They felt, that the deficiencies in the receipts of the American Board must be made up in some way, before the financial year should close in July. They felt, that the honor of God was concerned in this event. They could not calmly see the enemy triumph. They could not thus encourage him to come again and again, till he should take the whole ground, and rejoice in his victory. They could not think of that chapter in our future history, which should record the missionary decline—the missionary failure of 1843. They could not send forth the herald, which should tell it in Gath, and publish it in Askelon, and to all the enemies of God throughout the world. They could not see the cruel hand of retrenchment again laid on the very vitals of all our missionary stations. They could not again look on the tragic scenes of 1837. Each felt, that he had more to do with his own conscience than with that of any other one—more to do with his own duty, than with that of the church. Each felt, for himself, that there was no neutral ground in this matter. In his own case, to stand still, would be to lift the fatal dagger—not to do, would be to strike the deadly blow. Together they lifted up their voices and cried, Who of us can begin this dreadful work? Which of us can say to that right hand of the missionary heart, Write thou again the fatal deed, though thy fingers should cleave to their pen, and though thy blood should cease to flow in its veins. Who of us can unsheath the sword, and bathe it again in those bleeding wounds, not yet half healed from the last deadly stroke? Which of us can let down the pall of mourning on all our missionary stations, and on all the friends of Missions throughout the whole world? Not one of us. Each one cried for himself, Let not this deed be found in my hand—let not the blood be found in my garments. Sooner "let my right hand forget her cunning,"—sooner "let my tongue cleave to the roof of my mouth." Rather let me bestow my all—my most valued possessions—my last and best earthly treasure. Nay more, sooner would I give up my own life—sooner would I bow mine own head to the fatal stroke. Together they cried to the God of heaven, and prayed, that he would lift his holy arm, and make all the earth know, that there was a God in Israel, and that he reigned in the hearts of his American Zion.

There are times when philosophy is too slow for the occasion. Look at yonder building enveloped in flames. See that helpless widow and group of little children, just awakened from sleep, crying in agony at the window. The flames are making rapid strides. A few moments more, and it will be too late. Can the heart of that young man, determined on their rescue, wait for the actings of philosophy? Can he stay to divide out with exactness the danger, and the loss of the undertaking, between himself and his more phlegmatic neighbor? Can he wait to inquire, whether or not, he shall be ready, or able, or willing to do the like deed tomorrow? No. He leaps from the ground. He flies to their relief, and almost in the twinkling of an eye, he delivers one after another, till the last is safe in its mother's arms. So the occasion now seemed to these rare spirits. Each seemed to feel for himself, that there was no time to be lost. They had no time to calculate, no time to speculate. They had no time to censure the church, or to weep over her apathy. They were kindred spirits, indeed, but they had no time to sympathize, no time to unite. Each stood by himself alone in the strength of his God. They could not wait to inquire what others ought to do, or what others would do. Each seemed to take it for granted, that his neighbor would not do much, and that he must do the more. All their numerical calculations were by the rule of inverse proportion. Each did what his hands found to do with his might. More he could not have done, if the whole had rested on him.

We had now just entered on June. During this month, I witnessed many a social, and many a domestic scene of melting tenderness. I saw a devoted and faithful pastor of a little flock among the hills of New England. The neat but simple style of his house plainly showed, that he was not rich in the things of this world. But he was rich in faith and good works. I beheld that pastor with a burdened heart, reading that Circular from his pulpit on the Sabbath. He anticipated no warm response from his church as a body, but with anxious look, he followed every tearful eye, and every thoughtful face. I saw him go out on Monday with a downcast look, and with a trembling step, that he might find access to the house, and to the heart of a kindred soul. He found his friend, who was a friend indeed, and he addressed him in words like these. I thought that I had done all I could, this year, considering my peculiar circumstances, but since reading that Circular, my conscience has not been at rest. My dear wife and myself have been considering this subject a whole month. Last Saturday we came to the conclusion, that we must do something more. I shall send to Boston this week, and I have come to invite you to join me. I saw him go on a similar errand to a second, and a third, and I witnessed the over-flowings of his grateful heart, as he made out a purse of a few hundred dollars for the relief of the Board. Again, I saw a good deacon, asking of his minister the loan of that Circular a few days, that he might read it to his wife, and his sons, and his daughters, and to one or two neighbors, of kindred spirit; and the reading of it was not in vain. I saw, too, an aged mother in Zion reading that same appeal to two or three sisters in that praying circle, with whom she had been waiting thirty years for the consolation of Israel, and I witnessed her tears of grateful joy, as their little bounty was on its way as a messenger of mercy.

At another time, I saw a father and his two sons, with deep thought, looking each other in the face, till they mutually broke the silence, each revealing the same decision on the questions, which they had unitedly agreed to take into solemn and prayerful consideration. The propositions were the following; that the father should abandon the prospect of that addition to his little farm, which had long been with him a favorite object, that the eldest son should give up that improvement in the shop, which he so much needed, and that the youngest son should relinquish the long anticipated extension of his merchandize, which he had but just this season found himself able to meet. This subject had cost each a severe struggle. Such a course must alter all their plans for several years. The father had yet all his younger children to educate, and the sons had each a rising family to sustain. Besides there were circumstances, relating to their family connexions, of a very peculiar nature, which could not be told, and which none but themselves could know, but which were liable to make large demands on their purses. Not a neighbor of theirs, not a member of that church, could know aught of the amount of sacrifice, that such a step would cost that father and his two sons. But the struggle was now over. The decision was made. They were of the same mind. The sacrifice was brought in their hearts, and laid on the altar. They went about raising the money, and soon their united sum of a few hundred dollars was made out for the missionary cause. They committed the precious treasure to the hands of a safe messenger, and then they knelt down, and prayed together, and wept together, and thanked God together, and rejoiced, that they were accounted worthy to suffer for the cause of Christ.

Again I saw a family assembled at evening around the domestic altar. It was the appointed time for each to decide what sacrifices he would make for the cause. It was a solemn time—it was a tender scene. The thoughts of all were there revealed—the tears of all flowed together—the hearts of all mingled in sweetest sympathy. The united head of that household would not allow an opportunity like that furnished by the present state of the Board, to pass unimproved. The father stood pledged to convert all their offerings into ready money—whether they should be the labor of their hands, or their most valued treasures—whether they should be real possessions, or those of anticipation to meet the wants of the season. It was Saturday night, and what a week had they passed. Never was ingenuity more active than in those young hearts. Invention ever new, and ever busy, passed from one to another, prompted indeed sometimes by a gentle hint from the mother, and carried along by the sweet smiles of the father, as day by day they assembled around the family table. On Saturday, how slowly did the hours pass away. How often were the same inquiries, repeated and returned—how much do you think we shall make out? How much do you think father will give? How much do you think mother will give? But twilight came, and the lamps were lighted, and they met in that consecrated room—in that family Bethel. Each one spoke in his turn, from the eldest son, who had just been admitted as a partner with his father, to the youngest, who sat by his mother's side. The paper was before them. It was headed by the generous united donation of the father, and his partner son. Next came that of the mother, but it was not so far below, as might have been expected, for her husband had trained her to the work. He would even contend, that the wife ought to give a liberal example to her daughters, especially as the law allowed her one third, and as she must share a full third of the skill, the economy, and the self denial of keeping the family in a state for liberal giving. Then came the individual donations of four smiling daughters, the eldest, or youngest of whom, no one could have guessed. Next followed the united offering of two twin sisters, who were like one soul in two bodies, and never could be separated in any of their doings; and last of all, that of the little cherub-faced boy, the darling of the whole family. The sums were all added together, and the estimate laid on the table. Then they knelt around the family altar. What a prayer for Missions was that! What a cloud of incense ascended from those grateful hearts.

But the work was not yet done. The father and his partner son, must now raise all that sum of money. This was no small effort for those careful spirits. This was no small part of the self denial of this undertaking. But zeal and necessity will accomplish much. A part was raised by converting goods into money—a part was borrowed of a good old uncle, who was liable to have a few hundred dollars on hand—the remainder was taken up at the bank. When their offering was fairly on its way, think ye that they would have recalled it? As soon would we recall a loved friend, just safely landed in heaven. Who in that family can ever forget that week?—can ever forget that evening?—can ever forget that prayer? Think ye that the father and mother of that household would regard another special call from Missions as any calamity?

But the precious treasures were not all counted up by the hundred. The history of many a little purse—some of a few dollars, and some of a few cents only, would have power to draw tears from eyes, which seldom weep. The precious spirits of that day, and of that occasion, did not think it below their dignity to stoop to the latchet of a shoe, or to the falling of a sparrow. They thought it no condescension to commune with that spirit, which could take a piece of money from the mouth of a fish—with that Spirit, which on the approach of a cold winter, could take care about a cloak, to shield "Paul the aged" from the chilling damps of a Roman prison. I saw many a sudden little thought of mercy, which appeared like a precious gem, bursting forth from the solid rock. Once I heard an affectionate and devoted wife, waking her husband, while it was yet dark, that she might reveal her midnight plan of repairing her old carpet, that the money for the new one might be given to the cause. Again I saw a stripling youth, just entered on his college course, pleading with his mother to repair his old coat, that the money for the new coat might be added to the little sum just received of his father, as the result of a sudden thought of his, that he *could* substitute pedestrian excursions for rides during his vacations of the coming year. I beheld too, a beautiful daughter, not yet entered on her teens—an only child, and her mother in heaven—running with a throbbing heart to her widowed father, and asking that she might repair her old bonnet for the season, and send the money for the new bonnet to Ceylon, that it might save one little girl from the anguish of being torn away from her beloved school, and her new missionary home. And I saw the fountains of that father's heart stirred as never before. With what eyes of surpassing tenderness, did he look on that dearest image of her departed mother, as his flowing tears gave a silent consent. I saw that father too add a postscript to the letter, which was to bear away her little bounty. It was as follows;

"To the Treasurer of the American Board of Commissioners for Foreign Missions,

Sir,—In addition to what I sent you last week, please to place one hundred dollars more to my account. You shall receive the money safely before the close of July."

The work was carried forward with great haste, for "the thing was done suddenly." And such efforts to convert goods, and notes of hand into ready money, I never before witnessed. And such charges of despatch, as were given to the messenger of each one's bounty, I never before heard. I looked too, into the houses and hearts of those kindred souls; and I felt that even in this life, they had received a hundred fold. Every house seemed like the house of Obed Edom, which God blessed, because the ark of God was there.

CHAPTER IX
REVERSED SCENE AT THE MISSIONARY HOUSE—ANNUAL MEETING AT ROCHESTER—APPLICATION OF PERSONAL RESPONSIBILITY

But I hastened away to the treasure house in the temple of the Lord in the city of our solemnities, that I might know the sum of the whole matter. There I beheld longing eyes, such as were seen in Jacob's tent, stretching forth towards the land of Egypt, in quest of her long delayed, and long expected bread. There I witnessed too, those tears of gratitude, embalming each little parcel, as they came in one by one. And there I beheld all that pile of letters, written as in characters of blood, all signed and sealed. I saw the ships too, lying in the harbor, appointed to carry the fatal mandate to all our missionary stations. There I beheld those adverse winds and waves, angels of mercy, as they were commissioned by Heaven, to keep back those vessels in our ports, till the needed relief should come. And I heard the voice of Justice, crying, Stay thine hand, spare the stroke. The will of the people must be done. The voice of the church must be obeyed. At this voice, the sad decree was passed. At her voice; let it now be repealed. And I saw all that pile of letters recalled, and committed to the flames, ere one had left our shores. It was like the reversing of those "letters, written in the name of Ahasuerus, and sealed with the king's ring."

But the time for the next great annual festival drew near, and I hastened to the spot, that I might there witness the overflowings of joyful sympathy in behalf of Missions. It was a solemn place. Silence reigned—tears flowed—every heart was filled with humble gratitude. It was like that day of the month Adar in Shushan the palace, "which was turned from sorrow to joy, and from mourning to a good day." To those kindred spirits, that had "mourned in Zion, was now given, beauty for ashes, the oil of joy, and the garment of praise for the spirit of heaviness." As they gathered around the table of their blessed Redeemer, all lifted up their voices together, and cried, "Not unto us, not unto us, but unto thy name be all the glory." "What are we, and what is our people, that we should be able to offer so willingly after this sort?"

But I awoke from my pleasing reverie, and I felt the solemn truth, that the work was yet to be done—that the battle was yet to be fought—that the victory was yet to be gained. And I heard a voice saying, "Who is on the Lord's side?" Who will take his life in his hand, and rush in between the living and the dead? And I heard one and another cry, "Here am I, Lord, send me." Lord, teach me thy ways, show me the right path, that my willing feet may run therein. Then I heard the footsteps of Wisdom, sweet messenger of heaven. She cried without, she uttered her voice in the streets, she cried in the chief place of concourse, in the opening of the gates, in the city, she uttered her words, saying, "Unto you O men I call, and my voice is to the sons of men." To each inquiring soul, I heard her say, Come hearken unto me, and "I will lead thee in right paths. Attend to my sayings, and keep them in the midst of thine heart. Then shalt thou understand righteousness, and judgment, and equity; yea, and every good path." And she uttered a lesson of Personal Responsibility, and these were her words. Let each one look to his own work. "It is nothing with God to help, whether with many, or with them that have no power." But his blessing is delayed, so as to be given as a rich reward to the willing and obedient heart. Is the spirit of any one stirred within him in behalf of this cause, let him be faithful in his own place, and in his own way, and for himself alone. Let him carry his own petition, warm from his own heart, to the throne of mercy, rather than to seek for a friend to carry it in his behalf, and it shall prevail. Let him give *all—all* that he ought— either from his abundance, or from his scanty store, rather than to look to his neighbor to do it in his stead, and the deed shall be remembered in heaven, and his work shall not be in vain. Is he poor, let him be careful to give the last mite, which the Lord requires at his hand. That little pittance, which he has laid aside, which he really seems to need for his comfort, and on which his eye is now fixed with that anxious inquiry, may be more in the Lord's treasury than thousands in other hands. It may be of more weight in the counsels of Heaven, as this great question, relative to the funds of the American Board, shall there be settled. Is he rich, let him give—not a part—but all which the Lord requires. Though he may cast his thousands into the treasury of the Lord, it may weigh nought in the counsels of Heaven, if anything is kept back. But let him come fully up to his ability, let him come fully up to the urgency of the case, and he shall receive even a richer reward, than did the widow with her two mites. No one knows to whom, in this case, it shall be said, "Thou hast power with God, and with men, and hast prevailed." No one knows to whom the balancing power may be given, which shall determine this great question in the court of heaven. The balancing power was given to Achan, and with his wedge of gold, he could trouble the whole camp of Israel. The deciding power was given to Phineas, and with javelin in hand, he was able by a single act, to stay the plague, and save thousands from a speedy death. Let no one say, therefore, that the little which he can do, will have no avail. When God, in the court of heaven, shall weigh the offerings, which shall decide this great question, he may say, "This poor widow hath cast in more than they all." On the other hand, let no one, feel, that he can afford to consume treasures on himself, because he has already done so much for the cause. The little, that remains in his hand, which he can give, and which the Lord requires of him, may be the balancing power, which shall decide the whole case. But let each, in his own condition, be faithful unto the last iota, and he shall have his reward. With his faithful hands, and willing heart, and obedient spirit, and through that grace, by which he is what he is, let him go in the name of Jesus, and carry his petition to the mercy seat, and it shall be granted. Is his petition, that the hearts of others may be opened to go and do likewise? Then the hearts of others shall be opened, and they shall go and do likewise, and the work shall be done. "He that goeth forth and weepeth, bearing precious seed, shall doubtless come again rejoicing, bringing his sheaves with him."

These were the words uttered by the voice of wisdom, and as she ceased, my thoughts returned to my own bosom. A view of my own individual responsibility rested on me with an indescribable weight. I felt that my duty in my own little sphere, and with my own feeble ability, was more to me in the sight of God, than the duty of all the world besides. Could I throw my influence over the whole country, and bring thousands into the treasury of the Lord, it might not be so important a duty for me, as to give from my own little purse, that last farthing, which God requires. Could I make my voice heard from one end of the land to the other, and so plead in behalf of the perishing heathen, that all our missionary concerts should be filled with hearts bowing together in the presence of God, it might not be so important a duty for me, as to carry my own feeble petition myself to the throne of mercy, and there in the name of our blessed Redeemer, plead the promises with an earnestness, which cannot be denied. While I mused on these things, my heart seemed ready to sink under its load, and I fled away to the cross of Christ, that there my weak and fainting spirit might find support, comfort, and guidance. There I looked up, and cried, My dear Redeemer, make me "to know the fellowship of thy sufferings; make me conformable unto thy death." There, under the banner of the Saviour's dying love, I felt it to be the most precious privilege in the universe, to deny myself, to take up my cross, and to follow the Lamb whithersoever he goeth.

In view of this reverie, I can only say, I "have believed, and therefore have I spoken." I have written, because my heart was so full, that I could but write. Whether this feeble development of my own feelings, will ever find its way to any other heart, and whether it shall ever be permitted to touch a chord in any other soul, which shall vibrate to personal responsibility, and self-application, the Lord only knows; but that is enough. Let the will of the Lord be done concerning this little, feeble "missionary offering." If it shall seem good in his sight, to bless it to the cause of Him, who remembers a cup of cold water, let the praise all be rendered to the riches of his condescending love. But if it shall seem good in his sight, to lay it aside, and bury it in oblivion, and to supply its place from the rich stores of his providence, so let it be. Our only desire is, that hearts may be opened, and that hands may be opened, and that lives may be devoted to the salvation of men, to the service of Christ, and to the glory of God. Our only prayer is, that immortal souls, just ready to perish, may be saved from the horrors of the second death, before it shall be forever too late; and that our blessed Redeemer, who gave his life for us all, may enter into the full possession of that joy, which was set before him, for which he endured the cross, despising the shame—that he may see of the travail of his soul and be satisfied—that "the heathen may be given to him for his inheritance, and the uttermost parts of the earth for his possession."

IV

DETACHED SAYINGS AND WRITINGS

1

Behold How Great

1821

'Small sands, the mountains; moments make the years;
And trifles, life."

Proper conduct is generally considered of great importance. And no one, having attended to the subject, will believe that point easily gained. But do not some suppose, that the importance and difficulty of proper conduct, belong principally to the great—to those in the higher walks of life. Have we then, who fill the humble path of obscurity, whose lives no splendid acts will crown, whose names will never be known beyond the little circle of our chosen friends—have we, whose lives are made up of apparent trifles, nothing to do with conduct; or rather is our conduct all nonessential? If so, then in vain have I chosen this for my theme of meditation.

But have we not reason to believe otherwise? Judas betrayed the Lord of glory with a kiss; and David's sling, used in apparently playlike amusement, decided the fate of a kingdom. Who can tell the important events, which may depend on the most trifling act, even though at the time, we think nothing about consequences?

While the poor publican was directing his trembling steps to that place, where he offered up his feeble, humble petition; so intent upon himself and his guilt, and upon the holy character and law of God, that crowds might have passed him unperceived; little did he think, this act would be recorded in the sacred page, and there made an instrument of building up the kingdom of that God he had so deeply offended.

While the poor widow, with her heart raised in silent devotion, was pressing her way through the mixed multitude, that the treasury of the Son might receive her consecrated mite, little did she think, that this obscure deed would be so much commended by Him, "who went about doing good;" and ever to the end of time, would be related as a specimen of pure and exalted benevolence.

But, though no pen of an inspired recorder will hereafter add dignity to our conduct, and perhaps the minute consequences may not be singled out from the general whole by the finger of Providence, yet is it unimportant? The ocean is composed of drops; all created matter of particles, and the world, of apparent trifles.

In the intellectual firmament, truly here and there a Locke and a Newton have shone with resplendent beams; but have not many lesser lights cast the sum of their rays on this once dreary path? Have not many events, trifling in themselves, contributed to produce the wonderful revolution, here presented by the historic page? —events, known only to Him, "who telleth the number of the stars" and "calleth them by their names"; to Him, with whom one day is as a thousand years; and a thousand years, as one day.

Who of us, at the great day of accounts, shall be assured by Him, who notices the falling of a sparrow, and "numbers the very hairs of our head," that we have been faithful in the few things committed to our care?

2

Benevolence

1821

This is a virtue of celestial origin. It is a fundamental attribute in the character of Jehovah. He is the source of the heaven-born principle.

Here, in this cold, unfriendly soil, scarcely has this heavenly plant begun to bud. Briers and thorns impede the growth, and noxious weeds entwine around the very root.

But one perfect example have we witnessed on earth, and, then, he, who deigned to plant it here, soon bore it to its native home, and left the world in tears. But he left a promise; sufficient to dispel each despairing thought; a promise more valuable than all the wealth of India, or than worlds heaped on worlds. Though clouds of darkness now hover around us, though self-love now extends its empire from sea to sea, from continent to continent, the earth shall not always wear this gloomy aspect. Soon shall the "Prince of Peace" return and establish "a kingdom, which shall never be destroyed." Then the whole earth shall become a paradise, a genial soil for pure benevolence.

But human means are the ordained instruments, to bring about this great design. Does not each act, each word, and each thought, serve to roll on that happy day; or, on the contrary, to protract the gloomy period, which must yet intervene? Benevolence is the grand instrument in this great work; and this work should be the ultimate object of all benevolent designs and operations. Here is a pursuit, in which all are bound to unite. Each has his sphere of influence; each his sphere of ability; even the widow, the fatherless, and the orphan, are not excluded. Let none say, my path of life is humble. Must he, who is unable to influence the king on his throne, relieve the sorrow of a princely palace, or diffuse happiness around the court of nobles, despair of activity? No; the widow's mite is not forgotten. Can we enter the humble cot of poverty, there pour consolation into the bosom of the wretched; there embrace the helpless, prattling infant, guide his tender years and teach him to lisp forth the Redeemer's praise, and trace the truth of the sacred oracles, let us be thankful for such a privilege. Can we diffuse one ray of light to the degraded African, to mitigate his woe, and check that horrid darkness, which hovers over that hapless land, a "darkness, which can be felt," which swallows up all natural, moral and intellectual excellence, let us seek no higher honor.

What command is more evaded than this, "Love thy neighbor as thyself"? When motives and arguments press with the might of a torrent, each repels them with double force, while ingenuity is racked to form an excuse. "One" must go "to his farm; another, to his merchandize"; another is fettered by the chains of poverty; and the favorite maxim of a fourth is, "Charity begins at home."

Are any willing to relinquish the dearest personal enjoyments, part forever with a beloved native home, a christian, and a civilized land, encounter the boisterous deep, and endure the sufferings of a distant, barbarous clime, to carry the gospel to a heathen world. Enthusiasm will be almost indelibly stamped on the name of such. But, let wealth raise her flattering standard, and how many will enlist under her banners. The stormy ocean then becomes a calm; the trackless desert, a fruitful field; and Afric's wilds, a genial soil.

Let each examine his excuse, before he presumes to offer it to the "God of Heaven." Let all rise with new activity; and "work while the day lasts." May duty become a delight, and our hearts rise in gratitude to Him, who deigns to accept our humble efforts for promoting his cause.

3

One Beautiful Evening

1821

One beautiful evening, I walked out for meditation. The state of my mind, assisted by the nature of the range, through which I chanced to wander, prompted a gloomy train of reflection. I began to regret, that so little happiness is destined for man, —and indulge a great desire to know the cause.

Wherever recollection wandered, unhappiness seemed painted on every brow. My own heart, at the same time, evincing that no outward visage can fully describe the feelings of [the] soul.

To behold man, the only being in the universe capable of happiness, confined in the gloomy caverns of discontent, to a reflecting mind is very melancholy. What is the cause? who the author? and what the source? At one moment I was ready to father it on Deity, at another to conclude it must spring from man's own bosom, and again to class it with those hidden truths, which, as yet, lie buried in impenetrable darkness, far beyond the reach of the human intellect. All was anxiety to know the reason of this unhappiness. My eager curiosity seemed unwilling to be denied. Lost in thought, almost inadvertently I strayed far from my native cottage; but, loth to return still I bent my steps forward toward a scene far different from the preceding rugged forest through which I had been roving. With hasty steps, thither I proceeded, where, a multiplicity of objects presented, inviting my attention and curiosity, of which I shall relate a few sketches.

Here was a vale enriched and ornamented, by nature and art, by beauty, magnificence, and splendor. This was the vale of real life. Here was a superb idol seated on a lofty magnificent throne, before whom all the nations of the earth seemed to bow. Thousands were daily paying their adoration to this mighty god, and nothing could excel the sincerity of their devotion. Ambition to please this universal monarch, pervaded every soul, filled every bosom, prompted every act, and swayed the sceptre of the whole human family. The utmost exertion prevailed in every quarter, because all imagined, that to him who could present the most pleasing offering, would redound the most exalted happiness. But, notwithstanding, this undue respect, instead of increasing their happiness, tended to extinguish the very last rays, still their alliance was unbroken; their piety was genuine and incessant, and nothing could abate the ardor of their love. Their loyalty was bound by chains of iron, which nothing seemed able to sever. Never did adoration exceed this. No sacrifice was too great; no incense too costly. In their view, the interest of the whole human family sunk to nothing. Yes; and, were it in their power, gladly would they have hurled the God of heaven from his throne, to gratify the insatiate appetite of this haughty god. Various were their modes of worship, and various their offerings.

The first, a young lady, presented beauty, vainly imagining that the most acceptable offering. She appeared perfectly beautiful, nature had laid true foundation for elegance of form, and art had added her every ornament. But, alas! this was all her excellence. She was the only child of fond indulgent parents, who were then mourning in silence the conduct of their darling. Vanity filled her bosom. Each anxious thought pursued beauty with unwearied steps. Her parent's love was returned with neglect and cruelty. Unrelentingly could she have torn from her wretched parents, their last morsel of sustenance, to furnish some trinkling ornament. This, to gratify this haughty idol. O deluded worship! Next came an epicurean, dissolved in luxury, apparently past the meridian of life. His offering, pleasure, had been years in preparing, while it had buried in grief his loving, but disconsolate parents, and finally locked them, in the silent tomb; but, loth to stop here, this apparently gentle adder next thrusts his cruel sting into the bosom of his own wretched family, casting a hopeless wife, with her tender babes on a friendless world, helpless and forlorn. Then were presented wealth, honor, knowledge, wit, and prejudice, with many others too numerous to be related. Pity cannot restrain the votary of wealth, he reduces thousands to penury and want, and wrests bread from the hungry. No difficulty can retard his progress. He plunges himself into the bowels of the earth, traverses the trackless ocean, and pierces even to hapless Afric's shores, and sultry India's climes. Honor fell not beneath in his exertions. His sword had deluged the earth in blood. Thousands had fallen a victim to his rage. He had plunged whole nations into the gulf of misery and destruction. Many a promising genius had fallen a sacrifice to wit. When indulged and cultivated, it saps the mental powers and cuts short the intellectual progress. In short, to detail and describe their numerous ceremonies, their various modes of worship, the number, variety, and nature of their offerings, the manner in which they were procured, and the consequences, and evils, resulting there from would fill pages. But, —stop. A figure very different arrests my attention. She is of angelic form. Her name is revelation. She thus addresses these deluded worshippers. "You are all seeking happiness, but you seek it not in the right path. While you thus go on, not a ray of that heaven born light, will pierce your benighted souls. Forsake this idol worship; worship only the God of heaven, and happiness will come. Then peace and joy will possess each corner of your souls." And then turning to me, she replied, this, idol worship is the cause of that unhappiness, which has of late so much engaged your thoughts. Look at the foundation and you will behold the name. Instantly obeying I beheld written in indelible characters, "Self in Disguise."

4

The Bible

1821

This is a book superior to all others. Here are subjects the most important and interesting—subjects, worthy the noble nature of man—subjects, worthy of angels, and even of God himself. Here is a volume replete with instruction. Here each line swells with import, and from each sentence, might volumes be drawn.

And where else shall we find such a style? Where such striking language? Where shall we find a Homer or a Virgil, that can compare with the seraphic pencil of David and Isaiah?

Without the Bible, probably the general laws of nature might be known; and perhaps even Newton might have erected his fabric; but all would be comparatively a body without a soul. But with this guide, while travelling among the stars, we behold them first emerging from their original chaos; we behold the sun mounting his majestic throne; and the almighty finger meting out and wheeling the planets, in their respective orbs. Then we descend to the earth, and there behold order rising out of confusion. We traverse from pole to pole, witness the first limits of the sea, and first appearance of dry land. We behold this globe carpeted with green, and in every element, life starting into being.

New light the cheerer of creation, is spoken into life. And now wisdom, beaming from the noble council of the eternal Three, calls man into existence.

With this light, we behold Jehovah riding upon the stormy wind, and managing the seas. Ten thousand wheels are whirled on their axes by his continued touch. Are we anxious to know the character of the great first Cause, and the duty of man? Here then we may, enjoy meridian light, which can be but feebly reflected by the dim face of nature. Here alone is delineated the great, the gloomy, and the awfully interesting cause of the rivers of blood, which have drenched the earth, and of the wretched scenes, which have enveloped the world.

But here is still a subject, more noble, more wonderful and more interesting—a subject, before which creation sinks to nothing; infinitude of stars and worlds on worlds bow their heads. Angels halt amazed! man stands astonished! all nature starts from her seat! and none but the eternal God remains unmoved. This is no other than the redemption of man.

With the Bible, either by the historic or more noble prophetic page, we may trace time from her first dawn, down to the closing scene. Here we are introduced to the society of patriarchs, prophets and apostles. We ascend the awful mount with faithful Abraham; we drop a tear with weeping Joseph; we bow the knee with holy David; and mount the wing with enraptured Isaiah. We even dare enter the blood-stained Gethsemane, and climb the steep of rugged Calvary. We hasten down through the lapse of ages, hail the Millenial morn, and embrace her meridian glory. We finally witness the concluding scene; behold the earth wrapt in flames, the sleeping dead bursting their tombs, and the Judge descending in the chariots of heaven. The heartrending lamentations of the wicked, pierce our souls, as they are hurled into the horrid gulf. The songs of the righteous salute our ears, as they rise in the air, and attend their Savior to the realms of bliss.

5

Motives for Engaging in Teaching

(Date Unknown)

Motives which may induce young ladies to hire money, make extraordinary efforts to improve their education.

    1.   The prospect of doing more good through life may be a most powerful motive. This, if sufficiently strong, clear and well defined in the mind, may of itself justify the greatest effort and even those, which under other circumstances would merit the imputation of imprudence. When the desire to do the greatest possible good becomes firm and unshaken, I know not what may not be attempted. But this desire must be firmly fixed, or the career of doing good, will end in selfishness under the cloak of benevolence. But I do believe there is such a thing as knowing our own hearts, and becoming unalterably fixed in our purpose, and in the strength of going forward till the day of our death unchangeable in our pursuits. To such I would say, Go forward, attempt great things, accomplish great things.

    2.   The anticipated pleasure of an elevated education, for an elevated object may form another motive. There are peculiar sweets derived from gaining knowledge, from possessing a mind more elevated and soul more enlarged, and from having a greater and nobler object of pursuit. There are delights

known only to those who have tasted them, they are not coveted by others. Those who have tasted may thirst for an abundant supply at the fountain. This motive is lawful and may be allowed a place in the argument urging forward to the accomplishing of the desire of the heart.

3. The hope of future, and final pecuniary advantage may have another motive operating on the heart. This is a very strong, very common motive to action in the pursuits of life. It is so tangible, and so material in its character, that the soul need not be raised above the very dust to be under its most powerful control. But this is a motive, which ought not to be allowed at all to bear on the question under consideration. Suppose a young lady, who is without property, and without parents to aid her, and who already has a respectable education, is considering the expediency of attempting by extraordinary efforts to avail herself of additional means, to prepare herself for future usefulness, with a hope that she shall be thus enabled to do more good all the remainder of her life. In weighing the arguments and considering the motives let not a hope of pecuniary advantage have any place in her heart. Let her not go forward with such an undertaking, encouraged by the hope, that in consequence, she may be able to lay up a little more annual income for a time of sickness—or be able to support herself more handsomely—or that she shall be less liable to embarassment and difficulty in providing for her own support. This is my candid opinion on mature consideration. It is a point on which every lady considering such a subject ought to be fully settled. She ought firmly to resolve to be always in future satisfied, provided that after her entire efforts to prepare herself for future usefulness, her pecuniary prospects should be as favorable as they were before she commenced. This opinion is not founded on belief that it is positively wrong to regard the pecuniary advantages of different situations, provided this is subservient to the plain dealings of Providence, and a supreme desire to do the greatest possible good. This opinion is founded on an observation of the common dealings of Providence—on

the situation of things as they are—on the real wants of the world.

For a young lady to indulge such an expectation is both visionary and inconsistent with the highest standard of benevolence. It is visionary because there is but very little probability that it will be realized. It would be visionary for a man to emigrate to the west with the expectation that wealth would flow in upon him because here and there a case occurs. It would be visionary for a young man to prepare for the ministry with the expectation, that that should be favored with a large united church, and a wealthy, prosperous and benevolent parish, because here and there one is to be found in the U.S. To ascertain what would be reasonable and what visionary for an educated female teacher to expect of pecuniary favor, we must enumerate all the spots, which need the labors of such teachers and their pecuniary advantages. In counting up those which hold out anything flattering in this respect, we shall find a few at the South, which [looks] to the North for teachers, but from those few, it is often found, on examination, that large deductions must be made for hazard, difficulties and dangers. We shall also find a few high schools at the west designed for the daughters of wealth, which we may add, and also the schools in our few cities and large villages in New England and perhaps also here and there a large seminary. When we have made out the whole number of this class, let us count up and compare the multitude of other schools among the hills of New England and the plains valleys of the west, amidst an immense population, which have enough to eat and to drink, but scarcely know by experience for what money is made. I mean simply day schools for those over the age of children, each composed of a little handful, and each needing a teacher of power and influence. And let us look at the multitude of other similar schools which need to be gathered together and brought into operation. And shall a reasonable young lady expect that her lot will be cast among the few in the first class mentioned or among the many of the last class. When I look over the whole field, it does seem to me visionary for a young lady to expect much pecuniary advantage from attaining high qualifications as a teacher.

Such expectations seem to me also to be inconsistent with the highest standard of benevolence. In the first place because there is now an abundant supply for a large proportion of the situations offering a flattering salary, and in some cases, such a superabundant supply, as to produce a rivalship degrading to the cause of education, and degrading to the profession of teachers. In the new place, I regard these so, because very many of these situations do not present the widest fields of usefulness. In many cases the pupils are in such a morbid state, produced by indulgence, luxury and indolence, and possess so much self-sufficiency and so little docility, that the field of usefulness cannot be very flattering to a large benevolent soul. In many cases, a good thorough teacher, who has a good mechanical and military tact at getting along, and who labors faithfully merely for the sake of the money at the end of the year, will do about as much good as the most benevolent teacher. But among the immense country population the case is very different. A teacher of superior talents, of high attainments, and enlarged benevolence, may often be the means of gathering together young ladies and little girls in one neighborhood enough to make a little school, over whose characters and future lives they can gain a most powerful control, and through them an influence over the whole neighborhood in favor of the great cause for which we should all labor.

The query very naturally arises, if teachers of such qualifications devote themselves to such schools for a very small compensation, and that frequently only a part of the year, what will they do, if they should be sick? I would say, let them do just what they would have done, if they had not received a superior education. Let them do just what other unmarried females, in good standing society, but without property, do, in case of sickness. Most of them, in time of health just live along, coming out even at the end of the year, and no more. And they may be very happy in living on mutual acts of kindness and perhaps those who by their good deeds, lay up a large store in hearts of others, are made as comfortable in time of sickness, and feel as little solicitude as any other females, also are dependent on their own exertions. It is often remarked that Providences are fitted to each other. That some hand of Providence which has closed almost every door to wealth and independence against the personal efforts of females, does provide for them in cases of sickness and dependence much more comfortably and respectably than for the other sex in similar cases of sickness and dependence.

6

MARY LYON~Will

WRITTEN 1846, PROBATED 1849

I, Mary Lyon, native of Buckland, Mass. now resident of South Hadley, County of Hampshire, State of Massachusetts, do now this twenty seventh day of November, 1846, solemnly make this my last will and testament.

I give to each of the children of my deceased sister Jemima Wing ten dollars, namely, to Electa Wing, ten dollars, to Rosina Cook, ten dollars, to Elisha Wing, ten dollars.

I give to each of the children of my deceased sister Lovina L. Putnam, ten dollars, namely, to William Putnam ten dollars, to Lydia Putnam Haydon ten dollars, to Daniel Putnam ten dollars.

I give to each of the children of my deceased sister Rosina Ellsworth, ten dollars, namely, to Stukely Ellsworth, ten dollars, to Hazelius Ellsworth, ten dollars, and to Franklin Ells, ten dollars, and to Henry Martin Ellsworth ten dollars.

I give to my brother, Aaron Lyon of Stockton, New York the use of all my property in his hands, at my decease, during his life, and I give the use of the same property to his wife during her life, if she survives her husband. At the decease of my brother and his wife, I give the same property to the American Board of Commissioners for Foreign Missions, namely the property in the hands of my brother at my decease.

I give to my nieces & nephews, any debts, they may owe me at my decease.

If my nephew, Mason Moore shall not have completed his course of study before my decease, I give him thirty dollars, for each remaining year of his pupilage.

I give my watch to my niece, Rosina Lyon.

I give my miniature portraits of Mrs. Z. P. G. Banister, Mrs. Eunice Caldwell Cowles, and of Mrs. Abigail Moore Burgess to the Trustees of Mount Holyoke Female Seminary.

I give all my notes and money, not otherwise named in this instrument to the American Board of Commissioners for Foreign Missions.

I give to my sister, Electa Moore fifty dollars.

I commit to Miss Mary C. Whitman my associate in the Mount Holyoke Female Seminary, the disposal of all my clothing, books, and furniture, requesting her to retain a part of each for her own use and to dispose of the rest according to her own judgment, and her knowledge of my wishes. Where there is no special reason for a different disposition, it is my wish to have all such property retained for the use of those connected with the seminary.

All other property not covered in this instrument, I give to the Trustees of the Mount Holyoke Female Seminary.

I hereby appoint and constitute Dea. Andrew W. Porter of Monson, Executor of this my last will and Testament.

In witness hereof, I the said Mary Lyon, have to this my last Will and Testament set my hand and seal, this twenty-seventh day of November, in the year of our Lord, one thousand eight hundred and forty six.

Signed, sealed, and published by the above-named Mary Lyon, as her last will and testament, in the presence of us, who at her request and in her presence and in the presence of each other, have subscribed our names as witnesses hereunto.

Mary Lyon.

S.   *Mary C. Whitman*
       Mary M. Stevens
       Persis G. Thurston.

7

From the Mary Lyon Yearbook

Compiled by Elizabeth Storrs Mead
Mt. Holyoke College
May 6, 1895

Our relations to God are the most important subjects of study and thought. We should consider them very often, for all our other relations flow from these.

The friends of God have the feelings and conduct of friends. They regard and love the character of God; they feel that they have sinned against a friend; they have confidence in God as a friend; they are grateful to him, they seek to honor him, they delight in having his will done, they do his will. In eternity, they will be forever with the Lord; will never sin again, never do a wrong or careless deed again, never see any one sin again, never know sickness or sorrow.

When God has a great work for anyone to do in the world, he usually gives him a peculiar training for it; and that training is just what no earthly friend would choose for him, and sometimes it is so long continued that there seems to us to be but little time left for him to work. We should not have led Moses into Midian to prepare him to guide a nation, and certainly we should not have left him there forty years. But God knew that the life of the humble shepherd, and in the desert, too, would best fit him to lead his people like a flock, and that he needed to be in that school no less than forty long years to be the truly meek Moses...He must have long years of quiet, under the shadow of Sinai, for meditation on the character of God, before he could meet that God on the top of the mount, and there receive the lively oracles to give to us.

All the essential conditions of our existence will doubtless continue through eternity, but we shall follow out the shades of condition fully in another world...Happiness, whether great or little, is important here, but it will be vastly more important there. We are not perhaps aware how much of our happiness and misery consists in remembering. There would really be but little enjoyment here were it cut off with the moment and blotted out of our being. How much happiness do we sometimes now enjoy in remembering the past! What will that happiness be in eternity? There we shall remember with joy all that was endured to some purpose.

What a place does Christ occupy as an atoning sacrifice in all the great things of Divine Providence! What a book is there yet to be opened and read in the glorious doctrine of the atonement!

I would not desire anything that would not be for the glory of God and in accordance with the will of my Saviour.

We must not be careless of what we have, but remember that God's blessing depends, in no small degree, on the manner we use what he has committed to us for his cause.

Our minds are so constituted that nothing but God can fill them. He is the only object suitable and capable of satisfying the immortal mind. And the mind craves a spiritual satisfying almost as the physical system does food.

Remember, the command "Thou shalt not kill" means not only outright, but slowly; it means not only others, but yourself; not only this generation, but the generation to come. It is probable that many of you are now suffering from the fact that those who have gone before you have not properly cared for their health. Your mothers, when at your age, were not living for themselves alone...they lived for you, even as they have done in later years.

If the Bible only take the lead in our schools, I care not how closely the sciences follow.

Seek to give at least two hours of every Sabbath to the careful study of the Scriptures. Read the Bible in course. There is an advantage in this, especially for those who are weighed down with cares or literary pursuits, or those whose minds are undisciplined. Disinclination to reading is thus overcome.

Study the Bible so much that every week you can perceive that you are increasing in knowledge of the sacred Scriptures.

We should look carefully to the manner of performing not only our religious duties, but also our temporal duties, for this also is to affect us through all eternity. Let us remember that time is really a part of eternity. This is our sowing-time and the reaping-time is at hand.

The feeble efforts which I am permitted to put forth in cooperating with others in laying the foundation of this new seminary will probably do more for the cause of Christ, after I am laid in my grave, than all I have done in my life before.

When in doubt which of two courses to take, follow that which involves most self-denial. You will then find yourself in the safer and happier path, and walking with Him who denied himself for our sakes. We are told many times in the Bible that we are not to seek our own ease; that our life does not consist in the abundance of the things that we possess. We are taught to renounce self. We should first give ourselves to Christ, and then seek, like him, to do good to all about us.

I think that proper parental government is a beautiful

illustration of the principles and spirit of the divine government, and I think that school government should be made the same. It is indeed sometimes more like the divine government than the parental, because the latter is more liable to be vitiated by parental fondness.

Never plead native character as an excuse for your faults. The Bible gives no such excuse.

It is not wise for a Peter to try to be a John, but rather to be the best Peter possible, and John to be the best John possible, rather than seek to be a Paul.

Humility consists not so much in thinking meanly of one's self as in feeling one's dependence on a higher power for success. There is no better time for the exercise of humility than when we succeed.

Do not allow pride to make you silent. Some think they can say nothing worth saying. Probably none of us can; but if communing together is appointed as a means of good, we should not neglect it.

Could I plead in behalf of the perishing heathen that all our missionary concerts should be filled with hearts prostrate together before God, it might not be so important a duty for me as to carry my own feeble petition to the throne of mercy, and there, in the name of our blessed Redeemer, plead the promises with an earnestness which cannot be denied.

Economy and self-denial are the two great springs which feed the fountains of benevolence. Practice them for Christ's sake, but talk very little about them.

Our grandmothers were not housekeepers only. True, they read but few books, but they read those thoroughly, thought deeply; and many of them had much mental culture.

The honor of God demands a public profession of religion. It is essential to honor God before men. The authority of God demands it; peace of conscience requires it; no one can be for Christ in the protracted neglect of this duty; God will not bless the labors of those who live in this neglect, and whoever lives in the continued neglect of this duty must destroy instead of saving souls.

What is more desirable than to have such a frame of mind that the habitual and uniform desire of the heart shall be: "Lord, what wilt thou have me to do?"

It is a blessed life to be conscious of doing all we do because God would have it done, and feeling that all we possess is his, and if taken from us will still be found in safe keeping.

Decide whether you will be selfish or benevolent characters.

Selfishness contains within itself a canker-worm. Loving self supremely continually disappoints. Selfishness is our greatest enemy. We may be in danger of following the advice of friends who would lead us to practice less self-denial.

At the close of each day carefully review your conduct. Avoid unpleasant looks. Be sincere in your professions of friendship. Cultivate a pleasant countenance. Learn to bear disappointments cheerfully. Never smile at the infirmities of others. Never be a minute too late. Never make sport of an intoxicated or an insane person.

There is much in the Bible to establish the belief that a certain proportion of our property should be devoted to the Lord's service. In the Old Testament the system of tithing is fully explained. The clearer light which shines in the New discloses our duty without any need of specific directions…It seems probable that the Jews gave at least four-tenths of their income. Shall we, under the gospel dispensation, with increased light and ability, do less?

In choosing the Lord, what do we choose between? Love

of forgetting sin or the pleasure of pardoned sin; the strength of Christ or the weakness of self; the presence of Christ in the closet, or alone, without any access to God; Christ's presence through all this dark world, or a wandering alone; Christ's presence as death approaches, or a dread of death; Christ's presence in the last struggle or passing alone through the solemn scene.

General faith implies confidence, trust, reliance, belief in God and in Christ. In special faith, the heart is filled with great truths, such as the great atonement by Christ; the infinite, the eternal condition in eternity; the helpless condition of men; the fullness of salvation; the power of the Holy Ghost; the promises of the Holy Ghost.

When the Bible speaks we are not to parley. It is our statute-book, and when it makes known our duty we are not to answer back, any more than Abraham when he was commanded by a voice from heaven to offer up his son, his only son, Isaac.

The law of the Lord is perfect. It is so because if changed in the least it would be imperfect. The best laws for nations, communities, schools, or societies are capable of improvement. Not thus with God's law. It is perfect because it treats all alike.

When curses are denounced upon children for parents' sake, it is upon wicked children for wicked parents' sake.

It is a sweet relief to my mind that you have a Father in heaven, and I do believe that all things will work together for your good, though the way in which this is to be effected may seem to us very undesirable. You may not be saved from trials, but I believe you will be supported under them; and after all, I trust you will find more enjoyment even in the present life than the worldling who has no such support.

I believe that my schools here have been more and more interesting every winter, and we all think this has been most so of all. I have never witnessed such an improvement in moral character, in ardent desire to possess meekness, humility, patience, perseverance, etc. But more than all, we have been visited by the influence of the Holy Spirit. Soon after the commencement of the school the gentle dews began to descend, and continued to increase until the last week, when we were blessed with a plentiful and refreshing shower.

Christ has died for us, has given us his Spirit, has adopted us as his own, has forgiven us all our sins, has engaged himself and all he has in our behalf, will give us his presence and sympathy, will allow us to partake in all which he has and does; he will never leave us, he will stand by us in death, will shield us at the judgment day, will take us home to glory, and will teach us the new song.

We are placed here for a little while and then go away and live in another world. How shall we live, and how shall we use what God has given us?

I believe that I do have some foretastes, from time to time, of what I think heaven is, though between these seasons there is much of strange stupidity. These little foretastes, too, as they return again and again, become more and more enriching to my soul, and ravishing to my heart.

From all eternity Christ had the plan of salvation before his infinite mind. He never turned aside from his work. In the fullness of time he came into the world; his whole temporal life was given to the work. He is now seated on the right hand of God to make intercession for us. For whom? Among others, for us here. For those who have recently been born again; for those who are anxious for their souls; for those who desire to be more deeply interested than they are, and for those who care not for their doings.

Cultivate foresight and a habit of looking on the bright side. Nothing except a good conscience contributes more to an habitual cheerfulness.

Never feel that you cannot get good from ordinary preachers. If you are where God has placed you, he can and will bless you ever and always in his house. Your duty is to hear.

It is important for young ladies to decide early in the school year whether or not they can be cheerful and contented. Homesick people I do not place very high in the scale of character.

※

Christians should be solemn, penitent, prayerful; they should bear their own sins and the condition of sinners on their hearts as they enter the holy place, and lay them on the head of the Lamb of God.

※

It is a divine requirement to "take fast hold of instruction." This implies something more than to sit still and merely receive what is brought to our minds. You must seek for knowledge; for be assured the heavenly stranger will not force herself into your possession.

Christ is the grand theme of the Bible; the grand subject presented to the heart by the Holy Spirit; the grand object of opposition by the powers of darkness and by wicked men; Christ is everything to us; we live in him, for him, to him.

※

We may, perhaps, be submissive to the will of God in great events, where we can see his hand, but when his will is made known through the agency of man, find ourselves unsubmissive. This should not be so. His providence makes known his will and not his audible voice.

※

There are two reasons why we ought to give…it is right and it will do good. Thus it is in God's government. He is guided by absolute right and infinite benevolence. The manner in which we act this year is like investing capital. Its influence will be increasing from year to year.

※

It seems to me more and more important that the professed followers of the Lamb should commence their Christian course guided by the pure and perfect standard of truth. Is it not too true that many take their standard from those around them, and on that account live a life which leads others justly to inquire "What do ye more than others?"

God knows our unworthiness, guilt, dependence, and want. God can forgive sin.

The vagueness of my own mind is often most trying, as connected with religious things. I often enjoy the anticipation of its not being thus in heaven. What a wonder of mercy if I shall at last find a seat in that glorious world where the will of God shall be known and loved and obeyed!

My own strength is weakness. I am a sinner, a great sinner. I can have no hope but in the infinite mercy of God.

I am weaker than weakness itself, and my wisdom is altogether folly. May I be more and more sensible of the preciousness of the direction, "If any of you lack wisdom, let him ask of God."

God has a vineyard and it is a great privilege to be called into it. He rewards, and his rewards are gratuitous. Those called into the vineyard are often most unworthy. They are sometimes called at a late period, late in age or late in having refused invitation. Service in the vineyard is not idle service. There is encouragement to all who ask for a place, and there is a necessity for a spirit of entire consecration to God, as is illustrated in the life of Abraham.

A uniform, serious Christian deportment can be obtained only by having the heart deeply impressed with eternal things. A want of uniformity in this respect is a great hindrance to Christian usefulness.

If God wants me to succeed, I shall succeed.

The privilege of laboring is to me more and more precious. I would not choose the spot. I would not choose the circumstances. To be able to do something is a privilege of which I am altogether unworthy.

Early rising is not rising at any particular hour; for what is early for one may be late for another. Early rising for any individual is rising at the earliest time proper for her under the existing circumstances. The hour of rising should not be decided on in the delicious dreaminess of the half-waking and more than half-dozing state of one's morning slumbers, but the decision should be made when you are up and awake, with all your powers in vigorous exercise.

I have recently been reading, or rather am now reading, McCheyne's "Life, Letters, and Lectures." It is just what I need…the sincere milk dealt out in childlike simplicity and godly sincerity. It is just what I need when I am so tired that I can do nothing with strong meat.

No missionary can give up as much as Christ did when he came to earth. We have none of us such a Father's house to leave.

Christ was never seeking a place where to live, but a place where he could deny himself for others.

We have a great work to do. Let us be faithful to these dear children. How many parents' hearts are beating with anxious hope for our dear charge! I like to think what a number of Christian parents are connected with our school. It is a privilege to spend and be spent for their children; above all, let us seek their spiritual welfare. Let us keep in mind that our great work is to seek the salvation of souls.

Every confirmed habit of doing little things well will have an influence on our future…Good habits will enable mothers to have greater moral power over their daughters, and daughters should come up to their mothers' standard in everything, thus inciting the mothers to higher and higher endeavors, so that each generation will increase in moral perfection till the dawn of millennium.

Taste should be made a subject of practical education. Those articles of dress that are in the best taste do not change as much from year to year as others.

※

Generally I feel that the dark cloud which hangs over the future is under the direction of Him who led his people by a pillar of cloud and of fire.

※

How little we read our Bibles! Might we not find time to read some chapters more every day?

Always have a plan for studying the Scriptures. Make a plan that you will like to follow for years.

Let us think for a moment how we should feel if a voice from heaven should tell us that we could never open a Bible again.

※

How many do we see around us seeking for ease, honor, pleasure or improvement, just to gratify self! If their object is attained, there comes little of happiness with it, because all is expended on self. We ought to turn the current of feeling toward others. Let it flow out in a thousand streams. How much happier you will be to live in a thousand than to live in yourself alone!

We ought to appear benevolent, as well as to be really so. This is the reason I think it best to have our missionary contributions in the form of subscriptions.

We can train benevolent workers only by being benevolent ourselves. The Levites had no portion among the tribes; the Lord was their inheritance; but out of their living they gave their tithes to the Lord.

※

I have lived to see a body of gentlemen venture to lay the cornerstone of an edifice, which will cost about fifteen thousand dollars, for the education of women. Surely the Lord hath remembered our low estate. This will be an era for the cause. It may have to struggle through embarrassments for years, but its influence will be felt. The work will not stop with this institution.

What a wonder that the Infinite God is willing to take thought for us, and it is a greater wonder that we are not willing to trust him. With God to take thought for us we need never be sad. We have only to go on and do present duty, and God will take care of the future.

I have been asked if it would not be well for our young ladies to give an example of economy, and throw their influence in favor of it by pledging themselves to wear certain articles of dress. I would not like to have you do anything of the kind. I do not wish you to be singular in your dress. Your time is too precious to be given to such an object. Neither do I think it best for you to confine yourselves to the cheapest articles of dress. It is not economy to do this. Nor do I believe that you will thus accomplish the greatest good.

A wish to be remembered after we are dead is not wrong, not pride, unless excessive. The Bible presents this as a motive for action.

Any lady—and the cases are not rare—who has occasion to excel in guiding her household; in being the active head of all her various departments of domestic labor...and, besides all, who finds it desirable to be intelligent on most subjects of practical interest, and it may be, too, to be literary without vanity, and scientific without ostentation...will have great reason for gratitude that she ever enjoyed the privilege of sitting under the instruction of my dearly beloved and highly revered teacher.

Self-control is never perfect till we can cheerfully meet our own government. Nor is a child really governed until he can smile under government.

Some easily find dark hours. They are perpetually seeking enjoyment, assurance, or some remarkable manifestation, instead of seeking to do just what their heavenly Father appoints. They want to be able to look to themselves, to get through with the conflict.

Never be boisterous; treat all with respect. Let the Bible have its full influence upon your hearts and you will be gentle and at the same time happy. I am always afraid of those who talk a great deal about what they are doing. Some of the most efficient characters in the world are the most quiet.

How foolish to yield to temptation and forget that we are to live forever! How changed will our views of life be in another world! What views of the Divine character will be revealed to us when we reach the eternal shores!

It is one thing to approve, and another to love; one thing to disapprove, and another to hate. Much of our unhappiness arises from loving what we most disapprove.

It is easier to judge without reason than to stop and think.

Seek to be always in such a state of mind, and to so spend each day that you will be prepared for afflictive intelligence and even for death itself.

The mind may have a pressure of care, and yet the heart may be on the things of religion.

Rest here, my child, and we will ask God to take care of the whole matter.

It is nothing with God to help, whether with many or with them that have no power. But his blessing is delayed so as to be given, as a rich reward, to the willing and obedient heart. Is the spirit of any one stirred within him in behalf of some benevolent undertaking?...Let him give all...all that he ought, either from his abundance from his scanty store, and rather than to look to his neighbor to do it in his stead, and the deed shall be remembered in heaven, and his work shall not be in vain.

Let us cheerfully make all due concessions, where God has designed a difference in the situation of the two sexes, while we plead constantly for the religious privileges of woman, and for equal facilities for the improvement of her talents, and for the privilege of using all her talents in doing good.

The way to increase your evidence is to increase in faith and love and conformity to the divine will.

Drink in divine truth, obey all your heavenly Father's commands. "Then shall we know, if we follow on to know the Lord."

We may perform our daily tasks with or without prayer; with the feeling "If the Lord will," or without this feeling; with the impression that this earth is the Lord's and the fullness thereof or without it; with a connection in our feeling between the commands of God and a perfect standard of doing what we undertake, or without this; and with or without the feeling that eternity is the end of everything in time.

Pardon is not to be purchased by our contributions; but when the gift of grace is secured, the precious casket may be filled with enduring treasures.

During the few months past, I have learned a little of the minor prophets. I am now reading Hosea. The figurative language in the second chapter is exceedingly forcible. How strikingly are described the treachery, ingratitude, unreasonableness, and wickedness of spiritual departures from God!

This sordid money, what is it? Why, we may perhaps keep it till we go to the grave, and then we must give it up. This dust, what is it? God suffers us to show by it how much we love him. He has thus put his stamp upon it; so it has become very precious. Yes, we can give it to Christ, and so secure a never-failing treasure in heaven.

The reason that the Ten Commandments are given in so little space, is because the willing-hearted understand easily. They understand duty by the general spirit of the Bible; e. g., the spirit of the fifth commandment is, that we observe all relative duties.

We should economize in nothing more than in time and be very careful of the time of others. Young ladies are in great danger of using the time of others too freely, and perhaps never more in danger than on recreation day.

We may become like little children, willing to be led just where God would have us go. When we find ourselves ready to give up even lawful pleasures and possessions, how happy is our life! When we can relinquish health and friends and our smile not be disturbed, how much we enjoy them! I think our feelings are somewhat like those of Abraham and Sarah when Isaac was given back to them from Moriah.

The law of the Lord is perfect. Its requirements are in accordance with the principles implanted in our natures. It treats all alike. Thou shalt love the Lord thy God with all thy strength and thy neighbor as thyself. This is as easily obeyed in sickness as in health, in weakness as in strength, by the wise as by the ignorant, by the child as by the adult, by the poor as by the rich. It is exactly adapted to the wisdom of the wisest, to the poverty of the poorest, to the conditions of all. Obedience is easy where there is first a willing mind, a conscience void of offense, enlightened by the spirit, is the best exposition of this glorious law.

What was Achan's sin? He disobeyed the express command of God. Have you not many times done the same thing? He robbed not man, but God. He took for himself that which belonged to the Lord. Have you never done the same? Have you never spent on yourself, on your appetites, on your dress, the time or the money that belonged to the Lord?

It is easier to obey God than anyone else.

Promptly and faithfully to perform every duty in the place where you are, as a member of a family, or of a school, is the best way to prepare for the duties of any and every station in life.

※

I am not indifferent to enjoyments. Your society seems to me a greater blessing than ever. If I should enjoy it, may my soul be filled with gratitude to God; if, in His providence, He should deprive me of this in a greater or less degree, may I never complain in my heart of Him who does all things well.

※

To be left to doubt is one of the greatest chastenings of the young Christian. Some are thus chastened to try them, to make them solemn, humble; to make them love the gospel for its own sake. *The* hope instead of *my* hope should often fill the mind. Christians are also tempted to prepare them to entertain and give a consistent and uniform reason for the hope within them; to prepare them to be stable Christians, not changeable; to prepare them to enter on a Christian life as a subject of trial rather than of enjoyment; to prepare them to labor for the salvation of others; to prepare them to act in obedience to the commands of Christ rather than according to their own present feelings.

※

There is not a day in which I do not ask how can I enlighten the understanding and direct the feelings of my pupils aright on this great subject, the salvation of the world? The trial of giving my little is nothing in comparison with my anxiety on this point. And an important part of your work hereafter may be to lead others to give as they should.

※

Eternity is probably more like time than we imagine. All the essential conditions of our existence will doubtless continue through eternity, but we shall follow out the shades of condition fully in another world.

We should judge of the pleasure which anything affords,

not by the present delight, but by the remembrances it will bring; and these, to be truly delightful, must be increasingly joyous through time and eternity.

"Son, remember," said Abraham to the rich man in his place of torment.

※

Our God is faithful. The unfaithfulness of his rebellious creatures cannot exceed his mercy and long-suffering. His mercy endures forever, and his promises never fail.

※

It is a privilege to give even the widow's mite. I want you to meet all your treasures in heaven. But remember that riches may be corrupted. We shall find that they have been, in the last great day. We shall there find garments moth-eaten, gold and silver cankered, and rust that will eat flesh as fire. But, my dear pupils, you may sell all that you have and give alms, and you will find a treasure in heaven. And oh, what a treasure it will be! Redeemed souls carried to heaven through your instrumentality!

※

Oh, how immensely important is this work of preparing the daughters of the land to become good mothers! If they are prepared for this situation, they will have the most important preparation which they can have for any other; they can soon and easily become good teachers, and they will become, at all events, good members of society.

※

No one, let him do all he can for others, can make the sacrifice that Christ has made for us. His natural life was as dear to him as anyone's, but he gave it all for the good of others.

※

He who sows to the Spirit and denies himself will have an increase of happiness and great spiritual growth; while those who sow to the flesh, loving self, reap only corruption. The most wretched beings in this world are those who think only of themselves, having no interest in others.

※

It is giving but one view of the Christian's life to say it is a life of joy. It is a paradox that the more he suffers the greater will be his joy. There are three kinds of suffering—suffering for sin, for the common trials of life and those trials which we might avoid by going out of the path of duty. The last are those which, if met, give us an exceeding great reward.

Resist bodily temptation, affectation, love of ease, dread of pain, resist worldly friendships and intimacies, temptations of your own heart, dread of being watchful, love of excitement and of following it, and the love of approbation.

This world is to be used faithfully and diligently, but only as a way-mark to that better home, where, I trust, we shall rejoice together over many dear ones gathered into our Father's house.

I thought I knew something of self-denial in giving money, but I am thankful that I had something else to give, for there is an inner soul that was not reached before. If I have two idols, they are the seminary and the missionary cause, and they were both God's before they were mine.

Social or public prayer is like dwelling in the outer court; secret prayer like entering the inner temple. None enter the inner temple who are not found in the outer court. Every want, every grief, every anxiety, every temptation, every friend and every foe should be objects of prayer. But prayer for spiritual blessings for ourselves and others is the essence of prayer. And spiritual blessing consists chiefly in the gift of the Holy Spirit. Nothing is given us but by the Holy Spirit. He is the messenger. He takes of the things of Christ and gives them to us.

God is the supreme governor of the world and of everything that takes place in it. Every act as it is performed, every thought as it passes through the mind, takes its foreseen place in the infinite series of events out of which God will evolve the glory of His great name and the greatest good of the created universe.

At the judgment, the friends of Christ will enjoy His glorious appearance, the sweetness of His voice, His protection from the divine wrath; they will be forever with the Lord.

I have just commenced giving instruction on the epistles of Peter. We have had two exercises, three verses each. I have looked forward to studying and teaching these epistles as a kind of feast. But the commencement is more precious than I had anticipated.

I often feel that my days are rapidly passing and that I have but a few remaining, but these remaining days will be precious if spent in the cause of Christ.

I love to live for you, my dear children; but when I think of myself alone I want to go home.

Those around you look to you…they notice you in the room, in the class, in the prayer meeting, in your calls, your walks, at all times, your words, in your looks, in everything. The consistent life of the young Christian may be a more effectual means for the conversion of youth than all others combined. You may do much by religious conversation. I do not mean studied conversation, but by always having a heart to speak with Christians before others. Be free to speak of a passage of Scripture that has interested you, of a prayer-meeting, of doing good to souls.

If work needs to be done, and no one wants to do it, that is the work for you. Much of the work of the world, if done at all, must be done for love…not for pecuniary returns. Never decide hastily that you cannot do because you have not physical or mental strength. Everyone has something to do for Christ, and each is responsible for doing her part, and in the best way in her power.

If the citadel of the heart is once taken possession of by its rightful Sovereign, it can never be re-taken by Satan. It may be called the internal heart.

I have no definite spot in view where I may spend the remnant of my strength in behalf of an object which for a long time has seemed to drink up my spirits; yet I never had a prospect of engaging in any work which seemed so directly the work of the Lord as this. The present path is plain. The future I can leave with Him who doeth all things well.

It does seem to me a less evil that farmers and mechanics have scanty stores of knowledge, than that their wives, the mothers of their children, should be uneducated.

Most ladies can do more for the missionary cause at home than abroad. Wives, mothers, and daughters have much to do to elevate the standard of liberality in those they love. Perhaps as daughters you should not be willing to have so much lavished upon you, while there is so little given for the cause of Christ.

Now it seems to me that if God sees it to be best that we should live, it is important that we should labor with all our strength; but that whenever God may see it best to call us hence, we should cheerfully leave our work at a moment's warning. He who has given us our work to do, can easily commit it to other hands. It is my desire to be in daily readiness to leave all.

In reading for devotion, it is more profitable to read a few verses. Read a little, and let the truths fall into your mind. Receive them just as they drop, as it were, voluntarily into the mind, and see if some thought does not seem most precious. Many make a great mistake in making too great an effort to feel. You should not make much effort. Keep the mind on the passage without wandering. This is very important. If you have one thought peculiarly precious, just think why you have it: because you have your mind on the Bible. Perhaps these precious thoughts will be some of the same you will have in heaven.

Experience has taught me to fear the gratification of any ardent desire, unless I first feel a perfect willingness to yield my will entirely.

I have nothing to say but to ask that the will of the Lord be done, whether we are with or without means to carry on our plans. My only wish is for the furtherance of His kingdom. Some professing Christians depend on their plans for religious improvement, instead of depending solely on Christ. We must do all that God would have us because He would have us, and leave the future with Him.

The same omniscient God who gives the wayside violet its beautiful tints, and guides satellites and suns in their mighty courses, knows your circumstances. You know not how many hairs you have upon your head, but He has numbered them all. He knows everything about you. He knew, millions of years before you were born, just what you would need for guidance and food this day. He knew what chapter would come in course in your reading, and that it would just meet your case. In the counsels of eternity He arranged all the circumstances that surround you here.

Make many general acquaintances that you may lay a broad foundation for usefulness and influence, but be slow in forming intimate friendships.

We may, and should, ask the Lord every day to lead us where we shall not need to spend our time and strength in resisting temptation, but rather give them directly to his service. We should ask to be free from temptations of pleasure and comfort, no less than those of pain and sorrow. And when tried we should inquire if we have run into the path of temptation.

A lady's dress should be such as to please God, not laying aside taste; for is He not much more pleased when His children look well than otherwise? I have no idea that Christ was negligent of his dress. His garment was one counted worthy of casting lots upon. Taste should be made a matter of practical education. Self-respect is promoted by proper attention to dress.

Self-respect is acquired and retained by some attention to dress. I have only a few brief rules to give you on this subject, and may never speak to you of it again. Never be singular in your dress, but endeavor to dress so as not to be noticed. Never impress people as being fond of dress. Purchase good articles when you purchase any, and seek to use them to the best advantage.

Would we wish to live for any other than Him who has given His own life for us? We are bought with a price, and when we consider what that price was, can we ask to be our own?

There are three distinct things that we should bear in mind in reference to the Israelites. They were the recipients of the oracles of God; through them the Messiah was to come; they were the foundation of the Church.

I have now no mother or sister whom I can go and see, and alone I followed my dear mother to the grave. Her prayers, which I have had daily for so many years, I shall have no more. She, to whose comfort I have been expecting the pleasant privilege of administering for years to come, as almost the only child left her, will need nothing more. I feel my family loneliness, but with it, eternity seems very near, with all its precious privileges purchased by the blood of our glorious Saviour.

We forget in this life but shall remember in eternity. Our remembrances here, compared with those there, will be like the glimmer of a candle before the sun; this life is but a faint picture of eternity…The least word here is to live through those countless ages. How foolish to yield to temptation, and forget that we are to live forever! How changed will our views of life be in another world! What views of the Divine character will be revealed to us when we reach the eternal shores!

Act from principle in regard to going to church. Then you will do right, be it hot or cold, wet or dry. You probably know very little how much your vacant seat in church on the Sabbath affects your pastor. I am sure that it will always do the man of God good to see you regularly in your place of worship with the interested countenance which always goes with the interested heart.

No one will know how much he ought to give unless he has a strong desire to know. God will make our treasures, whether few or many, a touchstone, a test of the willingness of our hearts. If God asks a part of our pittance, we must not inquire how we can get along without it. We must not be careless of what we have, but remember that God's blessing depends on the manner we use what he has committed to us for his cause.

We will pray, but let us also do, and do now. By waiting you may lose the little desire you have. Feeling without action is exceedingly dangerous.

We are on the verge of another holy Sabbath. It is a great event for us to pass a holy Sabbath.

We hope to spend forty Sabbaths together, and will not those who love the Lord speak often one to another? Then will He write for us a book of precious remembrance, for He has said He will. After forty Sabbaths, we shall separate; we have dear ones here who have no hope of meeting us beyond this life. May not such a hope be given to some of them this first Sabbath morning?

The yielding of the will to parent or teacher is often the schoolmaster that leads to Christ. Thank God if you have learned to submit your will to that of your parents...You will often be called to yield your will where you least expected it, and perhaps to those to whom you would not naturally yield it. This is often true in the family relations. Unhappiness in domestic circles might almost always be avoided if there were only those found to say from the heart, "Not my will, but thine be done."

When you read the Psalms and the Epistles, dwell carefully on each word and pray over every verse. Let your soul sometimes delight itself in reading, meditating, and praying at the same time, over your open Bible.

I want to ask you to pray for me in a very special manner about one thing. It is for divine guidance and strength in giving religious instruction. Pray that I may have hid in my own heart all that I attempt to say. Pray that I may speak the words of truth, every jot and tittle…that which God sees and knows to be truth.

The same amount of talent will rise higher with benevolence.

Those who are most ready to give splendid presents are not, usually, the most ready to give to benevolent objects.

Before we take up our contribution, let us all take time in our closets to consider the worth of a single soul.

Trials for Christ's sake were different in different ages. We may not suffer persecution, but we may give so much as to suffer in the opinion of others; of those, too, whom we love, and the trials be the same in essence as of those who suffer persecution, and we shall not lose the reward.

I have often found myself attempting to preserve the manna till the morning, but I have never succeeded. How wise is the economy of Providence and the economy of grace! How should we rejoice that we cannot lay up stores for ourselves either of wisdom or of faith!

Do for and speak of these young ladies just as you would wish us to do for your own dear sister. They are our daughters… our sisters. We must never speak lightly of them. We must remember that we have them in a most precious trust.

I have suffered all my life from the want of regular habits. I wish you to accustom yourselves to be thoroughly systematic in the division of your time and duties. I know you have many interruptions and many little things to look after; but so it must be with ladies.

※

The love of grateful hearts is a rich treasure, and even a better resource for a supply of our bodily wants than coffers of gold.

God requires us to give without great ability. We should consider our circumstances, decide what proportion we will give and adhere to it. I regard it my duty to carry out in my own course of action what I have said to you. You will probably see it all true at the judgment, and maybe in the light of eternity you will find that I have fallen far below the true standard. Let us make no exceptions in our own favor, but rather, like Paul, make exceptions against ourselves.

※

While man looketh on the outward appearance, God judgeth righteous judgment. I now believe that the eye, which saw seven thousand in Israel who had not bowed the knee to Baal, has seen the effectual prayer rising continually from some hearts in towns around us, though I knew it not at the time.

※

By grace we are redeemed, by grace we are saved, by grace we are received and sanctified, by grace we have our work given us, and by grace, strength and a heart to do it.

※

Nothing helps the Christian more in the discharge of his duty than a sense of his responsibility; but who can duly estimate that responsibility! It increases with every beating pulse. An immortal spirit is committed to him, which is to be an inhabitant of heaven, a companion of Jesus Christ forever, and there is doubtless a very close connection between our religious character here and our state in the world to come.

※

Do something; have a plan; live for some purpose; be faithful and conscientious and understand what you are to do; but do not expect to make over this world, or to greatly change your condition in it; but seek, rather, to be ready to do and to bear what comes in your way. Be willing to do anything anywhere that Providence seems to lay upon you.

Let us not only have our hearts right, "sprinkled from an evil conscience," but "our bodies washed with pure water," our external conduct, on which our influence and usefulness so much depend, free from reproach.

If trials and perplexities come, then we may look for some comforting, consoling providence. We may always expect enough of trial and difficulty to make us love to sing "Is this, dear Lord, the thorny road/That leads us to the mount of God?" And enough of consolation and support and blessing to make us feel that Christ's yoke is easy and his burden light.

A stated time, a particular place and a punctual attention to secret prayer are necessary to keep up the life and power of religion in the soul.

I don't want you to spin and weave because I did. It was best for me to do it, but you may be thankful that this necessity is removed and that you may be able to finish your studies earlier and thus have more time to work for the Lord. I thank God every day for the hope and expectation that you will do a great deal more than I have done in the world.

I really think it requires more discipline of mind and more grace to meet a lady's duties than a gentleman's. He has little of minutiae to attend to. He can rise in the morning and go to his business without hindrance; but it is not so with a lady, and I would not have it otherwise.

The value of health is inestimable to a lady. Her appropriate duties are so numerous and varied, so constant in their demands, and so imperious in the moment of their calls, that health to her is above price. She cannot perform her duties faithfully and successfully unless she possesses a calm mind, an even temper, a cheerful heart, and a happy face. To possess all these will require a good degree of health.

What a delightful place will heaven be!...Shall we, being washed and made white in the blood of the Lamb, be permitted, through rich, free, and wonderful grace, to sit down in that holy place, where there shall be no more pollution, no more pride, no more selfishness, no more disobedience to God; where we shall no more be distressed with our own sin, no more pained with the sins of others?

In everything by prayer and supplication with thanksgiving, let your requests be made known to God. When He says everything, He means just what He says. Those who are Christians can accept this and those who are not may begin today to be Christian.

We should never think of Christ's trial as confined to the last agony. His was a life of constant trials and we may expect ours to be.

Perhaps the qualification for the highest influence is power to wield the pen, to write so as to make others desire to be better.

A day set apart by ourselves from its ordinary avocations to be devoted exclusively to religious purposes is like the alabaster box of ointment broken over our Saviour. Some may ask, What profit is there in it? Why was this ointment poured upon the Saviour's head? It is from love to Him. An hour spent in religious worship does not fail to meet its end. Time spent in earnest prayer, in sacred meditation, in absorbing adoration and praise, approximates more nearly to the felicity of heaven than that spent in any other way or manner.

Our amount of duty will always be equal to our amount

of strength or ability to perform it. We should be perfect in all we do, not merely for the present, but to help in the formation of a good character. We should not be like the soapstone, that crumbles as it is rubbed, but like gold, that shines brighter and brighter the more it is used.

Always remember that there is no possible making up of lost time.

Hasten on, young ladies. You are not aware of the habit of lagging that you are forming.

By grace I am the little that I am, and by grace alone would I do the little that I hope to do. The doctrine of grace, in all its aspects and relations, is more and more precious here; and what will it be hereafter, when we shall be permitted to join in that song of Moses and the Lamb to Him who has redeemed us, and washed our robes and made them white in His own blood!

Consider the meeting at the judgment of Cain and Abel; of Noah and the men who reviled him; of Pharaoh and Moses; of David and Saul; of Stephen and his persecutors; of Peter and Judas. Whom will you meet? Your father, your mother; your teachers; your brothers and sisters; your minister,—all whom you knew on earth who love Christ. Where will you be? Where will you go?

There is a standard of giving for every individual. And this we are to find out each for herself. If it were written on the walls of our rooms how large or how small a sum we should give, we should not be treated as moral agents.

All are to take part in the domestic work, not as a servile labor, for which they are to receive a small weekly remuneration, but as a gratuitous service to the institution of which they are members, designed for its improvement and elevation.

The sweet pleasure and satisfaction found in sitting down alone to read the Bible is evidence of being a Christian.

If there is so much that is delightful where there is sin, what must that state be where there is no more sin! What hallowed, what sublime affections shall we behold there!

Be sure to have your heavenly Father for your most intimate friend.

It is a great thing voluntarily to give up all our business for a whole day, that we may meet God in the inner sanctuary of his holy, spiritual temple.

When in doubt which of two courses to take, it is usually wise to choose that which involves the greater self-denial; as when, for example, you feel loth to rise in the morning or to go to meeting on the Sabbath.

When God, in the court of Heaven, shall weigh the offerings which shall decide this great question, He may say, "This poor widow hath cast in more than they all." On the other hand, let no one feel that he can afford to consume treasures on himself, because he has already done so much for the cause. The little that remains in his hand which he can give, and which the Lord requires of him, may be the balancing power which decides the whole case.

Young ladies can nowhere be so well cared for as in the family. There the government may be so mild, yet so undeviating and inflexible, that there will be only advice on the part of parents and compliance on the part of the child.

Always be in haste but never in a hurry.

May God give every one of you more for your heart and hands to do, and more and more fellowship with Christ in His sufferings.

Every success has been from His hand, and every discouragement has been such that when good comes we feel constrained to say, "This is the Lord's doing."

It is a fearful thing, young ladies, to disregard the laws

of health. You know not where the consequences may cease. This view of the subject makes life more noble and important. I should not dare speak to those of little cultivation of mind and heart as I do to you; but I expect you to appreciate what I say and to weigh the subject carefully before God.

There is one place of meeting, of sweet communion of spirit, when absent in body. There I love to ask our heavenly Father to bless you all, to bless you individually in your work, to bless the dear companions of your missionary joys and missionary toils, and to bless, too, the children whom God has given you in the land of your adoption.

I am very anxious in regard to your health and comfort. If you are Christ's now, or if you become His, remember that He has redeemed your bodies as well as your souls. He is to present them pure and spotless before your Father in heaven. These bodies are not your own. They are the temple of the Holy Ghost. Can you be negligent of them?

Be wise in diligence, in self-control, in choice of companions, in conversation, in seeking for Heaven rather than Earth, in seeking that others may be blessed, instead of thinking of yourself.

We give others much vexation and trouble by negligence. We should form a strong resolution to avoid, through life, trying the patience or irritating the feelings of others in this manner, and strive to possess those habits which will make us welcome visitors anywhere, and valuable friends.

During all these years I know not how many just commencing a life of godliness may have received an impression from me that will be felt all their lives. May I, in this, be saved from blood-guiltiness.

Practice would not be so diverse in respect to Christian liberality, if the hearts of all were right. Two Christians of equal means would not then be found, one giving five dollars and one five hundred. This contributing is the current money of the heart. It shows to an extent how much we love. And oh, what a privilege, by giving money to show our love to Him who has redeemed us! "Unto us who are the least of all."

We think of things of which we ought not to think. We often make ourselves unhappy by dwelling on our condition and prospects, and those of our friends. But it is our blessed privilege to commit all these to Him who will certainly take care of us, if he sees we are not afraid to trust him.

Regeneration is an entire change not of the mind but of the religious character. It is illustrated by the figures of the new birth and of raising from the dead. The change is as great as any miracle, and while not very obvious always to the individual, it is to God. The manifestations of increase in grace are like the growth of an infant. It is a work beyond the scrutiny of man, and the circumstances are not to be calculated upon, not to be predicted.

I fear that I ask more for you that is temporal than I do that is spiritual. I have been led to inquire whether it is not very common for my prayers to center on blessings which may end with this life. Three things I desire for you, and for these I daily supplicate the Father of mercies; that you may have wisdom from above to direct you to the best measures; that you may daily trust in your almighty Friend, and in Him find immediate and continual support in every time of need; and that you may be saved from overwhelming trials.

Sometimes I am almost ready to exclaim, "When will the work of my feeble hands be done that I may go home?" But through the mercy of God these seasons are not frequent and do not continue long. Generally I feel that the dark cloud that hangs over the future is under the direction of Him who led His people by a pillar of cloud and of fire.

The throwing out of your whole soul in powerful, disinterested, vigorous action for others, no matter how self-denying, will make you to receive a hundredfold even in this life. It is our duty to exhibit to the universe a being enjoying all the happiness for which we were created. How is this to be done? By a forgetfulness of self, and devotion of thought, time, feeling, and money to the interests of others. Thus there will be a constantly increasing inward realization of real happiness.

Parents are often more grieved by the dishonor shown them by their advanced children than by the disobedience of little children.

Let your letters to your mother be a picture of a warm-hearted, loving, confiding daughter. Bestow your choicest expressions of affection upon your mother.

I have often conceived very high respect, and even affection, for the parents of my pupils before meeting those parents. This has been given me by their faithful daughters.

However much we may labor and pray for souls, remember that Christ died for them. We must make effort for the salvation of souls, and that effort must be accompanied by an inward desire and love for the work. There is an internal feeling, which none know but those who have experienced it, that prompts to action and is never tired of the work, though one may feel that she cannot make the mental or physical effort requisite.

Pray that real Christians may be holy, as God is holy.

If we are grieved by what is unjustly reported, let us remember the example of our Saviour. He opened not His mouth. Let God in His own way and time vindicate His own acts. Let us commit ourselves to the covenant-keeping God, who doeth all things well.

The duty of sacred charity is plainly inculcated in the Scriptures. The highest form of this charity is that which goes out of ourselves, which is not concerned with ourselves or our interests. Other charities may partake of the true spirit of giving...while other motives are involved. If this great principle is paramount, other charities will flow out of it, as in the case of a church and an individual. The church that will give for the salvation of the world, will give for the salvation of her country.

Pray directly for the conversion of the world. Dwell on the promises that the world shall be converted; read them; pray over them; pray that the fulfillment of these promises may be hastened. Think of the multitudes who perish every year, and will continue to perish till the promises are fulfilled. Think of the truth, that the conversion of the world can be hastened by prayer, and that it can be delayed by unbelief.

Four excuses for neglecting to seek salvation: —It will do no good for me to try; I would try if I knew that I should succeed; I have once had a false hope and now I want a good one or none; what will others think of me?

Entire consecration to the service of God makes a person willing to take just the place to which He, in His providence, calls her, whether it be to a post of distinction or of humble and tedious labor. Outward circumstances neither greatly elate nor depress such an one.

Consider well what you can and ought to do, and be faithful in performing it.

Perfect punctuality in the time and manner of doing things is of great consequence.

I want you all to teach, if it is only your little brothers and sisters. I do not think a lady is educated till she has had some experience in teaching children. It is a valuable preparation for influence. In no other way can the principles of the human mind and heart be so well learned. If you do not succeed at first, teach till you do succeed. Prepare thoroughly for every exercise and for every recitation, but study the minds and hearts of your children more than any book. I do not expect many of you to give your lives to teaching; but she who can control the minds of the young happily and rightly, is all the better prepared for any sphere.

Young ladies at school with all the helps and comforts which they should have, naturally incline more to being ministered unto than to minister to others. To counteract this there is needed the special cultivation of an unselfish spirit, while opportunities for its cultivation are comparatively few.

Now hear God say, "There I will meet thee, and commune with thee from above the mercy-seat." Yes, there, from off that mercy-seat, the shadow of a good thing to come, even of Him who is now in the presence of God for us, we hear Jehovah speak…The faces of the cherubim are toward the mercy-seat, and thus the holy angels "desire to look into" that "way into the holiest" of all, where we may obtain eternal redemption. Shall we refuse what angels desire to know?

If you are unhappy, it is probably because you have so many thoughts about yourself and so few about the happiness of others.

Let ladies understand the great doctrine of seeking the greatest good, of loving their neighbors as themselves; let them indoctrinate their children in this fundamental truth and we shall have wise legislators.

It takes longer to learn a lesson for a lifetime than for a week, but it is the best economy to give it the extra attention necessary to make it a sure and lasting investment.

We should know by experience what hard study is. It would be well for all to have one severe study, like Latin or mathematics, through the year. All should have thorough discipline in these studies before taking the higher English branches. Let the roots grow and expand before we gather fruit. There is no reason why ladies should not faithfully pursue such studies as well as gentlemen.

All may be dark to us, but, like Noah's dove, we may find a rare, sweet resting-place with our God. He cannot fail us.

"Jesus has come for you, Adaline. Now, you will not be afraid, will you? He will carry you safely over. You have nothing to do but look directly to Him. You will suffer only a little while longer."

How sweet it is to be directed from hour to hour, with scarce a ray of light beyond! The darker the future, the brighter often is faith, and the more firmly do we rely on that arm that can never fail.

Can you not come and stay with me a few days? I am not able to go out of my room much, and it would be a great comfort to me to have you with me, Dear one! I have felt for you most tenderly in your trials. They have been mine...I want to talk with you of your loss...Rest, and rest here with me, if you can leave your mother. Arms of love wait to receive you.

I am more indebted to my mother than to all others except my Maker.

You can continue to seek mental improvement and still be good business characters. Versatility is given you for this purpose; and I hope I shall hear that you make your mothers' cares your cares.

There is a threefold duty in reference to the truth--to receive it, to believe and love it, and to obey it.

In the bestowment of temporal blessings God has a higher design than immediate good.

His mercy endureth forever is the great principle in the divine economy.

The benevolence of the Jews was, to an extent, expended on their ceremonies. God seemed to say to them, You are not strong enough to convert the world.

I have been interested in the lovely and perfect example of Jesus Christ. Though he loved all his own as the world loveth not, and though he laid down his life for his enemies, yet as a man we have reason to think that he acknowledged some as his particular friends. It is said emphatically that Jesus loved Martha, and her sister, and Lazarus; and among the twelve was found "that disciple whom Jesus loved."

Abel, being dead, yet speaketh. The dead in Christ send a voice after them. Abel speaks to the impenitent, he was penitent; he speaks to the unbelieving, he had faith in Christ; he speaks to the self-righteous, he was clothed in Christ's righteousness; he speaks to those who depend on a religion which does not purify the life, his works were righteous; he speaks to those who neglect great light, he speaks encouragement to the desponding, he magnifies the grace of God.

Pray for yourselves; for yourself as an individual. Connect your prayer with your duty in the great work of converting the world. What does God require of you, and what should you be to do it? Pray for the conversion of souls. Connect their conversion with their future work in the conversion of the world. God often connects great results with small things done in sincerity and faith.

He is not ashamed to call us brethren—brethren in labors, brethren in sufferings, brethren in gathering in the rich harvest of immortal souls.

"The secret of the Lord is with them that fear him." Girls have many intimates. Think of the grandeur of being admitted to intimacy with the King of kings.

When I can realize a little of the value of one soul, I feel that a great work has been accomplished; but when I remember that Jesus died for all our pupils I can but ask, why did not all hear his voice?

What shall it profit a Christian mother, though by her industry and discretion she clothe all "her household in scarlet, in silk, and in purple," if she refuse the robe of Christ's righteousness to the destitute heathen?

☙

Be very slow to depart from a Christian father's counsel. In your father you have a divinely appointed safeguard; trust him, lean upon him, and there learn your relation to your heavenly Father. If you can lose your will in your father's, you will much more easily say, "Not my will, but thine be done, my Father in heaven."

☙

When Jesus comes for one of my dear children, I want to go with her just as far as I can. I do not expect to pass over with our dear friend at this time, but maybe the Lord will give me a word wherewith to comfort her, and maybe, as I see Heaven open, I shall get a new view of its blessedness, to give to those who remain.

☙

Comfort and economy, good taste and true Christian liberality, are not incompatible, but their union requires care, forethought, and good judgment.

Never destroy anything that God has made or given skill to others to make; not even a kernel of corn nor a pin. Never think anything worthless until it has done all the good it can. This is the true sense of economy.

It is the plan of God that all should live on little. He has given, on an average, but little to the human family. Each, of course, must take but little and use it. By the great law of love, God demands of each much of the little that has been given him. God has opened a wide door into the field of his service and thus made a demand on the little.

☙

The influence of these pupils on each other, the influence from absorbing studies, and that which I may exert, may produce an impression which shall affect their whole lives.

❧

Settle some great principles of duty for life. All who have ever attained to any degree of perfection have had certain rules by which to abide. Doubtful cases cause us much trouble. In these refer to your general rule.

❧

It is the joy of the Christian that God is his Creator, that He lives in him and receives all good from Him. How full are the Psalms of this feeling!

❧

Perhaps that same Being, that could with a glance look through the course of the Israelitish nation, from the selling of Joseph to the coming of the Messiah, has designs of mercy on all the nations of the earth, through the unparalleled blessings which he has bestowed on this great people. And have not his dealings with our beloved country some connection with the causes which will bring forward that happy day, to which all who love the Lord Jesus Christ are looking with earnest prayer?

❧

This department [the domestic department of Mt. Holyoke Seminary] is too complicated, and requires too much care to continue it, were it not for the great advantage it is to the family... Had I fully understood how complicated its working must be, I should never have undertaken it, but a kind Providence hid many of its difficulties from me, and I can see so much in it that is for the comfort of our household and favorable to the young ladies individually, that I am willing to take all this extra care.

❧

How little do I know what is best! I can pray without reserve that the will of God may be done; that the Kingdom of Christ may speedily come; that the events which Christ sees to be best may take place, and that we may have hearts to do the whole will of God. But when I pray for particular blessings, I often feel that perhaps I know not what I ask, and it is a delightful privilege to refer the whole to God.

If you would be good teachers, you must seek to have your minds meet other minds. You must be able to take charge of any part of a child's education, try to lead in the path of universal wisdom.

Have we ever given and toiled and prayed for those in darkness till we felt the sacrifice? Are you ready to go yourself to the corners of the Earth for the salvation of others? If we send others to endure the toils, shall we not be willing to practice self-denial?

Our standard of giving must be different from that of those who have gone before us. The lowest of us ought to rise as high as the highest did thirty years ago. We ought to rise as much higher than our parents as we are younger. We cast no reflections on them. They will receive a crown if they labored and gave according to their light. We have greater light and greater opportunities to do good. The providence of God is opening to the Christian everywhere a way, a highway, a way of holiness, in which his willing feet may run, as on the wings of the wind, carrying the tidings of salvation to the remotest corners of the earth.

For a long time I have at intervals been anxious about my own state of mind. I have felt that if I were ardently attached to my Saviour, my desires to honor him would be more uniform. I had hoped that the Lord would direct to means which would effectually move my soul, so that I could no longer sleep when reflecting on the cause of our dear Redeemer. But let me depend on nothing but God.

Ever since vocal music has been introduced into our seminary, I have had an increasing sense of its practical importance. By our influence and the influence of our pupils on this subject probably hundreds may be benefited for a succession of generations. Those who have been able to sing from childhood do not know by experience the feelings which some have who cannot sing.

※

If you ever seek an interest in Christ you must make up your mind to begin. One time is more favorable than another, and the favorable time is known to God but is not known to us. There is a daily danger of meeting and passing the most favorable time.

※

Since last Friday morning our school-room has been a solemn place. During these five days four have had a change of feeling, which has led them to hope that they have passed from death unto life...Several are now deeply anxious and I know of only one entirely unaffected...Our state is most critical. I do not feel it to be a time for rejoicing, but for mourning, solemnity, and deep humiliation before God. I fear first, lest I shall grieve the Spirit, and then I fear for the friends of the Redeemer here.

※

An economical character is to be formed by precept, by practice, and by example. Example has great effect, not only in furnishing a model for imitation, but also in proving that economy is practicable, which is one of the most essential requisites for success. Let a young lady spend two or three years on intimate terms in a family distinguished for a judicious and constant illustration of this principle, and the effect cannot be lost...Proper economy will be an unostentatious habit, offensive to no one, because regulated by wisdom from above, and will greatly promote the cause of Christ. In practicing it we shall influence hundreds and they, in their turn, thousands. We cannot expect the blessing of God if we waste what he gives us.

※

Do not expect to be independent because educated. Ladies can never be independent; and those best educated most feel their dependence. They must expect great demands to be made upon their time and strength; and they should meet them in the spirit of Him who came to minister rather than to be ministered unto. You will find no pleasure like the pleasure of active effort.

Ask for a life of growth in all that is good, but do not ask for a life of ease. In asking this you may ask for eternal misery.

Little faith, few works, and a little treasure in heaven go together.

I should love to tell you how the Lord has led me since we parted; how one comfort has been taken and another given, and how the promise "As thy days so shall thy strength be" has never failed.

Some expect religion to free them from all their infirmities at once. But it will not be so. We groan in this life, being burdened. The evidence that we are renewed is in the effort to counteract everything that opposes our spirituality. We should not rest because the citadel is taken. We should rather make continued conquests on the outlying provinces. The Christian course requires exertion. It is a race which demands an effort greater than any physical effort we have ever put forth.

An obliging disposition is of special importance in forming a lovely social and domestic character.

Cultivate the habit of moving noiselessly, so that you will always be welcome in the chamber of sickness and suffering.

Young ladies should always speak with a gentle voice. Gentleness and sprightliness can walk hand in hand. Come to see me with a quiet footstep. I shall not care to know of your approach till you knock at my door.

The world is intended as a place of education for Heaven, and when it is not made such, it is perverted from true use. To this end, God has so arranged His providences, so planned His government, as to require unintermitting watchfulness, diligence, and effort. We are not to look for ease; as fast as we acquire a facility in accomplishing one task, we may expect that another more difficult will be assigned us. This world is not our rest.

※

Christians must often go forward in efforts for themselves and others also, when it seems utterly impossible. Efforts made in such a way cause us to grow rapidly in the strength that God gives. When laboring for souls we are often called upon to speak the last word we can speak, give the last bread we have, and then to look to Christ for more.

※

Never, under the plea of peculiar circumstances, allow yourself to do that which you know would be wrong in another.

Keep the mind in Christ. Follow him through good report and through evil report, not for the sake of getting certainty, of feeling security, but to please him. Seek more grace instead of seeking more assurance.

※

What an immense loss I must suffer through life on account of the misimprovement of so long a period of my existence! I humbly hope I shall finally be saved, although as by fire; but I have no reason to expect ever in this world all that spiritual enjoyment with which I might have been favored, if all these years had witnessed a regular advance in a life of faith and piety. Neither can I expect that satisfaction and success in laboring in the cause of the Saviour which I might have enjoyed if I had received that preparation which can be gained by no means but by a long course of active, faithful obedience.

※

All the sins of the Christian will be remembered in judgment to show the exceeding love of Christ in their forgiveness.

The great end of Christ's sufferings and death is to reconcile us to God and to restore us back to His favor and presence.

※

I am feeling more and more that it is much more important that all our powers, greater or less, should be devoted to God, than that our powers should be great; and that it is more important that all our time, whether longer or shorter, should be devoted to him, than that this life should be long.

It is a serious thing to live, to have responsibility not only for your own life, but for your conscious and unconscious influence. No act and no word can be known to be without future consequences.

❦

The aid of Christian sympathy in converting the world was appointed of God in infinite wisdom and in condescending love.

❦

Prayer for spiritual blessings for ourselves and others is the essence of prayer. Nothing is given us but by the Holy Ghost. He is the messenger. He takes of the things of Christ and gives them unto us.

❦

Death will come upon us like this meeting—some in readiness; some like the foolish virgins; some without God. You hear my voice for the last time; there will be a last time of hearing Christ's voice.

We are so constituted that we cannot, in this world, sustain a great depth of feeling continually; this is reserved for another world. But we should feel deeply at times. It has an influence upon our after lives.

❦

Young ladies, never ask to live simply for yourselves. Live for the good of others and you will find your cup of happiness running over in this world, and oh, what will it be in heaven! Be willing to do anything and go anywhere for the good of others, and remember that you are responsible for elevating the character of every one with whom you have to do.

❦

Shakespeare is not worthy of a place beside the Bible. How often some verse will come home to the heart as nothing else will! It seems to penetrate deeper than any sermon or religious instruction.

❦

No law is perfect without a penalty, otherwise it would be only advice…and no one but its divine Author can judge what

※

God has instituted laws for the regulation of health, and the difference between the moral and the natural and physical law is, that the former is right in itself and can never be set aside; and the latter derive their authority from God's appointment; but he has given us a certain degree of elasticity, which makes it safe for us to turn aside when duty requires it. We ought never to lessen this elasticity by using it for self-indulgence. This principle is illustrated by the difference between a mother's depriving herself of her accustomed sleep to care for her sick infant, and doing the same for self-gratification.

※

Economy can be equally manifested in the tasteful decorations of a palace and in the simple comforts of a cottage. If all ladies possessed it in a high degree, how much more would be found in families of comfort and convenience; of taste and refinement; of education and improvement; of charity and good works.

Economy for the sake of giving is never mean, but noble.

※

I would not attempt to point out to you any new resting-place for the feet of weary pilgrims on their way to the Celestial City. No, I would only repeat, if I could, a few of the many precious things which you already know, and in which your hearts now delight to dwell. I would only, while I am in this tabernacle, now and then write you a few words, stirring you up by way of remembrance.

※

Souls bought and redeemed from all this woe, how they should show forth the glory of God. How should they feel towards the multitudes in danger of perishing for lack of the bread of life! Who that has been redeemed and permitted to linger on the shores of earth a while to represent her ascended Saviour, would not wish to eat and drink and live to the glory of God? Who but would rejoice to give all her money, her time, her influence to this great cause the salvation of the perishing?

The great means of doing good, though we cannot tell why or how, only because God so directed it, is by example. We are to be ourselves what we would have others to be. And this not only when others know it, but in all places; for I believe that even what we do in secret affects others.

There are no Christians so young or so weak that they cannot labor. All are watchmen. We should all lift up our voice to warn those who see not the sword of God pursuing them. We should all seek to live consistent Christian lives. Perhaps it will be found, when the history of every conversion shall be made known, that there has been no louder and more effectual voice than this.

I will leave three thoughts with those who wish to be guided in the strait and narrow way. First, you must not expect others to do that which God requires of you. "Enter ye." He that is mine is mine for himself. Second, nothing relating to the soul which ought to be done today should be deferred until tomorrow. Third, God is your only strength. Go to him…depend on him…ask of him. Go through Christ.

Between the ringing of the doorbell and the response, I tried to roll all my care upon God the Lord, and to be willing to receive not one encouraging word, if so my God might be most honored. But He was better to me than my fears… God had prepared those hearts.

The dealings of Providence have been such toward me as to lead me to think most tenderly of all my friends.

Some suppose the strength of affection is greater in youth than in advanced life. This may be true of worldly love, but not of Christian love. Young ladies, I want you to love so tenderly, so deeply, that the roots will not be found spread upon the surface alone. Let them strike into your inmost souls. You need not fear loving too ardently, if you only love in Christ. You may show too much fondness for your friends in public, but you are in no danger of giving them too much true affection.

The present path is plain. The future I can leave with Him who doeth all things well.

It is a means of grace to be accustomed to seek and watch the guidance of Providence.

The man who cared faithfully for the sheep in the desert, led Israel to Canaan, and he who kept "those few sheep in the wilderness," was afterwards Israel's king and sweetest singer.

One minute lost by ninety persons, makes ninety minutes lost forever.

Time is often misspent in indefinite musings; in anticipating needlessly; in needless speculation; by indulging in reluctance to begin a duty; in doubtful cases by hesitating too long; by spending time in reverie when it should be spent in prayer.

In order to get an equivalent for the money and time you are spending, you must be systematic, and that is impossible unless you have a regular hour for rising. If that hour is five, and you are on your feet before the clock has done striking, then you are punctual; but if you lie five minutes, or even one, after that hour passes, you are tardy, and you must lose a little respect for yourself in consequence.

These precious souls have been sent here by the providence of God; but what to do I know not. I am weaker than weakness itself, and my wisdom is altogether folly. May I be more and more sensible of the preciousness of the direction, "if any of you lack wisdom, let him ask of God."

There is nothing more pleasant on earth than a cultivated, refined, well-organized Christian family.

In the family we get the first ideas of right and wrong, and there the most correct ideas of mutual relations, of obedience to authority, of treating equals with respect and affection.

Domestic life is little else but a continued scene of

conferring and receiving favors. And how much of happiness depends on their being conferred with the manifest evidence of a willing heart, and on their being received with suitable tokens of gratitude; these two lovely traits go hand in hand, not often to be separated.

※

A spirit of benevolence has seemed to reign among us to such a degree that selfishness has appeared to most of our little community somewhat in its own character. We have made it an object to gain enlarged and correct views especially relating to our own country, its present state, its interesting character, its wants, its prospects, as to what needs to be done, what can be done, what ought to be done, and, finally, as to what is our duty. Many intelligent, refined young ladies who have been brought up in the lap of indulgence, thought they should be willing to go to the remotest corner of the world and teach a school among the most degraded and ignorant, might it only be said of them by their Master, as it was said of one of old, "She hath done what she could."

※

It is as easy to improve five talents as one.

Character may be compared to a piece of embroidery, which is all accomplished stitch by stitch.

※

Poor persons often speak disparagingly of the rich Christian. If they knew all his trials, they would spend the time thus occupied in praying for him.

In observing how ignorant the disciples were on some points, I was reminded of our inability to determine the way by which Christ will be most glorified. How easy it would have been for Christ to make them understand that he should rise from the dead. But he knew that it was not then best that they should understand this clearly.

※

We should glory not in sins but in infirmities. Our greatest excellences have, by their side, some humiliating fault. Christ often employs the weakest instruments. We may be encouraged by this. There is often a needful thorn, needful to open the way for communications of glory, for blessed success in our work.

You must not call this Miss Lyon's school. I regard it so much a child of Providence, that I do not like to have my name made prominent. And you would look upon it as I do, if you could see a few of the many gulfs that were to me impassable made passable by a divine hand. All has sometimes seemed to hang upon some slight pivot without which the whole would have fallen to the ground. I can see a ruling hand in everything connected with its establishment, and I would have you ever remember that you are being educated in an institution built by the hand of the Lord, and that you are not to live for yourselves.

Loving self supremely continually disappoints.

It is not possible for a person to be thoroughly imbued with the missionary spirit who is not benevolent in other respects.

With a burden on my heart which I cannot describe, there is something in my soul like trust in God, which is like a peaceful river overflowing all its banks. Light can shine out of darkness, and I have great hope that we shall receive a blessing.

If anyone thinks he has no responsibilities, it is because he has not sought them out.

Trials give us most delightful sympathy with the dear Saviour, and help prepare us to go and dwell with him. Those happy ones who have been washed in the blood of the Lamb came out of great tribulation. We desire the result but shrink from the process leading to it. To have sympathy with Christ, we must take up the cross in the path of duty. We need not seek the cross, but we should never try to go around it.

It does seem this week as if we had nothing to do but to stand still and see the salvation of God.

I had many gracious visits from my blessed and glorious Redeemer. The word of God appeared very precious to me, and many times opened with abundance of clearness to my mind. The cry of my soul was, Lord, what wilt thou have me to do?

Some of you desire to be first-class teachers, others would be cherished wives; but, young ladies, if you are God's children, and his glory fails to be your highest aim, in that other ambition you will be disappointed.

I can see through a veil of forty years, in that mountain home growing on the perennial stalk of great principles, the buddings of sentiments, of customs, and of habits, which, if spread over the country and fanned by the gentle breezes of intelligence, influence, and Christian sympathy, would produce a rich and abundant harvest to the treasury of the Lord.

We can compare ourselves profitably with others sometimes, and we should be careful not to lose what we thus gain. From the unwise we may learn to be wise, from the impatient, learn to be patient; from the unreasonable, learn the undesirableness of such a course.

Make all you can of your intellectual and moral powers and of your influence over others.

Nothing helps a Christian more in the discharge of his duty than a sense of responsibility; but who can duly estimate that responsibility? It increases with every beating pulse. An immortal spirit is committed to him, which is to be an inhabitant of heaven, a companion of Jesus Christ forever, and there is doubtless a very close connection between our religious character here and our state in the world to come. There is a wonderful adaptation in this world to fitting us for our eternal home.

My daily desire for myself is, that I may know and do the will of God; that I may live by faith; that I may have a calm and quiet mind;…and that, in some way or other, I may be permitted to do something for the salvation of souls.

We have desired to educate you to go among the rich or the poor, to live in the country or the village, in New England, the West, or in a foreign land. And wherever you are, remember that God will be with you if you seek to do good to immortal souls.

Christ prayed that his disciples might be kept and not lost. Why should not we fall as Adam did? Why not fall as the angels did? And that they might be kept from the evil of the world. When you pray for this, think of Christ's prayer.

We shall doubtless be tried. It must be precept upon precept and prayer upon prayer. All may be dark to us, but, like Noah's dove, we may find a rare sweet resting-place with our God. He cannot fail us.

You are claimed and sought after by the inhabitants of two worlds, and your salvation is entirely dependent on the Holy Spirit. The Spirit can be grieved away.

It is a solemn thought, that a word or look may so influence another's mind as to lead her to grieve away the Spirit.

Spend time not only profitably but most profitably.

The commands of God in the first ages are definite and simple, like those of a parent to young children. Little children cannot infer their duties from general commands, but older ones can judge of parents' wishes from definite commands given to the younger. This renders their obedience higher, nobler, more gratifying to parents than if exact rules were given. In the same manner God leads us, His elder children, to infer our duty from directions given to the younger…those living in earlier ages.

Teach children to bear disappointments with cheerfulness. Convince the scholars that you are their friend. If you have a dull scholar, endeavor to gain his attention, even to the neglect of some others. Let your affection be manifested in conduct rather than in words.

A church needs a foreign mission to teach it to carry its prayers and efforts out of itself; so the man who will give to send the gospel to the heathen, will educate his son to promote the same cause. Pray over this subject while you are considering it; remember it morning and evening.

Seek for yourself a place where the flame of selfishness will not be fanned.

Should I be laid aside as a useless servant it would be just. I would humbly seek that I may be permitted to labor faithfully and successfully, that I may be saved from those temptations which my feeble heart cannot withstand, and that I may be blessed with whatever may be desirable for health of body and of mind and for general usefulness. For little else of this world do I feel at present that I ought to ask.

I used to wish that I could find some retreat in the woods where I could gather all the young women and explain to them the great principles of benevolence and set them to doing good.

How much we may accomplish in fifteen years in studying the Bible! It is an inexhaustible mine, and most precious diamonds are found in it after we think all the gems are dug out. The historical portions reward long-continued and oft-repeated study. We can hardly give too much time to the history of the Israelitish nation.

The study of the Bible gives pupils intellectual discipline, guidance, and control over the heart, and they really love their Bible lessons.

How many do we see around us seeking for ease, honor, pleasure, or improvement, just to gratify self! If their object is attained, there comes little of happiness with it, because all is expended upon self.

He who sows to the spirit and denies himself, will have an increase of happiness and great spiritual growth, while those who sow to the flesh, loving self, reap only corruption.

We may be led of God all the time, and like Moses, we should be content with the place where he bids us dwell. I doubt not that some of you may feel that you have been, and even now are, kept back from the greatest usefulness. The sickness of friends and other circumstances may have hindered you in your studies, and maybe you sometimes long for wealth, and other friends to help you rise in life. I would not have you feel thus, but rather use very carefully all that the Lord gives you. And don't be afraid of the "backside of the desert," and never think you are forsaken of God because kept long there. He knows just how much of quiet humble life we need to serve him in the best manner hereafter.

How easy it is to work with the Holy Spirit!

The wear and tear of what I cannot do is a great deal more than the wear and tear of what I can do.

Well, I may fail of heaven, but I shall be very much disappointed if I do, very much disappointed.

The duty of the present moment is of more importance than all future duty.

The spirit of prayer, the prayer of faith, may be sought by looking at the subject as an important reality; by living with the solemnities of eternity in our hearts; by giving up our own souls to God; by abiding in Christ and following in his footsteps.

It is one of the nicest of mental operations to distinguish between the very difficult and the impossible.

Happy is she who possesses the ability to live respectably on a little.

Wealth and extravagance have no necessary connection. There are three ways of furnishing a table—the luxurious, the scanty, and the comfortable. The first we often find among the fashionable—but not among the most intellectual. It causes depression of both mind and body. The second, the scanty, causes more depression still. Those who practice the third, think very little about their food. Eating is not their great object. It is desirable to give attention to our tables as well as to our souls. I consider bread-making of so much consequence, that, in giving attention to it, I am confident that I am serving God.

❧

The voice of the Lord from Sinai was a striking manifestation to the children of Israel. When they had not the Bible, the influences of the Spirit were then mightily felt. There were many circumstances that combined to give overpowering solemnity; they were not to come near; to wait for three days; the lightnings and thunderings that made them quake as they stood at the foot of the mount and looked up to see it rising to heaven; the sound of that trumpet, as if blown by God himself; the unearthly stillness of all else; Sinai on smoke. Is it not a fearful thing to break a law thus given?

❧

Superior gifts are very convenient but they are rare, and any institution that can be carried on only by superior persons would be likely to fall by its own weight.

❧

I would desire such a frame of mind that I might be ever ready to say, not my will but thine be done. I would not desire anything that would not be for the glory of God and in accordance with the will of my Saviour. Sometimes I almost feel that I am not my own; but then again, I find my heart desiring those things from which I had hoped it was forever separated.

Go where no one else will go, not seeking the praise of men, but the favor which comes from God only.

❧

Never read a book without first praying over it.

You feel a great deal more interested when you pray for particular individuals than you do in general petitions. Plead for God's Spirit on your teachers, your companions…on those who have gone out from the seminary, especially on those who are laboring far away among the heathen. You will find your half-hour entirely too short. How often when the bell rings for its close, it seems to me as though it had but just begun! You will not know how to leave your Father and your God. You will want to stay longer in his more immediate presence.

※

Economy should be strict and based upon principle. It should extend to the smallest things. Those who resolve upon economy on some sudden occasion, or from some unusual motive, are apt to misplace it and appear mean.

A lady who has the genuine missionary spirit will carry it to the kitchen as well as to the monthly concert.

※

Sin is everywhere a dreadful evil. It is committed against the holy law of God. The Spirit teaches us the displeasure of God with sin and sinners; the just condemnation of the sinner; a great dread and loathing of sin; a fear of future sin; and a fear of continuing to sin through eternity. But, on the other hand, it teaches that there is a Friend of sinners; the need and sufficiency of the cleansing and pardoning blood of Christ and a relying on Christ and Christ alone for strength to forsake sin and consecrate one's self to the service of Christ.

※

There is an awful and solemn delight in the feeling that God hates sin. When we struggle against sin, it is comforting to know that there is One who hates and abhors all sin as it deserves. God knows our unworthiness, guilt, dependence, and want, and he can forgive sin.

※

Do not excuse yourselves from improving your talents either because you are so rich or so poor. There are peculiar advantages in both conditions. Do not defer to the future what is to be done now; do not forget; never faint or be discouraged. Keep eternity and the worth of the soul in view. Keep your eye on the Saviour day by day, in this work.

The remembrance of wrong living causes us unhappiness here. We have feelings of shame for the moment, but throw a veil over such feelings. It is like looking at the burning sun. We can close the eyelids and shut it out. But imagine yourself without eyelids. That would be like eternity. There will be no veil there.

How exceedingly sinful is sin! How deserving of all the judgments denounced against it! But the boundless love and mercy of God, as exhibited in the promises, I think most wonderful, and so of all his promises to guilty sinners.

We should never hear a sermon or a prayer without gaining something.

The true penitent will fix his eye on God—an injured God, a forgiving God—more than on self; guilty, polluted self.

If I ever get to heaven, it will be the greatest miracle of grace. I am so unworthy—so unworthy. But I rejoice to be unworthy, and to owe it all to the atoning blood of Jesus Christ.

We love that cause best for which we suffer most.

Through the light of Christ's agony we get a glimpse of heaven. Having a love of others like Christ's love, we must look at him to feel the worth of their souls. A view of what Christ has done alone can give us that love of others which we must have.

God looks on the heart of Christians in sending the Holy Spirit. A worldly deportment is suited to draw the heart from God. The daily deportment is a channel through which God bestows or withholds his blessings.

Think of the multitudes who die daily on heathen shores. But we should pray for them, because there is yet room in the heart of the Saviour, and because our Father's house is to be filled. Sinners ought to believe that the Redeemer has died for them, and that they may occupy the mansions above. They should compel themselves to come in. Christ has prepared mansions for us and they will be filled.

the penalty should be.

As a great whole the punishment of the wicked seems wise and good—most for the glory of God; most for the glorious happiness of the created universe. With this view we can join in thanksgiving for his judgments. But looking at individuals, our hearts are filled with anguish and our feeble minds clouded with mystery. We may sympathize with Christ in his weeping over Jerusalem.

Heaven seems nearer to me than ever before, and labor on earth sweeter. A gentler and a safer hand than mine leads those who are gone. How comforting!

A good Christian hope will not grow dimmer and dimmer like the taper, but like the rising sun, brighter and brighter.

This thought often overwhelms me—God, the great God, taking care of me, and willing to let me trust him! If all is dark; if there is universal darkness and long continued, we may still trust God, if we are willing to obey him.

How safe it is to trust in God. How easily can he give counsel and assistance in all things, the smallest as well as the greatest.

But, beloved, you are spoken to, not from Mount Sinai, but from Mount Zion. Jesus speaks. See that ye refuse not him who speaketh from heaven and who would give you a kingdom that cannot be moved. If you will not do it, you shall realize that "our God is a consuming fire."

The providence of God is opening to the Christian everywhere a way, a high way, a way of holiness, in which his willing feet can run as on the wings of the wind, carrying the tidings of salvation to the remotest ends of the earth.

We should so live that it will be pleasant for others to think of us when we are gone.

Form such a character in this life as you will wish to possess through eternity.

We know not always when the Holy Spirit is present, but we can see his work; and we can feel that He was here, and has gone and left his great work, himself unseen.

Without the teaching of the Holy Spirit there is no possible hope.

Why should the Spirit be grieved from us when he is so much more easily invited to stay with us, to come and bless us?

What ought to be done can be done.

Why are some persons in a hurry? Simply on account of slothfulness.

Do the best that you can do today.

I am about to embark in a frail boat on a boisterous sea. I know not how I shall be tossed, nor to what port I shall be directed, but it is sweet in the midst of darkness to commit the whole to his guidance.

If you are Christ's, do not seek for certainty in this life. Jesus never led any of his children that way. We must trust him.

Remember, if you are God's children, your life, every hour of it, must be a life of care lest you sin against him.

There is a defect in our present system of education. Knowledge of books increases faster than knowledge of character.

Our course of study embraces much, but probably fifty years hence it will appear quite limited. We should not study to be pleased any more than we live to eat; and as it is an important part of discipline not to be fastidious about our food if we would be prepared for usefulness in any sphere, so we should study and not expect, for a long while, to find pleasure; but when we do reap the fruit it will be very sweet.

Spending time purely for religion is more nearly like the service of heaven than anything else. Let us seek to spend this day so as to have a realization of eternity. Depart far out of the world and may you come back profited.

Are you doing the best you can? Do you not wish to improve?

※

To bring every opportunity to bear on the character is a leading object in the arrangements of the family. The domestic work done by the young ladies, in the varied and mutual duties of the day, furnishes many little opportunities for the manifestation of a generous, obliging, and self-denying spirit, the influence of which we trust will be felt through life. It also helps to give a spirit of gratitude and a sense of obligation.

※

For a few days I design to study two passages upon prayer—Luke 11: 5-13 and James 1: 5-8; would you like to study these daily with me as you pray?

※

Heavenly Father, teach me to live more as Christ lived, to feel more as He felt, to labor more as He labored, to deny myself more as He denied himself, to pray more as He prayed, to agonize over a lost and dying world more as He agonized.

※

Our prayers are sometimes not answered, that we may desire more than we can ask or think. How much better to have the thorn and grace than to have no thorn and no grace! The thorn often grows in our own character. This gives it sharpness. There is a mystery in being reconciled to our own mistakes and missteps, and yet groaning to be delivered from all sin.

When I am about my work, sometimes called unexpectedly and suddenly from one thing to another, I whisper in my heart, "Lord, help me to be patient, help me to remember, and help me to be faithful."

※

We must often pray till we have not another petition that we can offer, and then, when in silence, we are resting on the Eternal Arm, our friend may be saved.

※

God has committed to us these earthly treasures, requiring a part to be devoted to spiritual purposes. He might have so supplied all that there would have been no opportunity for us to give, but he has seen it best for us to divide our treasures with others. The Bible is our guide in this, and when it makes known our duty, we are not to answer again.

Nothing in our mountain home was left to take its own way. Everything was made to yield to the mother's faithful, diligent hand. Early and late she was engaged in the culture of the olive-plants around her table.

If we would learn of God, let us read the history of His ancient people. If we would know ourselves, we shall find our hearts well portrayed there. More knowledge of human nature is to be derived from its study than from any other source.

We have great power over ourselves. We may become almost what we will. Portray to yourself a character in mind, heart, education, taste, and manners, such as you ought to be, and then aim to be such.

Benevolent objects assume different garbs. There are societies whose work must be planned months and years beforehand. Our home and foreign missionary societies must pledge support to those whom they may send out. We should be very careful not to have our contributions diverted from such objects even for a single year. Let us never go backward one step in such a work as this, but rather onward to the day of our death. If our parents are not benevolent, let us seek to supply their lack of service.

All difficulties and perplexities can be referred to God, and there left.

It is very sweet, in the midst of darkness and doubt, to commit the whole to his guidance.

I doubt not you have learned, to a great extent, to depend

on God day by day for your daily bread. This lesson I desire to learn.

※

When the mind is deeply impressed with eternal truth, there is no disposition to be frivolous or trifling.

All are not required to act in relation to the same laws. Angels are not called upon to obey their parents, for they have no parents. Every command must be obeyed so far as individuals are called to act in relation to it.

What is duty is duty, though ever so small.

Form little rules for the improvement of character, but do not speak of them.

※

Never say you have no faith or hope. Always think of God's strength when you feel your weakness, and remember that you can come nearer to Him than to any being in the universe.

※

Treasure up hints; they may prove the seed of principles.

Sometimes when I have been reperusing your letters, sentence by sentence, to see if there was not some idea expressed or implied which I did not at first apprehend, I have thought it would be well for me to read my Bible with like care.

※

Do not break a postoffice law to save a ninepence or a quarter of a dollar. There is a kind of reverence in keeping law, though it be too strict.

Now I trust you will be inflexible in regard to the right. Do not yield that, even to please kings; but be very careful to distinguish between the right and personal gratification.

※

You will not all manifest your Christian character in the same way; you are variously constituted. Perhaps some of you are inclined to be very silent. Now we wish you to correct this as far as it is an evil. But being a Christian will not make such a person talk all the time; neither should it cause a very lively person to be silent. Honor God with the constitution He has given you, keeping your peculiar temperaments and tendencies in perfect control.

Pray for us that we may not receive all our good things in this life.

We cannot depend on the strongest resolutions or the impulses of immediate feeling; we must be guided by the truth.

None can be honest to God who are not honest to man.

God has a plan for every farthing He has placed in our hands.

Never excuse yourself from administering Christian rebuke because the person in fault has been told, or because she knew her duty. The addition of your kind caution or reproof may be the means of saving her.

Remember, there is no kindness that you can show a poor person like helping him to do for himself to the extent of his ability.

Never write a foolish thing in a letter or elsewhere. "What is written is written."

Yes, I know she has a small mind, but we must do the best we can for her.

Our greatest happiness is derived from our interest in and labor for others. The Christian's greatest joy or sorrow is in regard to others.

All that is sent upon you is at his bidding, and he stands ready to help you to know no will but his.

Does anyone feel anxious about her examinations? Carry all to your Heavenly Father. You may thus get an acquaintance with him that will make you long to say to God, "My Father."

Five effects of glorying in infirmity: our guilt magnifies the grace of God; our corruption magnifies the power of the Spirit in our hearts; our weakness magnifies the strength of

Christ; our unworthiness magnifies the condescension of Christ; a conviction of our unfitness to receive the blessing sought overwhelms us with gratitude when the blessing comes.

The keeping of the first table of the law is expressed in one word,—worship. One command gives us the object of worship, another the manner of worship, and another still, the time of worship.

The work of cultivating Christian sympathy should be commenced in the earliest years of childhood and it should be carried on till the days on earth are finished and the soul is released to go home and dwell forever in a world of infinite sympathy, of infinite fellowship, of infinite love.

If a Christian is rich, let him give—not a part—but all which the Lord requires. Though he may cast his thousands into the treasury of the Lord, it may weigh nought in the counsels of heaven if anything is kept back. But let him come fully up to his ability, let him come fully up to the urgency of the case, and he shall receive even a richer reward than did the widow with her two mites. No one knows to whom in this case it shall be said, "Thou hast power with God and hast prevailed."

The Sabbath is of inestimable value. It is worth more than all other days in bringing thoughts into captivity to the will of Christ. In times of revival it seems to be the day he delights peculiarly to honor.

Sometimes it seems as though I should sink under this burden. How all can be done—I know not; but in view of what the Lord has done for us we have abundant reason to trust him.

My own heart was so filled with thoughts of the blessedness of the departing soul, that I could think of nothing else. That room where our dear Adaline left her body, to see Jesus as he is, is a very precious spot to me. I should love to go and stay there for a season—yes, there where heaven was opened to receive one of our number. Jesus has honored it, for He came there, just as He said he would, to receive one of His dear children to himself. I did not say good-by to Adaline when I saw her eye closing in death, for I am confident that I shall see her again soon. What glories burst upon her view in that room! It can never be to us like other rooms.

One great thing to be gained in an education is to be able to possess comfort and privileges without becoming selfish.

The most wretched beings are those who think only of their own little selves, who are always regretting the past and reproaching themselves, and take no interest in any one but themselves.

To be a good wife, it matters not what there is with a lady, but what there is of her.

We thank God that the last thing sin can do is to break up the family circle. It is wonderful how much better we are made by these family relations. The little child makes the father a better man, and the excellences of a woman are nowhere so marked, and they nowhere shine so beautifully, as in the wife and mother.

The Jews enjoyed a great privilege in being permitted to build an earthly temple; we are permitted to build a spiritual temple. If you have any desire to do good, act at once. In waiting, you may lose the little desire you have. These passive impressions are exceedingly dangerous. Feeling without action brings no reward. Do and suffer, deny yourselves for Christ, and then you will count it all joy in the end. I am saying what I wish you to remember when you are far hence and see me no more. May you remember it when I am laid in my grave.

There is a great, solemn, and real delight in feeling that God is incomprehensible. The wicked seek to comprehend God and deny what they cannot comprehend.

It is a duty to commit Scripture to memory and have a plan for self-teaching. Commit passages that interest you and commit them perfectly. Do not mutilate them. If you have committed them well, when you teach a child, repeat Scripture to a sick person, or pray, it will flow forth easily and be just what is needed.

The Jews all gave to the Lord, the rich and the poor; and we should count it a privilege that we may do a little if we cannot do much. How the Saviour honored the two mites of her who gave all her living! The Bible teaches us to give a portion of our income to the Lord, and we must give it before we expend anything for ourselves.

Many assemble in the outer court, but only here and there one will tarry long enough to find his way into the inner temple.

Everything I do is such a privilege! It is so blessed, too, to depend hourly for light and strength and for success on our Heavenly Father, through Jesus Christ our Redeemer.

I believe that the blessings of this life are very great and will continue to be so; and that trials are trials under all circumstances. But I think I can faintly see that there is a foundation for support when this world is not made all in all.

To accomplish anything valuable, it is necessary to divide time wisely and systematically. Many have no definite lines to mark out their time. If they occasionally accomplish a considerable amount in a day, they know not how it was done; and when they accomplish nothing they know not the reason why. Just so with speaking; many do not know the boundary where slander begins. Nearly all think it their duty or their privilege to speak against others.

The sympathy of the Christian is not left to wear itself out by its own perpetual corrodings. It is not shut up to become loathsome and stagnant for the want of fresh air. No. It can flow forth in living streams of active benevolence, fertilizing many a barren plain, till it mingles in the great ocean of love, and thence it can return to refresh the soul. The providence of God is opening to the Christian everywhere, a way, a highway, a way of holiness, in which his willing feet can run, as on the wings of the wind, carrying the tidings of salvation to the remotest ends of the earth.

It is a serious thing to live, to have responsibility not only for your own life but for your conscious and unconscious influence. No act and no word can be known to be without future consequences.

The last evening I was with you, a little cloud of discouragement passed over me, such as I have scarcely before seen for several months. But it was soon gone. Even before I left you, future duties seemed pleasant. Whatever God may appoint, it is enough if I can see the path of duty.

We can know much of Heaven. If we have ever had feelings which we believe to be in unison with our Heavenly Father's will, we then know something of the feelings enjoyed there.

The life that I desire for you is as much above the pleasure-seeker's as an archangel is above an infant. You have been accustomed to follow where I led you. Now you are to be seated on a throne of your own. You can sway a golden sceptre there. Be sure to do it.

We ought to attain to that standard of piety set before us in the gospel, and ever be enabled to say: I will do either this or that, whichever may seem most likely to promote God's glory. We may be called to honor him by patient suffering or in some prominent station or in some humble obscure station. But we may have that state of mind in which our first thought in making any change of circumstances will be, not, will it promote my own happiness (God can make any situation happy), but will it be most for God's glory?

We are said to be crucified with Christ—to be partakers of his sufferings; to weep with him; to rejoice with him; to reign with him. He is not ashamed to call us brethren—brethren in labors; brethren in sufferings; brethren in gathering in the rich harvest of immortal souls. We are to be conformed to His image, that He may be the first-born among many brethren. We are to be heirs of God, and joint heirs with Christ, if so be that we suffer with Him. Who could conceive of condescension like this? Is not a life of suffering for Christ's sake a great privilege?

Pray for a blessing on missionary societies, pray for missionaries themselves, mentioning them by name; pray for particular stations; pray for all who are laboring at home in an eminent degree, either personally or by their money; pray for a universal spirit of liberality and a universal spirit of prayer.

Union together in Christ is the most exalted union among created beings.

Could I make my voice heard from one end of the land to the other, and so plead in behalf of the perishing heathen that all our missionary concerts should be filled with hearts bowing together in the presence of God, it might not be so important a duty for me as to carry my own feeble petition myself to the throne of mercy, and there, in the name of our blessed Redeemer, plead the promises with an earnestness which cannot be denied.

Such is the value of immortal beings, that all who have the care of youth ought to make every sacrifice for their good and, if need be, perhaps, lay down their lives.

The teaching of the children decides the destiny of the nation.

All our statesmen, rulers, ministers, and missionaries must come under the molding hand of mothers and teachers.

※

The prospect…has appeared sufficiently pleasant; indeed, I fear too pleasant. I tremble more than if the path appeared more rugged.

※

All, even the weakest believers, are to feed his lambs. This agrees with the whole tenor of the gospel system; with the experience of every new-born soul; with the experience of every returning backslider; with the experience of every advanced Christian. It is a great privilege to deliver immortal beings from eternal death, to give them a place with the redeemed. They are Christ's lambs, his by creation, his by providence, his by purchase, his because he is seeking their salvation.

※

A teacher should be careful not to appeal to herself. Let your actions speak. Make the dull ones think once a day; make their eyes sparkle once a day. Let your punishments be such as will affect the mind rather than the body. Let the certainty, not the severity, of your punishments inspire dread. Never compare one child with another. Never be in haste to believe that a pupil has done wrong. Treat a forward child with apparent indifference. When children have been accustomed to bad habits, it is better to keep a record of what is right than of what is wrong.

※

Who can bear the thought of one retrograde step in the missionary movement? Who would not sooner give his last mite and divide his last loaf? Though the barrel of meal be ever so low, and the cruse of oil be ever so far spent, who will not run and first make a little cake for this servant of the Lord?

※

I am distressed with the apparent want of sincerity among Christians on the first and grand principles of duty; and, more than all, with my own real deficiency in this respect. I am distressed that so many momentous subjects of Christian duty should wear so different an aspect in the pulpit and in the solemn and attentive audience from what they do in the social circle and in the business of life.

※

Each one of you is now called to the supper of the Lamb, and I charge you not to put off repentance for anything else. You have only a little time in which you may compel yourselves to come in.

Seeking the Lord is a work of great simplicity, of great sincerity, a work alone with God, a salvation for yourselves as you are, not as you are not; such a salvation as is provided and not such as is imagined.

※

We must always consider the good of the whole.

※

The formation of a character that can be grateful is an object of special importance in a lady's education. Parents should seek to give their daughters privileges, and especially the means of an education, in a manner suited to lead them to realize that they are favors for which gratitude is due.

Keep your tears for your sins.

Be very thankful for a little and you will receive more.

※

I have had a short extra meeting for the impenitent every day. In these meetings I have no very definite plan; my waiting eyes are unto the Lord God. It is sweet to carry every burden and every care to him, and from day to day the path has been made plain. I have no knowledge of future duty and I ask for none.

※

You will become more Christlike by loving little children.

If you have the care of only one little child, never for a moment think that you have not a great work. If that child is spared to grow up, it may be that you will influence thousands through him. If he is early taken away, be happy in the thought that you have helped prepare a child for heaven. And we cannot know but the child in heaven does more for this world than the most devoted Christian minister spared to see his threescore and ten years on earth.

We ought to be solemn, knowing that the least thing that we do is not overlooked by God. His government extends over the universe; the winds and the waves obey him, the beasts of the field, the fowls of the air, and the cattle upon a thousand hills; but he has a law for his moral beings. This law is full of glory and it is easy to be obeyed by a willing heart and an obedient mind.

Winter is the seed-time of health. Take much exercise in the cold season if you would be well in summer.

A gentleman may possibly do much good without much health; but what can a lady do unless she takes the attitude of an invalid and seeks to honor Christ by patience and submission. I would not undervalue this, but if you can do good in another way by taking care of your health, will you not be happier in it? If a gentleman cannot do his work in one hour, perhaps he may do it in another; but a lady's duties admit of no compromise of hours.

It is certainly a calamity to have an unsubdued will, but a blessing to have strong desires yielded to a higher and holier will.

If we cannot yield our will in little things, God will almost certainly give us greater trials. He may not do it at once, but he will not forget that His child needs discipline and He will take His own time for giving it.

We know just as much of Heaven as we know experimentally of feelings, purposes, and employments in unison with those of the saints about the throne of God. Communion with God the Father, God the Son, and God the Holy Ghost here below is an earnest of the bliss reserved above.

If amid so many deviations, so much lack in our services, the little seasons of conscious sincerity, when we desire for ourselves and others that we may do just what God sees to be exactly according to his will are so precious, how glorious must heaven be!

The Christian's Heaven is being eternally with his God and in the enjoyment of that bliss of which his communings with him here are only a foretaste.

The friends of Christ have the feelings and conduct of friends; they regard and love his character, they have confidence in Him as a friend, they are grateful to Him as to a friend, they seek to honor Him as a friend, and they delight in having His will done.

You all possess great power of influencing others, and I am afraid that some of you are weaving webs of sloth, worldliness, or thoughtlessness which you are throwing around your companions.

None but God knows how the responsibility of giving religious instruction to these candidates for eternity weighs on my heart. Sometimes beforehand my soul is weighed down with fear, trembling, and anxious solicitude which finds no relief but in God.

Secular music gives spirit and zest. We should thank God that He has made us so that we can enjoy it. It is wonderful kindness.

Singing exerts a mighty moral influence, and, young ladies, I have no doubt that if you cultivate your musical powers here, you will sing and enjoy the song of Moses and the Lamb as those cannot who have hidden their talent.

How safe it is to trust in God! How easily can he give counsel and assistance in all things, the smallest as well as the greatest! And how ready and willing is He always to assist!

It would seem that I have too frequently tried my own strength, that I have experienced too many instances of the particular guardian care and protection of God to doubt in whom I should place my trust.

Never burn what a bird would open its bill to get.

Many persons are poor not because they have not enough, but because they do not know how to use what they have.

※

Other things being equal you are under more obligation because of your opportunities here. Privilege and responsibility go hand in hand.

※

On entering this seminary, young ladies can scarcely avoid feeling that they are sharing the fruits of benevolent efforts; that they are enjoying privileges which they cannot purchase; that they owe a debt of gratitude to the founders, which gold and silver can never cancel, and which can be met only by a useful Christian life.

※

If we would labor aright for Christ, our hearts must take in the whole world.

Our first great blessing is that we may be in Christ; the second, that we labor for him.

※

There is a definite time for everything. If it is not done at its time, a place can never be found for it without displacing something else. If an hour is lost, it is never regained. We may crowd its duties into other hours, but the day is worth as much less as that hour's value, and even more. This is true of the whole of life.

※

Before you kneel to pray, consider what you want to ask God to grant you. "Be careful for nothing; but in everything by prayer and supplication with thanksgiving let your requests be made known unto God." You need not be careful about your words. When you pray with others you have to seek out acceptable words, but when you are alone, use any language that comes easiest to you. Bring everything before Him; spread out all your wants. Confess your sins, your secret sins. Recount your mercies; thank God for His goodness. When love flows in upon your soul, tell your Saviour that you love him, that you will go anywhere and do anything for his sake, that you will receive what He sends, and submit to what He appoints.

Persons who run around all day after the half hour they lost in the morning never accomplish much.

Acquire the habit of accounting for time as well as for money. Yet avoid appearing too economical of time; as when taking a book or paper into company.

The Bible has no favorite duties, no favorite laws. The stress the Bible lays upon subjects is proportioned to their importance.

There is a beauty and strength in Scripture language that is found nowhere else. Treasure the words and truths of the Bible. Make these truths the subject of frequent meditation.

The Saviour kindly remembered our weakness when he taught us to pray, "Lead us not into temptation."

Sin is universal; with the cross in view it becomes an individual subject. There may be a general confession, but at the cross the contrite heart needs something more. A general desire to become a Christian often gives a feeling of complacency and a cloak for sins; at the cross this is lost sight of.

Who am I that so many parents should be willing to trust their daughters to me; and what was my father's house, that God should give me such blessed work from year to year?

My heart goes out very tenderly this morning to those parents who have entrusted you to my care. Those fathers and mothers have no choicer treasures than their precious daughters. We are ready to labor for you in love and fidelity, and may you all be faithful to us. And oh, what inexpressible tenderness in the thought that you may all be preparing for heaven here!

Follow judgment rather than impulse. Of all the leading-strings in the world the last to follow should be fancy.

There is a deficiency of grasp of mind if you do not think; a deficiency of moral power if you do not care. Want of business habits in ladies consumes their time, their hearts, and gives them much perplexity.

Of all the changes that take place, the changing of fellow-laborers, of fellow-travelers through this pilgrimage is the most painful.

Are you like the Lord Jesus Christ, willing to make yourself poor that others through your poverty may be rich?

Our time as well as our property belong to the Lord. We ought to take care of every hour, that we may have the more for communion with heaven. To be most exact in secular appointments and give only fragments to religious duties, is not seeking first the kingdom of God.

We should look carefully to the manner of performing not only our religious duties, but also our temporal duties, for this also is to affect us through all eternity. This is our sowing time and the reaping is at hand.

If you form the habit of being a minute or two late, it will grow upon you and you will become very uncomfortable members of society. You will find yourselves neglected, losing your influence, becoming very unhappy, and maybe doubting even whether you are Christians, just from the effects of the habit of being a little behind time.

The crowning work of Jesus Christ was the redemption of the world.

Through Christ we can behold the joy set before us—the crown of rejoicing.

Christ is the only door by which we can be admitted to the presence of God.

In one thing I can rejoice—that as long as the Lord of the vineyard hath any need of my feeble service, he will allow me the privilege of living and laboring, and when he sees it to be best that I should labor no longer in this dark, wicked world, which has been promised to the Saviour as his inheritance, then may I be prepared to lay down this tabernacle with joy and rejoicing, and go to dwell with Christ, which is far better.

God is glorified by having his plans accomplished. When man's plans are accomplished it proves His wisdom and skill. Just so with God. One way of honoring God is by increasing the happiness of ourselves and friends. Every time we diminish happiness we dishonor Him. When we appear unhappy and dejected, we imply that He made us to be unhappy.

Always be within a half minute of the time appointed for any exercise or duty. Carry this habit through life, and always let your influence be felt for good in punctuality in attending church. Our own punctuality will greatly assist us in the care of others.

God has given us a certain amount of elasticity within which we can safely venture beyond the strictest regard for our health. We must take care never to lessen this elasticity by using it in self-indulgence.

I often look forward to the day when we shall hear it said, "Inasmuch as ye did it not to one of the least of these." Let us do it unto Christ, first of all giving to him our own hearts. I seem sometimes to look out through the crevices of my prisonhouse and see something of the work given us to do here.

The body and the mind each strives for the mastery; the body is of the earth, the mind ranges in eternity. The mind should not sit down and wash the body's feet. The master should have the master's place. Take an illustration. In the morning the mind says, It is time to rise. The body says, It is cold. The mind listens to the body. Servitude and degradation follow. When you know it is time to rise, do it at once. And will you remember it all your lives, and how I stood here and asked you to do it?

※

None have more responsibility than others. Teachers have no more than scholars, except comparatively. Absolutely considered in reference to God, all are alike responsible.

www.ingramcontent.com/pod-product-compliance
Lightning Source LLC
Chambersburg PA
CBHW030359100426
42812CB00028B/2768/J